Cambridge Middle East Library

Urban notables and Arab nationalism

Cambridge Middle East Library

Also in this series

Medicine and power in Tunisia 1780–1900
NANCY ELIZABETH GALLAGHER

Egypt in the reign of Muhammad Ali
AFAF LUTFI AL-SAYYID MARSOT

The Palestinian Liberation Organisation: people, power and politics
HELENA COBBAN

Urban notables and Arab nationalism

The politics of Damascus 1860–1920

PHILIP S. KHOURY

ASSISTANT PROFESSOR OF HISTORY
MASSACHUSETTS INSTITUTE OF TECHNOLOGY

CAMBRIDGE UNIVERSITY PRESS
CAMBRIDGE
LONDON   NEW YORK   NEW ROCHELLE
MELBOURNE   SYDNEY

Published by the Press Syndicate of the University of Cambridge
The Pitt Building, Trumpington Street, Cambridge CB2 1RP
32 East 57th Street, New York, NY 10022, USA
296 Beaconsfield Parade, Middle Park, Melbourne 3206, Australia

First published 1983

Printed in Great Britain by the University Press, Cambridge

Library of Congress catalogue card number: 83–5289

British Library Cataloguing in Publication Data
Khoury, Philip S.
Urban notables and Arab nationalism.–(Cambridge Middle East library)
1. Damascus–Politics and government
I. Title II. Series
320.95691′4   DS99.D3
ISBN 0 521 24796 9

TO MY MOTHER AND FATHER

UP

Contents

List of maps   vii
Note on transcription   vii
Preface   ix

Introduction   1

1 The political configuration of Damascus in 1860   8
The notables: some qualifications   10
The religious establishment   13
The secular dignitaries   18
The *aghawat*   20
The impact of the 1860 crisis   23

**2 The consolidation of leadership in Damascus after
1860**   26
The development of private landownership   26
Modernization and centralization of administration   29
Religious families in the recomposed leadership: the
   landowning-scholars   30
Landowning-bureaucratic families in the recomposed
   leadership   35
The size of the political élite in 1900   44
The position of the minorities   45
The behavior of the political and social leadership   46

**3 Damascus notables and the rise of Arab nationalism
before World War I**   53
The Young Turk revolution and the Arabs   55
'From Ottomanism to Arabism'   58
The social origins of Arab nationalism   67

**4 Notables, nationalists and Faysal's Arab government
in Damascus, 1918–20**   75
The impact of the Arab Revolt of 1916   76

Contents

The political configuration of Faysal's Arab state   78
The fragility of government: nationalist pressures   82
Elections to the Syrian Congress   86
Failure of diplomacy   89
Final days   91

Conclusion   93

Notes   101
Bibliography   133
Glossary of Arabic, Persian and Turkish terms   144
Index   146

Maps

1 Damascus *c.* 1920   24
2 Geographical Syria *c.* 1914   51

NOTE ON TRANSCRIPTION

'Ayns and *hamzas* are the only diacriticals included in the transcription of Arabic technical terms, personal names and sources. Otherwise commonly accepted English forms are used, especially for Arabic place names. Turkish technical terms, personal names, place names and sources are generally kept simple in the text, notes and bibliography.

Preface

No idea has captured the imagination or expressed the hopes of the Arabs in the twentieth century as has Arab nationalism, and perhaps no subject has received so much attention from historians of the Middle East. But while many historians have explored its sources, few have considered the social and political environment in which Arab nationalism evolved as an ideological movement. This study attempts to correct the imbalance.

Its focus is on the social and political life in Ottoman Damascus and, in particular, on the great notable families of that city who were to play a disproportionate role in politically activating the Arab nationalist idea before World War I. Chapters 1 and 2 explore the ways such long-term factors as the Ottoman reformation, European economic expansion and agrarian commercialization in Syria encouraged rival and socially differentiated networks of locally influential families in Damascus to merge into a socially cohesive upper class. Under the umbrella of a reinvigorated Ottoman central authority, this class of landowners and bureaucrats produced a new urban leadership which dominated local politics after 1860.

Although this leadership faced no serious challenges from further down the social scale in Damascus, it was by no means free of internal conflicts. Economic and political competition between and within upper-class family networks was always rife. Chapter 3 focuses on the ways this factionalism comes to be expressed in ideological terms, after the Young Turk revolution of 1908 shook the established balance of power between the Arab provincial élites and the Turkish authorities. In Damascus a number of local leaders lost their offices and suffered material losses under the impact of Young Turk centralizing reforms and 'Turkification' policies. It was this disaffected group of urban notables who seized the recently available but still dormant idea of Arabism and molded it into an ideological instrument with which to re-establish its political position.

The final chapter offers a new interpretation of political life in Amir Faysal's short-lived Arab state in postwar Syria by emphasizing the continuity of factionalism between rival groups of urban notables expressed in ideological terms. But now the scale of the Arab nationalist movement has widened to include other major towns in the Syrian interior. Moreover, nationalist notables now have the upper hand in politics, that is until France occupies Syria in 1920, checking this trend for nearly a generation.

I should like to express my appreciation to a number of people and institutions whose assistance has helped to make this book possible.

I am most indebted to my teacher, Albert Hourani, who supervised my graduate studies at Harvard University from the beginning and who encouraged the making of this book.

I wrote much of the text for this book in Oxford where I spent two years as an Associate of St Antony's College. I wish to thank the Warden and Fellows of St Antony's for offering me this unique and wonderful opportunity. Roger Owen and Derek Hopwood of the College and its Middle East Centre were especially helpful. I completed the final draft of the book in the warm and familiar environment of Harvard's Center for Middle Eastern Studies where I spent a postdoctoral year in 1980–81. Muhsin Mahdi, A. J. Meyer and Dennis Skiotis were my generous benefactors. Finishing touches were added after I moved to the Massachusetts Institute of Technology in 1981–82, and I thank my colleagues in the History Section of the Department of Humanities for their steady encouragement as I attempted to smooth out the manuscript's rough edges. I conducted most of my research in Lebanon and Syria where I was hospitably received by the staffs of the Jafet Library of the American University of Beirut, and the Institut Français d'Études Arabes and the Center for Historical Documents in Damascus.

Many other friends, teachers, colleagues and family members assisted me at one stage or another in completing this book. I would like to mention Diana Grimwood-Jones and Aziz al-Azmeh in Oxford; Nadim Demichkie and Salma Mardam-Beg in London; Dominique Chevallier in Paris; Hanna Batatu, Wajih Fanous, Rashid Hamid, Yusuf Ibish, Salma Jurdak, Samir Khalaf, Zafir al-Qasimi, Khayriyya al-Qasimiyya, Edmond Rabbath, George and Rose Tomeh, and Qustantin Zurayq in Beirut; Thierry Bianquis, Dawn Chatty, Hasan al-Hakim, Samir Kahalah, Colette al-Khuri, Jean-Paul Pascual and Regina Heinecke, Abdul-Karim Rafeq, Fu'ad Sidawi, and the late Farid Zayn al-Din in Damascus.

I reserve for last a special debt of gratitude to two very special people – Ramez Tomeh and Mary Christina Wilson. Ramez personally introduced me to Damascus, its old social classes and families, led me through its ancient and modern quarters, and instructed me in the ways landownership conferred power and influence in Syria. This book has profited immensely from Mary's profound understanding of Arab nationalist politics, her keen editorial skills and steady and selfless support.

Cambridge, Massachusetts   P.S.K.
September 1982

Introduction

Intellectual histories of the origins and content of Arab nationalism abound and insofar as these histories deal with the birthplace of Arab nationalism they must discuss political life in Syria just before World War I. Few histories, however, investigate the social conditions which gave birth to this ideology and which rendered it uniquely useful to Syrians, enabling Arab nationalism to become the reigning political idea in the Arab East after the War.

This study will attempt to situate Arab nationalism in the social and political environment in which it evolved in its infancy. It is a study of one social class in one town, Damascus. It is my argument that Damascus supplied a disproportionate share of the leading lights guiding the growth of the Arab nationalist movement in the early years of the twentieth century and that most important nationalist politicians in Damascus emerged from a single class in that city.[1] This class, which I shall call the 'landowning-bureaucratic class', began to assume its shape in the last half of the nineteenth century – that of a fairly well-integrated network of propertied and office-holding urban families which was to produce the political leadership in Damascus and other Syrian towns for several generations. And it was out of a struggle for power and position between two factions of this leadership that the idea of Arabism emerged as a political movement, one ultimately with widespread appeal in the Arab countries.[2]

The city as the locus of political power and influence in Syria dates from antiquity. Owing to the urban monopolization of administrative, judicial and commercial services, the city enforced an interdependence between itself and its agricultural and pastoral hinterland in which the hinterland was generally subordinate. This balance of power came increasingly to favor the city as it grew in size, for along with it government also grew. Pastoral nomads ultimately depended on the city as a commercial outlet for the hides, meat and dairy products derived from their herds of camels, sheep and goats. Hinterland villages depended on the city for protection, economic facilities and social services. By controlling these services the city was able to control the mode of production in the countryside, decide what was to be produced, gather the surplus, and direct its flow. The Syrian city also lay on international trade routes and was an organizing center for commerce and industry. In the case of Damascus, it served as the gathering center for Muslims from the North and East who wished to make the pilgrimage, itself both a pious and a commercial activity. As a regional capital with a concentrated and preponderant population, it was also the nexus of political life between the province and the imperial capital.[3]

During the four centuries of Ottoman rule in Syria, officials were sent from Istanbul to administer the provincial cities and, from there, the respective regions or administrative districts. Ottoman governors were usually perceived as outsiders; often they stood at a distance from the peoples they ruled and did not speak Arabic. Just as often, their superiors in the imperial capital placed checks on their authority such as preventing governors from having at their disposal the standing forces required to impose absolute control over the cities and their hinterland. Consequently these officials of the state had to make use of local elements with independent political and social influence in order to supplement or disguise the power they derived from Istanbul and to fill gaps in their local knowledge and experience. The need to tap local sources of influence allowed a particular type of politics to emerge which gave a degree of stability and continuity to political life in Syria. This mode of politics operated throughout the Ottoman era (and has been identified in earlier periods such as the Mamluk era) but perhaps most vividly in the eighteenth and nineteenth centuries. Albert Hourani has called it the 'politics of notables,'[4] as the notables or patricians were the local sources of influence in Syrian cities recognized and utilized by their externally imposed governors.

A notable recruited to aid the ruler must already be a leader in his society, hence his recruitment. Recruitment was not generally effected by coercion, for the notable's self-achieved position of leadership was enhanced through access to a legitimate authority. Indeed, one goal of achieving an independent local position of power was often to attract the notice of the imperial authority so that influence could be enhanced and aggrandized far beyond the local capabilities of a notable on his own. The notable–politician served as an intermediary or a broker for the imperial authority and for the society from which he came. To be a successful broker the notable could not appear to oppose the interests of the overlord for he risked being deprived of his access to authority; nor could he jeopardize the interests of his local clientele, for he risked losing his independent influence and thus his usefulness to the ruler.

The norm was for the notables to defend the social order and political status quo by supporting the government. Indeed, urban leaders acted in partnership with the government to ensure stability. But there were also occasions when the notables could be found leading protest movements against the government by mobilizing those popular forces from which they derived their independent influence. Such occasions might arise when a particularly strong government sought to dissolve the partnership or compact or when it became too weak to uphold its end of the bargain. Rarely, however, did the notables seek to overthrow, by some revolutionary act, the Ottoman system of rule. In any case, their political role was never institutionalized and, as Hourani suggests, it remained informal and often 'ambiguous.'[5]

The independent influence of some urban leaders was rooted in the 'inherited prestige of an ancient socio-religious position.'[6] These notables belonged to ranking families in the local religious establishment, controlled tax farms, and were often intimately tied to the Muslim commercial bourgeoisie. In the last decades of Ottoman rule these urban leaders and their families were to successfully transform their traditional type of influence into a stabler type of power based on landowning and office-holding in the growing secular wing of the state bureaucracy, a base far better suited to turn-of-the-century Ottoman realities. Meanwhile, other urban leaders had gained local influence comparatively recently. Their influence was rooted in military and commercial position (often the two went hand-in-hand) which they also were able to transform into a landowning and office-holding base of power. The point to emphasize here is that the vast majority of urban leaders in Syria came from the network of powerful and influential city families that constituted the landowning-bureaucratic class.

Before looking more closely at the formation of the landowning-bureaucratic class in Damascus, the political leadership it produced, this leadership's style and behavior, and its critical contribution to translating the idea of Arabism into a political movement in the early twentieth century, two important questions require at least tentative answers. First, what is meant by the use of the term 'class' in this study? And secondly, why were members of the landowning-bureaucratic class and not members of other classes able to assume seats at the summit of political life in Syria in the nineteenth century alongside representatives of the Ottoman government and an increasingly active group of European consular officials?[7]

Drawing on Hanna Batatu's conceptualization of class with regard to an Arab (Iraqi) society, a class is first of all 'an economically-based formation, though it ultimately refers to the social position of the constituent individuals or families in its varied aspects.'[8] It must be defined with respect to property or, more accurately, in its relationships to the means of production. Furthermore, the existence of a major class presumes the existence of at least one other class with a different set of relationships to the means of production. But like Batatu I accept at least two other qualifications. First in each major class a certain degree of internal differentiation exists such that the class may be composed of a hierarchy of subclasses which, in turn, 'may be related to one another as are distinct classes.'[9]

Secondly, the existence of a class should not presuppose that it need at 'every point of its historical existence act or feel as a unit . . . it need not be an organized and self-conscious group.'[10] Even though the behavior of class members may be 'class-conditioned,' they may not be 'class conscious,'[11] despite a strong similarity of interests and inclinations. For instance, within a single class we may find elements such as big landowners with interests on the rise and big landowners with interests on the downgrade lining up on different sides of the political fence on specific issues, especially in the absence of direct external threats or challenges to their class. Indeed, for class members to feel obliged to close their ranks and clarify their common interests as a class on 'crucial' political issues, there has to be a need.[12] Otherwise, intra-class (or even ethnic) conflict, expressed in terms of vertically structured factionalism, rather than conflict between classes, is likely to be the active force behind the emergence of particular social and political movements.

In the case of Syria (as well as Iraq) it is only in the nineteenth century that we begin to witness the formation of classes on a significant scale, the outcome of Syria's gradual economic integration into the world market. Classes undoubtedly existed before this time but they were much more difficult to identify and their lifespans much shorter mainly because their relations to the means of production and especially to property were much less stable. Indeed, security of non-urban property and the legal right to pass this property on from generation to generation, free of the regular threat of state confiscation or nomadic disruptions of settled life, are phenomena which appear widely for the first time in the nineteenth century. However, the crystallization of classes in Syria under the impact of capitalist development was a very uneven process. Before World War I few classes were 'sharply identifiable' or constituted relatively stable formations. Few evinced signs of strong political consciousness. The formation and consolidation of classes were still in process and some classes could still be differentiated along ethnic or religious lines, or by income level, or by degree of access to the state, or by the character of their interaction with Europe.[13]

4

One class in Syria, however, seems to have been relatively more stable and more easily identifiable than others; it also happened to dominate the local political scene. The emergence of the landowning-bureaucratic class in Syria correlates with the process of the private appropriation of property which proceeded without interruption in the second half of the nineteenth century, not only in the towns and their immediate hinterland but on the margins of cultivation as well. Agrarian commercialization coupled with the development of modern means of communication and transport helped to create the framework for the private appropriation of property and its consolidation in the hands of an increasingly inter-related network of urban families with ties to the imperial capital through the provincial bureaucracy. Indeed these families received the support of the state, which itself was supported by a new more efficient military and civil administration. Land, when combined with public office, produced for a family and its individual members unrivalled power on the local scene. And this was particularly so in the interior towns of Syria like Damascus where a high degree of social and cultural homogeneity existed between the urban masses and the local upper class. Here a socially cohesive network of urban families not only provided vital goods and services to the urban masses, but they also defended their faith and posed as the natural guardians of their culture. In other words, in Damascus and other towns an integrated Sunni-Muslim upper class both patronized and represented a predominantly Sunni-Muslim populace, providing it with its sociopolitical and cultural leaders who embodied and articulated its beliefs and enforced its code of moral behavior. As a result political culture in the cities was relatively unified and integrated, and politics was defined by the interaction of the local upper class with the Ottoman administration.[14]

By contrast to the relative ease with which the landowning-bureaucratic class consolidated its power locally after 1860 nearly all other classes witnessed a steady erosion of their positions, some completely dissolving in the face of intensifying European economic pressures and the forces of Ottoman centralization. In the countryside, small peasant proprietors were caught up in the mesh of capital. As market-oriented agriculture displaced subsistence agriculture and farming methods changed, the small peasant family or village community found itself besieged by land- and profit-hungry city notables-cum-moneylenders. Many peasants and, in some cases, whole villages lost their lands to the notables and turned to sharecropping; others, less fortunate, were completely dispossessed and either became wage laborers on the estates of big landowners or fled to small towns and cities. Similarly, the traditional bonds binding nomadic tribes to their chiefs were gradually broken under the increasing weight of a reinvigorated Ottoman state which sought to impose stability in the countryside by subduing and sedentarizing marauding tribes. Two methods were employed side-by-side: military force; and financial inducements to the chiefs in the form of land grants and special tax concessions, which eventually were to turn chiefs into big landlords and their tribesmen into cultivators on their lands.[15]

Urban life also underwent important changes in the course of the nineteenth century. Not only was there a shift in the relative power of Syrian cities from those in the interior to those on the coast (especially Beirut) in conjunction with the dramatic growth of trade with Europe, there was also a gradual shift in the location of power within the city from the old quarters and bazaars to new quarters with a European ambience and some of the physical amenities of the modern European city. In the old city, the traditional crafts found it increasingly difficult to compete with the flood of cheaper and often higher-quality European-manufactured goods; many crafts disappeared altogether. It is true that some crafts in towns like Damascus and Aleppo did enjoy a revival in the late nineteenth century by concentrating on special or restricted markets; ultimately, however, they were unable to develop new, cheaper production techniques.[16] Similarly, Muslim merchants engaged in regional trade also suffered heavy losses in their competition with European trading houses and their local agents.

These agents belonged to the indigenous religious minorities, Christians and some Jews with whom the European felt most comfortable. The protection these religious minorities sought and received from the European Powers and the education afforded them by European and American missionaries, specially prepared them to serve as agents of European commercial and diplomatic interests. The Capitulations were eventually extended to permit foreign consulates to offer Christians commercial protection that included special privileges such as paying lower rates of duty than Muslim merchants paid for exports and imports. And though Christians occasionally faced waves of persecution by the Muslim majority, after 1860 they began to enjoy a new era of security and prosperity owing to increased European pressures on the Ottoman state to guarantee their protection. As a result the Christian commercial bourgeoisie not only deepened its involvement in the export–import trade, but these protégés of Europe also established themselves as the moneylenders and bankers for Muslim artisans, landowners, and peasants.

Apart from the landowning-bureaucratic class, the only other class in Syria whose interests can be said to have risen in the second half of the nineteenth century was the Christian commercial bourgeoisie. One question, however, remains to be posed: if indeed it is true that the Ottoman system was working to the distinct advantage of both classes, why then did they both appear to be working against the system by the early twentieth century? Why were Syrian Christians among the earliest proponents of the new idea of 'Arabism' while members of the Muslim landowning-bureaucratic class were the first to translate this idea into a political movement with nationalist dimensions before World War I? As we shall see, both classes were unable in fact to enjoy the full benefits of the Ottoman system. Syrian Christians were already threatened with a loss of position by the end of the nineteenth century while a fraction of the landowning-bureaucratic class actually experienced a relative loss of position in the early twentieth century. In other words, their interests could not keep pace with their rising expectations. And any systematic explanation of the rise of Arab nationalism must take into consideration the widening gap that was developing at this time between both classes' interests and their expectations.

Chapter 1

The political configuration of Damascus in 1860

In the heat of July 1860, an outbreak of violence rocked Damascus. Mobs of beduin, Druzes and other neighboring villagers, Kurdish auxiliaries, and street toughs perpetrated eight days of massacre and pillage mainly in the ancient Christian quarter of Bab Tuma—eight days that would have resounding effects on political developments in Damascus for generations.

This event gave the Ottoman government an opportunity to reassert its control over Damascus. Fu'ad Pasha, the reformist Foreign Minister who had negotiated a temporary settlement of the civil war in Mount Lebanon, followed the newly appointed Ottoman governor into Damascus, backed by four thousand troops. Fu'ad knew his task well. In order to obviate French intervention in the name of 'oriental Christendom' he hammered out a settlement which compensated the demoralized Christian community and distributed the burden of guilt equitably and swiftly. On one hand, he set up a committee of prominent Damascenes, both Muslim and Christian, to assess compensation for the vast losses suffered by the inhabitants of Bab Tuma. On the other, he jailed, exiled or hanged scores of high-ranking Muslim notables and functionaries for their failure to prevent the bloodbath that had caused some six thousand deaths.[1]

The Christian committee members formed a powerful lobby under Fu'ad Pasha's protection and managed to gain ample compensation for themselves and their clients. Reconstruction in Bab Tuma commenced immediately and the inhabitants were encouraged to return.[2] However, thousands who had made a hurried exodus to the safer confines of Mount Lebanon and Beirut could not be convinced that the climate in Damascus was suitable for return. Meanwhile, the Christian leaders on the committee took advantage of their position to divert a considerable portion of the allotted indemnity to their immediate families. Nevertheless, Christians who remained were generally satisfied with Fu'ad Pasha's generosity, derived by unlining the pockets of wealthy Damascus Muslims.[3]

By the end of August the task of meting out punishment was complete.

The list of those exiled or executed read like a *Who's Who* of the town. The top political figures to suffer Fu'ad Pasha's condemnation were mostly members of the local *majlis* (council). This formidable body had caused the Ottoman government many headaches during the previous twenty years due to its stubborn resistance to a series of centralizing reforms instituted by Istanbul that conflicted with the interests of its members. Fu'ad Pasha was cautious enough, however, not to send the leading lights of the *majlis* to the gallows.[4] Banishment caused less local reaction than execution, yet helped to shift the balance of power in Damascus from the *majlis* towards the Ottoman authorities.

Christians witnessing the events of July and August 1860, but chronicling them several years later, blamed the leaders of Muslim society for failing to carry out their traditional duty of protecting the Christian minority in accordance with the *shari'a* (the revealed law of Islam). For such dereliction their punishment was fitting.[5] Writing in retrospect, when relations between Muslims and Christians had been smoothed over by outside pressure from Istanbul and Europe, these Christian chroniclers saw nothing peculiar in Muslims rushing to defend Christians against Muslims.

Another account, quite different in its focus from the Christian narrations, was written by a member of one of the leading Muslim families of Damascus. Abu'l Su'ud al-Hasibi was a young man-about-town in 1860, the scion of a wealthy family claiming descent from the Prophet. Writing some eight years after the events, he was more interested in describing the reaction of local Damascus notables than in providing a blow-by-blow account of the massacre itself. Al-Hasibi posited that the leading notables of Damascus were shocked and dismayed by the massacre in Bab Tuma, but that they could in no way be held responsible for the ugly actions of mobs run amok as they had not been 'consulted or notified' at the time of the disruption. He went on to defend the notability for trying to control the course of events once they had become known, though he admits that the notables were largely unsuccessful.[6] The interesting point is that the Damascus notability – believed to be the strongest social and political force in the city – proved to be incapable of controlling the situation.

Abu'l Su'ud al-Hasibi considered the Damascus notability or 'honorable citizenry' (*ahl al-'ird*) to be composed of members of the prominent religious families of the day. He did allow, however, exceptions from a long list of secular dignitaries to pass for 'honorable citizens.' For instance, he included his relations, the Rikabis, wealthy landlord-merchants of noble beduin origin, and the 'Azms, descendants of the powerful eighteenth-century governors of Damascus.[7] Al-Hasibi went to great lengths to absolve his notability of all guilt in the massacre of 1860, and severely censured other groups for bringing Damascus to its knees in front of the Ottoman authorities. These other groups were, according to al-Hasibi, the merchants, tradesmen, local military leaders, and the recent Kurdish and Hawrani immigrants living in the suburbs of al-Salhiyya and al-Maydan.[8]

The notables: some qualifications

The political configuration of Damascus during the Ottoman period suggests two areas of political power: one was external in the guise of the Ottoman state and included the governor and imperial troops, and the other was internal, filled by local groups possessing varying degrees of independent social and political influence who acted as intermediaries between the state and the populace in the town. (We could add here a second kind of intermediary that asserted itself in the nineteenth century, the European consul.) Historians regularly refer to these local inter-mediaries as 'notables' (most commonly *a'yan* in Arabic) and the historical record suggests that their relations with the state were rarely stable before the late nineteenth century. Recently, Karl Barbir has out-lined the changing character of relations between the Damascus notables and the Ottoman government in four consecutive periods of Damascus history: (1) from the Ottoman conquest of Syria in 1516 till the end of the sixteenth century when 'notables conformed to the norms established by Süleyman the Magnificent,' that is, when Ottoman central authority was at the height of its effectiveness and therefore commanded the support of the notables; (2) the seventeenth century when 'notables first tested their strength vis-à-vis the central authority and won important tax concessions,' including the right to hereditary tax farms; (3) the first sixty years of the eighteenth century when a reinvigorated 'provincial governorship' checked the independence of notables; (4) the period after 1760 when a weakened central authority came to rely on notables as 'semiindependent surrogates rather than as intermediaries' in Damascus and elsewhere in Syria.[9] But to complete Barbir's periodization of the history of relations between Damascus notables and the Ottoman government, it is necessary to add four more periods: (5) the 1830s when the Egyptian occupation of Syria inaugurated an unprecedented era of intensified state control in Damascus (and other Syrian towns) which severely checked the authority of the notables; (6) 1841–60, when the return of Ottoman control was accompanied by a series of centralizing reforms that were not, for the most part, warmly received by the notables of Damascus whose resistance helped to precipitate the crisis of 1860;

(7) 1860–1908, when a reinvigorated central authority drew the notables more completely into the state administration as a provincial aristocracy of service, especially after 1880; (8) from 1909, when the Young Turks imposed rigid centralizing reforms and 'Turkification' policies that caused resentment among a growing number of notables, who began to demand greater autonomy for their province and, in some cases, to agitate for separation from the Ottoman Empire.

In considering the Damascus notables and their evolution under Ottoman rule two qualifications are necessary. The first has been made by Albert Hourani and amplified by Barbir. They point out that even in the late eighteenth and early nineteenth centuries, when Damascus notables enjoyed their greatest measure of independent power, their authority could still be checked by the state if it got too far out of hand, either by playing notables against one another or by direct military intervention. The point is that there was always some measure of Ottoman central control over Damascus.[10]

Our second qualification concerns the very use of the term 'notables.' Historians have used this term primarily as a political concept to describe those local forces in provincial society with independent influence in the urban population and access to the government who can act as intermediaries or 'brokers' for both. Moreover, historians have been mainly interested in the period 1760–1860, when a 'politics of notables' was perhaps most active and visible. In our opinion, however, the use of 'notables' as a political or sociological concept with which to analyze the configuration of power in Damascus and other Ottoman-Syrian towns before 1860 can create serious analytical problems, unless the category of 'notables' is given more precise dimensions.[11] The term 'notables' generally corrals the *'ulama'* (Muslim religious experts), including the *ashraf* (descendants of the Prophet), a group of secular dignitaries composed of wealthy merchants and tax farmers who did not belong to the Muslim religious establishment, and the *aghawat* (chiefs) of local military garrisons into one stable. This implies that the 'notable estate' constituted an identifiable political unit, if not a socially homogeneous one. Yet, our historical evidence suggests that these three groups, each in the possession of a certain degree of independent influence, often did not possess similar power bases or even similar modes of political behavior. Before 1860 they rarely took political action in unison and they clearly did not belong to a single social class, either 'in itself' or 'for itself.'

Rather, the religious establishment, the secular dignitaries and the *aghawat* were politically organized on an informal basis; they were factionalized along family, kinship and economic lines; and they were

11

rooted in different and often competitive sections of Damascus where their power and influence were most strongly felt. Although these groups always sought to control the active forces of society and to have access to the state, they tended to attract different local followings, and their relations with the state differed, sometimes radically.

Thus, prior to 1860, it may be more useful to discuss the internal distribution of power in Damascus in terms of the socioeconomic and political orientation of three groups. On one hand, there were the *'ulama'*, including the *ashraf*, who constituted for al-Hasibi the acknowledged social and political leadership of Damascus—his 'honorable citizenry' or 'notability.' Mostly they resided within the city walls and dominated the religious, judicial and educational institutions and, along with a few well-placed laity, were found in the upper echelons of the local bureaucracy. On the other hand, there were the *aghawat* of the local garrisons who resided in the socially heterogeneous suburbs of the town and played active roles in the grain and livestock trades. Meanwhile, an intermediate and pivotal third group, composed of tax farmers and merchants resident within the city walls and the newer adjacent quarters, had not as yet acquired a base in local government. Until the 1830s these groups were socially differentiated from one another. But after 1830, and particularly in the 1840s and 1850s, a gradual social merging evolved in Damascus, encouraged by the Egyptian occupation, the Ottoman reformation and the increased commercialization of the Syrian economy.

With the reassertion of Ottoman control over Damascus in 1841, a growing number of secular dignitaries started to compete for posts in both the local and the imperial bureaucracy. They then used their offices to strengthen their material resource base in the commercialized sector of the economy. In the process they enhanced their social status and political power. Achievement of status and power is symbolized by their becoming eligible to marry into the leading families of the religious establishment.

Likewise, after 1840, the chiefs of the local garrisons had an opportunity to aggrandize their position. Although the *aghawat* had already begun to lose their traditional power base as garrisons were disbanded, first during the Egyptian occupation of the 1830s and then in the 1850s by a reinvigorated Ottoman central authority, they were left two outlets by which to preserve and enlarge their influence in their quarters. Through their control of the grain and livestock trade the *aghawat* managed to entrench themselves in the commercialized sector of the economy and to penetrate the middle layers of the expanding provincial bureaucracy. Some acquired the status of established notables in their own quarters and broadened their social and political influence in the city by intermarrying with other locally influential families. By 1860, the merchant *aghawat* and middle-level bureaucrats had gained influence with the general populace such that during the events of that year they proved to be a more effective force of social control than the more prestigious group of religious families.

The 1860 crisis contributed to the restructuring of the political configuration of Damascus; by the end of the century political and social leadership in the town emerged from a single, comparatively cohesive, social class. To understand how and why this change occurred it is necessary to look more closely at the political configuration of Damascus on the eve of the 1860 crisis.

The religious establishment

Before the 1860s, the Damascus notability was drawn almost exclusively from families in control of the key religious positions in the city. These scholarly families, many of whom claimed descent from the Prophet and thus constituted the only acknowledged 'aristocracy of blood in Islam,' emerged in the seventeenth and eighteenth centuries to form the heart of al-Hasibi's 'honorable citizenry' by 1860. Members of these families had competed for over 150 years for the most important religious posts in Damascus: *Khatib* (Preacher) at the Umayyad Mosque, Hanafi *Mufti* (jurisconsult), and *Naqib al-Ashraf* (doyen of the descendants of the Prophet). The ability to control these posts and their respective endowments (*awqaf*) determined each family's position in the social hierarchy of the city.[12]

The provincial '*ulama*' in the eighteenth and early nineteenth centuries depended as much on factional machinations in Istanbul to secure and retain their posts in the judicial, educational and religious institutions as they did on their reputations as scholars and teachers of the religious sciences and interpreters of the *shari'a*. Indeed, as local military leaders and secular dignitaries became increasingly independent from Istanbul during the course of the eighteenth century, ranking Damascus '*ulama*' were unable to maintain position without a powerful patron in the imperial capital.[13].

Competition for the posts of *Khatib* and Hanafi *Mufti* was especially fierce. As the most important preacher in Damascus, the *Khatib* at the Umayyad Mosque served as an important link between imperial government and local leadership, a conduit for information and a molder of public opinion, and this gave the incumbent considerable political and religious leverage.[14] Taj al-Din al-Mahasini, a prosperous merchant with an interest in theological questions, used his stature in society to gain the ear of the *Shaykh al-Islam* in Istanbul.[15] By 1650, two of his sons had served as *Khatib* at the Umayyad Mosque, and links with Istanbul during most of the eighteenth and early nineteenth centuries kept the post an al-Mahasini preserve.[16] But by the 1860s the Mahasinis were challenged by another family with powerful connections in Istanbul and on the death of Khalil al-Mahasini in 1869, the post devolved on the Khatib family.[17]

To be selected by the *Shaykh al-Islam* as *mufti* of one of the four schools (*madhhab*) of *Sunni* or 'orthodox' Muslim law was as high an honor as a member of the '*ulama*' could hope to attain within the religious establishment. A *mufti* would issue his legal opinion (*fatwa*) in a case, according to his *madhhab*'s particular interpretation, and was available for legal consultation. The position of Hanafi *Mufti* was especially sensitive to Istanbul.

Until the eighteenth century nearly half of the Damascene '*ulama*' belonged to the Shafi'i *madhhab* (school of law) while the official Ottoman *madhhab*, as sanctioned by Istanbul, was Hanafi.[18] Throughout the seventeenth century the 'Imadi family controlled the post of Hanafi *Mufti*, but during the course of the eighteenth century they were challenged by newcomers to Damascus, the Muradis, who originated from Samarkand and belonged to the Naqshabandi *sufi* (mystic) order. The Muradis reached Damascus in 1685 after residing several years in Istanbul, where they had forged links with powerful viziers and the Sultan.[19] These links enabled the Muradis to acquire villages near Damascus in the form of hereditary tax farms (*malikanes*). By the middle of the eighteenth century they had used further connections to replace the 'Imadis as *muftis*.[20] The Muradis retained this post till the end of the century when they lost it to the Hamza family, though they continued to hold important juridical and administrative positions in the religious institutions throughout the nineteenth century.[21]

The local religious post which conferred the most social prestige, though not necessarily the most political influence, was the office of *Naqib al-Ashraf*. Throughout the eighteenth and nineteenth centuries the post of *Naqib* alternated between two families, the Hamzas and the 'Ajlanis.[22] Both families claimed the position on historical evidence accumulated over several centuries. The 'Ajlanis acquired *malikanes* in the early eighteenth century[23] and by the turn of the nineteenth used this source of wealth to successfully challenge the Hamzas.[24] The latter were versatile, however, and their family members often managed to find employment in other branches of the religious institution. Although Istanbul did not find it necessary to impose its own candidate as *Naqib*, probably because no threatening independent power stemmed from this position, both the Hamzas and the 'Ajlanis conveniently switched from the Shafi'i to the Hanafi *madhhab* in the eighteenth century to counter any possible Ottoman interference.[25]

The prominent families of religious scholars in the decades leading up to the events of 1860 gradually broke with localist tendencies and jumped aboard the Ottoman bandwagon. Most switched from the Shafi'i to the Hanafi *madhhab* and began to depend as much on influence in Istanbul as on local sources of support in Damascus to gain high office. The contemporary accounts draw attention to the fact that the chief *sufi* orders in the city (Qadiriyya, Naqshabandiyya, and Khalwatiyya) were often controlled by shaykhs from these noted scholarly families.[26] It might be expected that leadership of these orders would have yielded some sort of independent influence as a countervailing force to Ottoman pressures. However, the little evidence available points to the orthodoxy of the largest orders and suborders and their rather subdued political activity. It may be that the religious dignitaries dominated these orders merely to gain a trump in the competition for access to patrons in Istanbul.

The top layers of the religious establishment seem to have been comparatively wealthy. Before gaining office many of the families had already enjoyed imperial favor in the form of hereditary tax farms in the vicinity of Damascus. Others had control over artisanal workshops in the city and the retail trade in manufactures for local consumption and for regional export. The Damascus *'ulama'* did not constitute an official group; rather their families had been rooted for generations in the provincial economy and their patronage of certain kinds of commerce and the guilds only enhanced their social position and influence.

The religious establishment was by no means a closed group; mobility in and out was common. Upstarts might be frowned on, but in a few generations they could gain full-fledged membership to the club. There is no better example of how a family could ascend to the apex of the local religious establishment than that of the Hasibis. Sometime in the late seventeenth century a man calling himself al-'Attar (the perfumer) came from his native village south of Homs to settle in Damascus. By the third generation certain members of the family had entered the scholarly professions, though there is no evidence that other members had given up their trade. In the fourth generation 'Ali al-'Attar (1742–1827), who had gained some degree of notoriety as a man of learning and a jurist, set out to establish his family as descendants of the Prophet. He even changed his surname to al-Hasib (the nobly born).[27] 'Ali's son, Ahmad (1792–1876), furthered his father's ambition by acquiring large landholdings near Damascus in the form of grants from the Ottoman government.[28] He became a member of the *majlis* and felt obliged to move his residence from the popular 'Uqayba quarter to the more

15

aristocratic al-Qanawat.[29] By 1860, Ahmad al-Hasibi was a wealthy member of the Damascene *ashraf*, a revered notable in the inner city, and the patron of his quarter.

In general, the higher *'ulama'* adjusted easily to new Ottoman pressures in the eighteenth and early nineteenth centuries. While they remained an important force in local society through their control of religious institutions, judicial and educational systems and charitable endowments, they also became more closely tied to Istanbul.[30] By becoming more 'cosmopolitan,'[31] however, they began to lose their traditional position of independent leadership over the local populace.

The Egyptian occupation of Syria in 1831 was the first shock wave to rattle the religious establishment in Damascus. On behalf of Muhammad 'Ali, his son, Ibrahim Pasha, inaugurated a series of reforms that led to the placement of Greater Syria under a single administration with headquarters in Damascus.[32] Ibrahim tried to reorganize the Syrian economy into a supplier of raw materials for Egypt's nascent government-owned industries by establishing monopolies over silk, cotton and soap. He also enforced stricter taxation measures including a new personal income tax. Although his measures fell hardest on the popular classes in the cities, Ibrahim also placed the urban notables and especially the religious establishment under stricter supervision. For instance, he limited the religious court system (*mahakim al-shari'a*) to cases involving personal status, a move which the *'ulama'* rightly perceived as a direct assault on their authority. Ibrahim Pasha also placed charitable endowments under direct government supervision, putting religious leaders in financial straits. Meanwhile, the new *majlis shura* (advisory council) in Damascus denied them adequate representation. And Ibrahim Pasha was not opposed to arresting and even executing dissident urban notables.[33]

The most objectionable development witnessed by the religious establishment and other members of the Muslim upper classes in Damascus (and other towns) concerned the growth of equality for religious minorities and the opening of their sacred and socially conservative city to direct European influences. Christians could now be found on the *majlis shura* and they were allowed to trade in grain and livestock, 'previously the exclusive domain of Muslims.' Meanwhile, European and especially British commerce with Syria expanded in this period to the benefit of the minorities and at the expense of the Muslim merchant classes.[34]

A decade of Egyptian rule had clearly damaged the interests of the Muslim upper classes of Damascus and in particular those of the religious establishment. Unable to resist the occupation, they rejoiced

16

widely when the European powers on behalf of Istanbul forced Ibrahim Pasha to withdraw his troops from Syria. They did not realize, however, that the return of Ottoman rule would result in efforts to continue many of Ibrahim's reform projects.

The return of the Ottomans to Damascus was accompanied by a program of reform, the *Tanzimat*. Although one of the major goals of the *Tanzimat* was to centralize administration in Istanbul, the *walis* (governors) sent out from the capital to govern the provinces were so inhibited by central government checks on their power that they were forced to align themselves with provincial factions in order to exercise any authority. The reforms were to be enacted by the *wali* through a new local *majlis*. Its membership included familiar religious and secular dignitaries. The *majlis* was given powers to 'set taxes and customs, supervise their collection, register and regulate land transactions, approve appointments of petty officials, oversee the recruitment of police and adjudicate civil cases.'[35] *Majlis* members were also able to increase their personal and family fortunes by granting themselves tax farms around Damascus.[36] With such powers the notability was able to return to its former standing.

The *majlis* used its powers to block those reforms promulgated by Istanbul which were inimical to its interests. Most objectionable were measures giving minorities more equality with Muslims. The *majlis* did implement, however, certain unpopular reforms to bolster its position vis-à-vis Istanbul which coincidentally improved members' financial situation. A compulsory draft scheme was directed at the masses while the *'ulama'* and secular notables secured exemptions for their sons and relatives. The burden of taxation was distributed unevenly, primarily on the backs of artisans and peasants.[37] Already the *'ulama'* had sacrificed some of their independent influence in the city prior to the Egyptian occupation; such unpopular reforms only served to widen the gap between the city's traditional leadership and the populace in and around Damascus.

To return to al-Hasibi's comments on the inability of the 'honorable citizenry' to control the outburst of violence in July 1860, one factor stands out. The traditional urban leadership, by using its domination of the new *majlis* to consolidate its political strength also became increasingly estranged from both the local populace and Istanbul. This allowed other kinds of leaders to emerge and to display their independent influence with the populace and before the Ottoman authorities.

The secular dignitaries

During the late eighteenth and early nineteenth centuries, as the traditional socioreligious leadership in Damascus grew more dependent on Istanbul, other families in the city capitalized on the weakening of imperial control to establish themselves as provincial leaders. The most prominent family to secure significant independent political power in Damascus was the 'Azm family.

Ibrahim al-'Azm, a rural notable possibly of Turkish stock, went to Ma'arrat al-Nu'man, a trading center between Aleppo and Hama catering to beduin, to restore order in the mid-seventeenth century. Although he was killed, his sons, Isma'il and Sulayman, completed their father's task and were rewarded with hereditary tax farms in Homs, Hama and Ma'arrat al-Nu'man. Using their new wealth and an important connection with an Ottoman agent, they obtained successive governorships of the Damascus province in the eighteenth century. In the process they brought a certain measure of stability to that province.

The 'Azms settled in Hama and Damascus and through high offices in the Syrian provinces increased their wealth and their independence from Istanbul.[38] They also purchased vast urban properties which, in addition to their hereditary tax farms, kept the family and its various branches financially secure for generations.[39] To symbolize their wealth and power the 'Azms built mosques, schools, public baths, coffee houses, *khans* and elaborate palaces in Damascus. The family was also interested in securing the support of the Damascus establishment. Indeed, to enhance their social and political prestige, the 'Azms developed trading alliances with leading merchant families, some of whom belonged to the religious establishment, and did not hesitate to contract marriages with such families. Moreover, to counter the growing challenge of the local janissary garrisons in the eighteenth century the 'Azms successfully played them against the imperial troops, siding with the latter. This enabled them to carry out perhaps their single most important function as governors of Damascus: to guarantee the safe passage of the annual pilgrimage caravan that originated in Damascus and had to pass through its southern suburbs where the *aghawat* of the local janissaries were most firmly entrenched. The pilgrimage also provided the 'Azms and the families of the old city and northern suburbs, to whom they were linked, with significant commercial opportunities from the long trading season that accompanied the pilgrimage.[40] And though on the death in 1783 of the 'Azm *wali*, Muhammad Pasha, the family's political star dimmed, the 'Azms remained the most influential family of secular dignitaries in Damascus for generations. The 'Azms, for instance, were one of the few non-scholarly families to sit on the local *majlis* between 1841 and 1860, and thus al-Hasibi included them among his 'honorable citizens.'[41]

There also emerged in the eighteenth century a group of non-scholarly families composed of merchants and tax farmers resident in the old city. They derived their influence from their position in the economy of the Syrian provinces but not from the upper echelons of the provincial administration or their social status.

As merchants (*tujjar*), they concentrated on organizing artisanal production by supplying traditional industries with raw materials and by selling manufactured goods on the regional market. These merchants had less of a stake, however, in the international and transit trade in spices, silk and other luxury goods in which the Christian and Jewish minorities featured prominently as agents of European trading houses.[42]

In addition to their monopoly of regional trade, the Muslim merchants of Damascus were active as provisioners of the annual pilgrimage to the Holy Cities. The 30,000–50,000 pilgrims who joined the caravan in Damascus each year required provisions for two to three months including vast supplies of grain and preserved foods such as dried fruits, which Damascus was eminently suited to supply. Some of these merchants travelled with the caravan and returned 'with merchandise from Africa, Yemen and India such as coffee, spices, textiles and slaves.'[43]

Many of these same merchant families acquired hereditary tax farms in the eighteenth and early nineteenth centuries. After the Ottoman conquest of Syria in 1516, a new method of revenue collection was imposed from Istanbul –the *iltizam* or tax-farming system.[44] During the following two centuries prosperous Damascus merchants, some religious dignitaries and local janissary chiefs acquired tax farms. Their acquisition was not always a sign of particular imperial favor, however, as tax farms were also auctioned to the highest bidder. Originally these auctions were held annually, but in the eighteenth century the Ottoman government, now increasingly burdened by financial malaise and the inability to impose firm central authority over its provinces, was obliged to extend one-year occupancies of *iltizams* to lifetime tenures (*malikanes*). Damascus merchants were among those with the capital to purchase the hereditary rights to tax farms.[45]

By dominating the agricultural surplus–both from the irrigated gardens (al-Ghuta) around Damascus and in the more distant grain-producing plains–the cultivators and the local and regional markets in which the surplus was sold, the merchant-tax farmers became a powerful group in the city and its hinterland. In the period 1760 to 1830, when Ottoman central authority in the Syrian provinces suffered a serious loss of control from a variety of internal and external pressures, these secular

19

dignitaries took advantage of the situation to assert their independence from Istanbul. Some merchant tax farmers even married their daughters to the Ottoman governors in Damascus, enabling them to assert their influence over these officials in such fragile circumstances. Thus while the *'ulama'*, including the *ashraf*, grew more dependent on Istanbul for their positions, the secular dignitaries were able to distance themselves. And though both groups depended for the most part on similar sources of material wealth (trade and hereditary tax farms), the secular dignitaries still remained socially differentiated from families in the religious establishment and do not seem to have built a significant base in the provincial administration. The religious notables do not appear to have welcomed integration with the secular dignitaries, though a gradual merging process had begun to take place at the instigation of the 'Azms.

With the Egyptian occupation and the subsequent Ottoman efforts to revitalize state authority before 1860, the secular dignitaries found it increasingly difficult to defend their local independence from the forces of centralization. Some were encouraged to assume administrative positions in an expanding bureaucracy in order to protect and expand their material resource bases. In this way, some families distinguished themselves within the group of secular dignitaries. Indeed, al-Hasibi saw fit to include members of such families with greater political clout and enhanced social status as members of his 'honorable citizens.'[46] However, most of the group of merchant tax farmers remained socially differentiated from the religious establishment.

The *aghawat*

In the popular quarters on the outskirts of Damascus the local janissary garrisons were another source of independent authority. Throughout the sixteenth century the imperial janissaries had kept aloof from local life; they were stationed in the Citadel and took their orders directly from Istanbul. In time, however, they became lodged in Damascus (and other provincial towns like Aleppo) on a permanent basis and were actively involved in local and regional commerce and craft production. They also became closely identified with certain quarters of the town.[47] Their chiefs (*aghawat*) enlisted auxiliaries from these quarters and regimental membership became hereditary.[48] By the last half of the seventeenth century these local garrisons (*yerlıyye*) had become local paramilitary forces with independent means for political action. Indeed, their strength obliged the Ottoman state to appoint some *aghawat* as commanders of the pilgrimage. Yet Ottoman-appointed governors tried to check the power of the *yerlıyye* by playing them against their replacements in the

Citadel, the imperial janissaries or *kapıkulları*.[49] They were not always successful. Contemporary chroniclers and biographers of eighteenth-century Damascus suggest that whenever the town fell under local control, the *yerlıyye* were the effective rulers. If this suggestion was exaggerated, it does seem that the *yerlıyye* at least ruled their quarters.[50]

One stronghold of the *yerlıyye* was the Maydan, a long suburb stretching southward towards the Hawran and composed of numerous subquarters of immigrant peasants from Hawran, Druzes, beduin tribesmen, Christian artisans and prosperous grain and livestock merchants. There were also garrisons in the Shaghur quarter, northeast of the Maydan, and in al-Salhiyya, a northern village.[51] Little can be said about the ability of the *aghawat* to mobilize their quarters for political action. The sources suggest that the *aghawat* may have penetrated *sufi* orders and artisanal corporations (*asnaf*), such as the militant butchers' guild. But what support they consistently derived from these orders and corporations remains a mystery. In the Maydan some *aghawat* became protectors of the grain merchants, and we find *aghawat* entering the grain trade by the end of the eighteenth century. By the early nineteenth century some *aghawat* from the Maydan and other suburbs extended their military and political control into the Hawran and served the Ottoman government there in return for the right to hold tax farms.[52]

Local scholars from the religious establishment writing in the eighteenth century frequently mentioned their disdain for the *aghawat*, and other forces like the 'Kurds' (many *aghawat* were Kurds) and the 'riff-raff' of the popular quarters, who created a situation of instability in Damascus. Indeed, the general trade recession experienced in Syria in the late eighteenth century probably caused a deterioration in the conditions of life of the city's popular classes, who were most capable of revolting.[53]

In this period Damascus was swelling both topographically and demographically owing to a steady stream of beduin and peasants from Hawran and Kurdish tribes from eastern Anatolia. As village insecurity increased because of beduin raids and famine, hordes of Hawrani peasants were uprooted and driven towards the security of Damascus.[54] The Maydan was one of the few areas where these peasants could settle; it was on the Hawran side of Damascus and the guild system which excluded newcomers from working and residing in the older established quarters, was not as firmly entrenched there. The immigrants resorted to animal husbandry or farming and sought protection wherever available. As *aghawat* of local garrisons were also establishing roots in the Maydan at this time and looking for auxiliaries, they were in a position to offer newcomers protection. In a section of the sparsely settled suburb of al-Salhiyya, to the northwest of Damascus, a similar process was under way. Kurdish immigrants unable to penetrate the old city set up home there.[55] Their chiefs created paramilitary forces composed of their tribesmen, and the state awarded them the title of *agha* for policing the countryside. The anger and fear generated in the minds of the traditional urban leadership in Damascus as they confronted these new forces only become understandable when it is realized that this old guard was unable to muster political support with a growing proportion of the city's population.

In the first half of the nineteenth century the growing independent power base of the *aghawat* was enhanced by a series of factors. First, the *aghawat* came to dominate more completely the grain and livestock trades of the Maydan and other quarters, and to acquire *iltizams* and *malikanes* in the Hawran.[56] Secondly, through marriage with other *aghawat* families and the daughters of secular and religious leaders, they formed prestigious households in their respective quarters.[57] Finally, this movement towards integration on the periphery of Damascus was encouraged first by the Egyptian occupation of the 1830s and then by the revitalization of Ottoman central authority in the late 1850s. Although reform in the military establishment gradually checked the autonomy of local garrisons, the Ottoman state did open up careers in the army, local bureaucracy and police force to the *aghawat* and their auxiliaries.[58]

Many *aghawat* had taken advantage of two economic developments to become part of the corps of secular dignitaries. Through land grants or outright financial exploitation, the *aghawat* acquired control of agricultural production in the Hawran and dominated its peasantry. In the process they had seized a very powerful weapon: the ability to dominate the supply of grain to Damascus and to fix prices. Meanwhile, within the old city, traditional industries, such as cloth weaving, were being hard hit by the influx of manufactured goods from Europe. For generations Damascus handicrafts had been patronized by a powerful group of inner-city merchants and moneylenders involved in regional and long-distance trade. With the decline of these industries many merchant-moneylenders turned to cash crops and tax farms for profit. Some *aghawat* did the same, and were quick to enhance their own social status in Damascus by striking up financial relationships, and occasionally cementing these relationships through marriage, with city merchant families. By 1860, a number of *agha* households in the Maydan, Shaghur, and in al-Salhiyya had become established dignitaries in their quarters. Some had acquired posts in the local administration and controlled a diverse network of financial relations. Moreover, they had successfully combined both resource bases to extend their patronage networks. They had yet to acquire, however, the social status or the approval of the 'honorable citizenry.'

The impact of the 1860 crisis

The crisis of 1860 derived in part from the social and political upheaval in Mount Lebanon during the previous two years.[59] Its roots can be seen, however, during the Egyptian occupation of Syria. Ibrahim Pasha's centralization and modernization schemes opened the doors to European political and economic influence, gave minorities more equality with Muslims, 'drained sources' of local military strength and, above all, weakened the independent political power base of the *'ulama'*.[60] With the return of Ottoman central authority in 1841, local *'ulama'* and secular notables were given a bigger share in local administration. Istanbul hoped that they would now draw closer to the state and support the new reform program, which they did, in part. Indeed, these dignitaries used their positions on the *majlis* to back those reforms that enabled them to defend and consolidate their many personal interests. However, they tried unsuccessfully to block one set of important reforms that gave minorities more equality with Muslims. Minority leaders were given positions of local administrative authority, including seats on the *majlis*, and their communities began to feel increasingly secure.[61] They also began to establish connections with and receive protection from European consuls and merchants. The economic impact of Europe was heightened during the twenty years leading up to the events of 1860, and many Christians and Jews enriched themselves by serving as agents of European interests.

Damascus Muslims of all 'classes' felt considerable resentment over these developments. The violent explosion in July 1860 may have been ignited by certain resentful *'ulama'*, linked to anti-*Tanzimat* factions in Istanbul who encouraged anti-Christian agitation as an expression of their opposition.[62] The mobs certainly consisted of many unemployed Muslim artisans, especially textile workers, out of work owing to the displacement of their crafts by European manufactured goods, who vented their anger on the more prosperous local Christian community, popularly identified with European interests.[63] Though prominent center-city notables may have been pleased by the riots, it is unlikely that they actively conspired in large numbers to incite the violence.[64] In fact, when the leaders of the *majlis* learned of the strife between Druzes and Christians in the regional market center of Zahla, they put out the lights in their quarters and market places to discourage troublemakers.[65] When the violence erupted they made efforts to subdue rowdy elements in their own quarters, but without much success. Their failure to prevent the

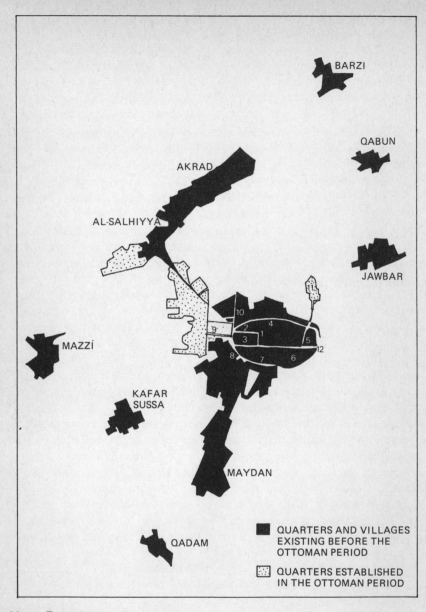

Map 1. Damascus *c.* 1920.
Key: 1. Great Mosque (Umayyad); 2. Citadel; 3. Suqs (al-Hamidiyya and Midhat Pasha); 4. al-'Amara; 5. Bab Tuma; 6. Jewish Quarter; 7. Shaghur; 8. Bab al-Jabiyya; 9. al-Qanawat; 10. Suq Saruja; 11. al-Qassa'; 12. Bab Sharqi.

outburst of violence or to control it was symptomatic of their gradual loss of independent social influence in the city.

The failure of the traditional leaders to control their quarters can be contrasted to events in the Maydan. When news of the violence reached the Maydan, gangs began to rush to the scene. But when they learned that their leaders, Salim Agha and Salih Agha al-Mahayni, 'Umar Agha al-'Abid and Sa'id Agha Nuri, were protecting the Christians of Bab Musalla, in the northern Maydan, these gangs turned back and assisted their leaders.[66] By 1860, the Maydan[67] and other suburbs of the city supported established patrons who, while still socially differentiated from the traditional leaders of the inner city, could rival them in their ability as patrons and quarter bosses.

Fu'ad Pasha levied sentences on Damascenes from all walks of life, though as a group the religious and secular notables on the *majlis* bore the brunt of his displeasure. These leaders were sentenced either for encouraging the violence in Bab Tuma or for their inability to control the riots. But there were deeper reasons for Ottoman severity. The *'ulama'*, having seemingly identified many of their interests with the state, in fact used the state apparatus to further their own ends while fundamentally rejecting many of the secular reforms emanating from Istanbul. With tunnel vision, conservative and suspicious, these leaders understood neither the nature of Ottoman efforts to centralize and reintegrate the Empire nor the extent of European pressures on the state to accelerate these processes. Moreover, they miscalculated their strength in relation to the Ottoman central authority. Proudly assuming that they were the only 'natural' leaders of the city, they manipulated the state apparatus to suit themselves while cutting off their traditional support from below. In August 1860 they could not understand why Istanbul had punished them or why the local populace had shown them such 'disrespect.'[68]

In general, the punishment of the traditional leadership took the form of banishment, rather than execution. Exile was only temporary and economic interests were usually left untouched. Social prestige suffered but the damage was not irreparable, providing their leadership agreed to toe the Ottoman line more faithfully and to acknowledge leaders outside of the 'honorable citizenry' and integrate them into the local social and political élite.

Chapter 2

The consolidation of leadership in Damascus after 1860

The immediate political impact of the 1860 disturbances was a weakened traditional leadership in Damascus. During the next forty years two new developments – the spread of private landownership and the growth of the state in the life of the town and province – stimulated the recomposition and integration of urban political forces. By the turn of the twentieth century a reconstituted political élite had emerged in Damascus, the product of a recently consolidated, fairly well integrated and socially cohesive landed upper class, which had aligned itself more closely with Istanbul.

The development of private landownership

During the first half of the nineteenth century the Syrian economy began to feel the impact of commercialization. Dislocations in the urban economy caused by the competition of European manufactured goods, coupled with the spread of cash cropping, helped to stimulate land acquisition.

In the Biqa' Valley and the Ghuta, members of the religious establishment and a group of secular dignitaries, who were center-city merchants and tax farmers, controlled the land system.[1] Some had used their posts on the *majlis* to extend their holdings by auctioning tax farms to themselves and their families. There also emerged another group of merchant-moneylenders – recently enriched by the forces of commercialization – who acquired lands through the manipulation of usurious capital in these areas and in the Hawran grain belt. *Aghawat* in the peripheral quarters of the city or lesser dignitaries from the center city, these merchant-moneylenders came to dominate the Hawran and joined the more socially prominent notable tax farmers in the Biqa' and the Ghuta. By the 1850s some families had already begun to establish claims to private landownership in these three regions.

They were encouraged by rapid commercialization in grain-producing regions throughout Syria, caused by the Crimean War and its aftermath.

26

A series of good harvests and the 'suspension of grain shipments sent prices soaring in the West and made Levantine grain temporarily competitive.'[2] Syrian tax farmers and merchant-moneylenders took advantage of the increased demand for grain to transform their land-holdings into outright landownership.

The push towards the formation of large privately-owned estates also accompanied the expansion of the agricultural frontiers in Syria which opened up new lands for settlement and cultivation. In any case, a combination of forces prompted the Ottoman government to enact a new Land Code in 1858, not least of which was its growing desire to increase its land revenues. And this was, in part, a response to mounting European pressures on Istanbul to repay the debts it had incurred as a result of ongoing efforts to centralize and modernize the Empire.[3]

The impact of the Land Code was not felt, however, in the Damascus area until after the events of 1860 and especially in the 1870s when a commercial depression obliged more and more notables to invest in land.[4] The aim of the Land Code was to encourage peasants to register state-owned land (*miri*) in their own names to prevent any intermediary between the state and the cultivator from dominating production at the expense of both. Designed to ensure a steady flow of revenue to the state and to tilt the balance of power in the province towards the central government, the Land Code proved an ironic failure; its local interpretation and execution facilitated the acquisition of land by the very intermediaries Istanbul had set out to enfeeble.[5] Although the balance of power in the province shifted in the direction of Istanbul after 1860, the Land Code proved to be an obstacle rather than an aid to this process.

The Land Code was predicated on two false premises: that peasants would be willing to register their land and able thereafter to hold on to it, and that the administration of the land registry (*defterkhane*) would be efficient and impartial.[6] However, the system of land registration, based on title deeds, registration fees and a census, frightened peasants from the outset. Believing that it was instituted to facilitate taxation and conscription, peasants ignored the potential benefits of the system and registered their lands in the name of deceased family members, big city patrons, or rural notables. By promising peasants protection from state interference, a number of powerful Damascus families acquired legal rights to large tracts of land.[7] Even when peasants sought to register their lands in their own names, the required registration fee was often prohibitive. If peasants were unable to pay the fee, their lands reverted to the state and were put up for auction by the local or provincial *majlis*, whose members were then able to fix the bids or simply outbid all other contenders.[8] Peasant landholdings also reverted to *majlis*-directed auctions for various infringements of the Land Code.[9] One of the most common transgressions was the peasant's failure to cultivate his lands for three consecutive years, usually owing to his inability to buy seed or implements. In this event a fine in the form of an additional land tax or registration fee was imposed. If the peasant could not afford to cultivate his plot, neither could he pay the fine, and so lost his land to auction. In this way, many peasants became tenants or sharecroppers (*métayers*) on the lands they previously controlled, and the fate of the small peasant proprietor became increasingly precarious.[10]

The real purpose of the Ottoman government in instituting the Land Code was thus deflected to facilitate and legalize land accumulation in the hands of a few wealthy Damascus families. By the turn of the twentieth century a powerful group of large-landholding families had emerged on the Damascus social and political scene. Many were upstarts, having climbed the social ladder after 1860, and most acquired land through their posts in the local administration and through usury in the Damascus hinterland. Wealth, once acquired, opened doors in local political circles and in Istanbul to even wider networks of administrative offices for themselves, their relations and their clients. Land grants from the Sultan and the extension of patronage in the countryside abetted the accumulation of agricultural land while urban real estate continued to attract investors. Some families even dabbled in local industrial enterprises, although most of the newly acquired fortunes were used for conspicuous consumption.

The large landowners of Damascus were not all upstarts, however. Some families from the pre-1860 élite converted their hereditary tax farms into outright landownership while retaining control of charitable endowments. But those of the old guard who managed to maintain their political power came to rely more on their material resource base than on their social pedigree. After 1860, political power became increasingly secularized and some of the new landowning families came to rank as high on the social ladder as any member of the religious establishment.

Within the post-1860 leadership, traditional scholarly families were a minority. In their antipathy to the *Tanzimat*, many *'ulama'* ensconced themselves in their traditional religious networks as secularization eroded religious prestige and office as a power base. The central government, comprehending the innate hostility of the *'ulama'* to reform, turned to other groups to carry out its policies in the province. The religious families that held on to their positions after 1860 owned large tracts of land and held both secular and religious posts. Unlike other scholarly families, they compromised and diversified to maintain their position of paramountcy.

Modernization and centralization of administration

Before 1860, the *'ulama'* monopolized the Muslim educational system. In the early 1860s, however, state secondary schools (*rushdiyya*) were established in Damascus. While the traditional network of Muslim schools (*maktabs* and *madrasas*) continued to be the mainstay of Muslim education, an increasing number of children from the Muslim élite were sent to the new secular schools. This provoked the *'ulama'* to take control of the *rushdiyya* administration although they were unable to impose a completely religious curriculum. Also, teachers were no longer all religious experts. Towards the end of the century landowning-bureaucratic families began to send their sons to Istanbul for a secular professional or military education that would enable them to secure high posts in the civil administration or army.[11] Public administration, civil law and military science were taught in Turkish at the expense of the traditional Islamic sciences. In fact, as the religious establishment lost its monopoly over education some of its more farsighted members adapted to the changing times and began sending their own sons to Istanbul.[12]

After 1860, Christian missionary schools began to have a visible impact in Damascus, though by 1880 there were still only four such schools in the city. These catered primarily to the city's religious minorities, but in due course a sprinkling of the Muslim élite also enrolled.[13] Students in these schools obtained a sound secondary education which included modern sciences and European languages. This enabled them to fill key technical posts in the provincial administration, to expand their financial connections with European merchants and manufacturers, and to secure important positions in European consulates. Missionary education also contributed to the revival (*nahda*) of the Arabic language and, despite its sectarian nature, promoted a cultural atmosphere with secular undertones in Damascus.[14] Nevertheless, European cultural influences penetrated the Syrian interior much more slowly than they did the coast.

Another traditional preserve of the *'ulama'* was the judicial system. However, after 1850 the Ottoman government set up, alongside the traditional religious court system (*mahakim al-shari'a*), special courts of summary justice and appeal composed of Christian, Jewish and Muslim judges.[15] Mixed courts containing an equal number of foreign and native judges were also established to adjudicate both criminal and commercial cases between foreigners and Ottoman subjects. Thus the *'ulama'* lost their monopoly of the judicial system and were left, for the most part, to adjudicate cases concerning matters of personal status. Some of the higher-ranking *'ulama'* actually began to encourage their sons to enter new professional schools in Istanbul to study law and public administration in order to gain a foothold in the ascendant secular judicial system.[16]

Meanwhile, in the 1860s, in conjunction with the *Tanzimat* and, in particular, with the 1864 Law of the Provinces, the Ottoman government established new councils on which Damascus notables could sit. And alongside such reforms, new salaried posts were created, most notably for the Commander of the Pilgrimage (*Amir al-Hajj*). The highest council–the Administrative Council of the Province (*Majlis al-idara al-wilaya*) which was based in Damascus–included three appointed Turkish officials (the *wali*, *qadi* and *defterdar*); two Muslim religious dignitaries who held permanent seats (the Hanafi *Mufti* and the *Naqib al-Ashraf*); and six elected members (three Muslim notables, two representatives of the Christian community, and one representative of the Jewish community). The next most important councils were the Administrative Council of the District (*Majlis al-idara al-liwa'*) and the Municipal Council (*Majlis al-baladiyya*) of Damascus.[17]

Religious families in the recomposed leadership: the landowning-scholars

The heads of the leading religious families continued to monopolize the posts of Hanafi *Mufti* and *Naqib al-Ashraf* though both positions carried less political weight after 1860. By that time seats on the Administrative Councils of the Province and District (*wilaya* and *liwa'*) conferred more clout on the local political scene than did high religious posts. No Damascene '*alim* held an elected seat on the Provincial Council between 1870 and 1900, and only a handful could be found on the District Council in the same period.[18] High-ranking '*ulama'* elected to either the District Council or the Municipal Council after 1870 often came from large-landowning families.

The religious dignitaries of Damascus maintained control of the administration of charitable endowments, though after 1860 notables in the secular branches of government also sat on the Council of the *Awqaf*.[19] Moreover, as the population of Damascus gradually began to increase, after a noticeable decline between 1820 and 1860,[20] the income from charitable endowments had to be spread among a larger number of inhabitants. Consequently, this left less income for the religious establishment. As the formation of large privately owned estates proceeded, some non-scholarly families established a family endowment (*waqf ahli*) to protect their families from the possibility of state confiscation. Some religious leaders did become trustees (*nazirs*) of these *awqaf*, but usually this function was entrusted to the head of the family.[21]

Although the power of religious institutions in Damascus was over-shadowed by the emerging secular institutions in the last third of the nineteenth century, competition for religious posts was as fierce as ever. In 1860, ten of the sixteen leading scholarly families of the eighteenth century were still at the top of the religious hierarchy, but they had to jostle for position and influence with at least twenty-five other families.[22] Since the number of religious posts was less than the number of office-seekers, many lesser religious figures found it necessary to seek employment outside the religious institutions. One alternative was found in the new secular institutions.[23]

Several families among the 'honorable citizens' – notably the 'Ajlanis, the Ghazzis, the Kaylanis and the Hasibis – merged with a group of non-scholarly landowning families to form the cream of Damascus society in the late nineteenth century. This upper class, in turn, provided the town's political élite. The Jaza'iri family, newcomers to Damascus, was another scholarly family that acquired sizeable landholdings. These five families, though not the only ones in the religious establishment to own land, appear to have been among the biggest landowners and the most socially and politically influential members of that establishment.[24]

AL-'AJLANI

The 'Ajlanis, a family belonging to the *ashraf*, came to Damascus from Mecca, possibly in the fifteenth century. In the eighteenth and nineteenth centuries they shared the post of *Naqib al-Ashraf* with the Hamzas, holding the post at least five times between 1769 and 1898. The most prominent 'Ajlani in the second half of the nineteenth century was Shaykh Ahmad Darwish. He was *Naqib* in 1860, and was one of the leading notables exiled by Fu'ad Pasha.[25] Soon after Fu'ad's departure he returned to Damascus and resumed the post of *Naqib*, which he held until his death in 1898, along with a number of other posts. In 1871, he served on the Council of Petitions of the Province,[26] and in 1876, he was elected to the short-lived Constituent Assembly in Istanbul.[27] He also held the position of *Shaykh al-Mashayikh*, or patron of the guild system in Damascus, though by the early 1880s this post had been 'reduced to a rubber stamp.'[28] Shaykh Ahmad's son, Muhammad, held offices in both the civil and religious courts, becoming a judge on the Court of Appeals and on a *shari'a* court in the early 1890s.[29] In 1909, Muhammad was elected to the Ottoman Parliament in Istanbul.[30] On his death two years later, his cousin, 'Ata, assumed the leadership of the 'Ajlani family.[31]

The 'Ajlanis acquired hereditary tax farms in the Ghuta and in Duma in the early eighteenth century. These were probably converted into privately owned estates after 1860.[32] Part of this land was held as a family *waqf*.[33] In addition, members of the family often served as trustees of other charitable endowments. The 'Ajlani patrimonial home was in the 'Amara quarter of Damascus where many prominent religious families lived, owing to its proximity to the Umayyad Mosque.[34] Social prestige, landownership and administrative position combined to keep the 'Ajlanis at the summit of the Damascus political élite.

AL-GHAZZI

The Ghazzis, an old family of religious scholars, arrived in Damascus from Palestine in the fifteenth century.[35] They soon became Shafi'i *Muftis* and monopolized this post till the twentieth century. Shaykh 'Umar al-Ghazzi, the Shafi'i *Mufti*, was exiled for complicity in the events of 1860. Though the family temporarily lost this still important post in the religious establishment, they were able to regain it soon afterwards.[36] Meanwhile other family members continued to hold important religious and secular posts throughout the late nineteenth and early twentieth centuries. 'Abd al-Rahman al-Ghazzi was a prominent member of the Municipal Council in the early 1870s, and of the Public Works Commission and the Chamber of Agriculture in the 1880s.[37] Between 1878 and 1893, Shaykh Husayn al-Ghazzi was a chief magistrate on a *shari'a* court and in 1894 became a *qadi*.[38] His brother, Isma'il, was a judge on the Mixed Commercial Court in 1884 and a member of the Municipal Council in the early 1890s.[39] Another Ghazzi, Salih, was a religious court magistrate while moonlighting as shaykh of the Qadiriyya *sufi* order at the end of the century.[40] Like the 'Ajlanis, the Ghazzis lived in the 'Amara quarter, administered charitable endowments and seem to have acquired tax farms in the district of Duma, which they registered as private property after 1860.

AL-KAYLANI

The Kaylanis belonged to the *ashraf* and claimed descent from the famous ascetic and founder of the Qadiriyya order, 'Abd al-Qadir al-Gaylani (1078–1166 A.D.). The family spread throughout the Fertile Crescent with its most prominent branches in Baghdad, Hama and

Damascus.[41] Found in Hama in the early sixteenth century, by the following century the Kaylanis had acquired tax farms there. Ruthless tax collectors, part of the family was driven out of Hama by a revolt of the populace and settled in Damascus.[42] In the eighteenth century two Kaylanis held the post of *Naqib al-Ashraf*, though the family seems to have fallen out of the competition for this post by the end of the century.[43] Sa'id, the son of an assistant magistrate on a *shari'a* court, was a leading member of the *majlis* in 1860, and was exiled along with its other members.[44] He soon returned to Damascus, however, and re-established himself in the local administration. In the early 1870s he became President of the Municipality, a post he held for many years.[45] Sa'id also managed to place his four sons in high posts in the local bureaucracy: 'Atallah was on the Commission of Public Works and was a member of the Chamber of Agriculture and the Council of Education; 'Abd al-Latif was on the Administrative Council of the People (*Sha'b*); Sharif inherited his father's seat on the Municipal Council and served as a judge on the court of Summary Justice; and Ibrahim became a magistrate on the Commercial Court.[46] Finally, their relation, Faris, was a wealthy notable involved in agricultural and commercial enterprises, including the Hijaz Railway scheme.[47] As a scholarly family the Kaylanis were unusual in that after 1860, the Damascus branch showed no apparent interest in religious posts, concentrating their efforts on offices in the civil administration.

No specific information was found on how or when the Damascus branch of the family accumulated land; however, it is possible that Sa'id's grandfather, Muhammad (d. 1821), acquired tax farms in the Duma district through his position in the local *diwan*.[48] Sa'id may have added to these later, when he was a member of the *majlis*. The Kaylani holdings were then registered after 1860. The family also maintained its main residence in al-'Amara.[49]

AL-HASIBI

The Hasibis, as mentioned, had successfully wedded wealth to title by 1860. In that year Ahmad al-Hasibi, a member of the *majlis* and the leader of al-Qanawat, was banished.[50] His son, Abu'l Su'ud, was spared this humiliation and became a leading member of the Municipal Council between the late 1870s and 1900.[51] In the early eighties he was elected Vice-President of the Chambers of Agriculture and Commerce and, in 1898, crowned his social career by being elected *Naqib al-Ashraf*, after the death of Shaykh Ahmad Darwish al-'Ajlani.[52]

The Hasibi lands, situated in Qatana and al-Judayda, were granted to

33

Ahmad by the Ottoman government before 1860.[53] After 1860, the family registered these holdings, adding to them during the remainder of the century.

AL-JAZA'IRI

The Jaza'iris, who also claimed descent from the Prophet, were the most recent addition to the Damascus religious establishment. The head of the family, the Amir 'Abd al-Qadir, became a noted warrior in the faith by resisting the French occupation of Algeria in the 1830s and 1840s. Forced to surrender in 1847, he was briefly imprisoned in France before moving to Istanbul and eventually to Damascus, in 1854, where he resided in the 'Amara quarter with his family and some of the armed retainers he brought with him from Algeria.[54] The family was subsidized by the French as a condition of surrender and received large handouts from the Sultan as well.[55] During the 1860 events 'Abd al-Qadir enhanced his reputation throughout the Islamic world and Europe by protecting the Christians of Bab Tuma.[56] The Amir and his offspring – outsiders who considered themselves socially superior to the local notability – took little interest in local administration.[57] Instead, they focused their attention on political intrigue in Paris and Istanbul. They did find time, however, to dabble in Islamic learning and in mysticism, and to convert their subsidies into vast estates in northern Palestine, al-Qunaytra, and Hawran. They settled Algerian tribesmen on their estates and maintained an armed retinue in Damascus.[58] The Jaza'iris were somewhat peripheral to local politics but, with their wealth and personal Algerian bodyguard, they participated in factional infighting, particularly after the outbreak of World War I.

In the last third of the nineteenth century the 'Ajlani, Ghazzi, Kaylani, Hasibi and Jaza'iri families enhanced their influence in Damascus along with several other families in the religious establishment, including the 'Attars, Hamzas, Mahasinis, Ustwanis and Muradis.[59] Greater wealth concentrated in land and keener interest and ability in acquiring posts in ascendant secular institutions distinguished them as the most influential scholarly families in the city, since the dual processes—Ottoman centralization-cum-modernization and agrarian commercialization—had redefined the nature of *real* power in Damascene society.

In this period a lesser group of scholarly families, including the Bakris, Ayyubis, Malkis, Halabis, 'Umaris and Maydanis, all with suitable pedigrees but generally unsuccessful in competition for the highest religious posts, turned to the secular bureaucracy, landownership and/or business enterprises to augment their local power.[60] They thus became full-fledged members of the political élite. By 1900, though still deriving some degree of social prestige from their scholarly origins, most of these families could be categorized more accurately as part of the landowning-bureaucratic group than as part of the religious establishment. Of this group, the Bakri family proved to be the most important. They were an old family that claimed to be *ashraf* but only became prominent in political affairs towards the end of the nineteenth century. 'Ata al-Bakri began his career as a judge on the Court of Appeals and by the early twentieth century had become a member of the prestigious District and Municipal Councils. Thanks to connections with a prominent Damascus merchant close to Istanbul, 'Ata was awarded the title of *pasha* in 1905. Four years later he became a member of the Administrative Council of the Province. More importantly, he accumulated a sizeable fortune through the acquisition of lands in two villages in the fertile Ghuta, and built a large palace in the Kharrab quarter behind the Umayyad Mosque. In the early twentieth century his sons, Fawzi and Nasib, expanded their family's wealth and influence, becoming politically active in their own right.[61]

Landowning-bureaucratic families in the recomposed leadership

The dominant partner in the Damascus political leadership of 1900 was a group of non-scholarly landowning-bureaucrats whose families ascended to the summit of political life in the town in the wake of the 1860 disturbances. By successfully monopolizing the most influential political and administrative posts in the civil bureaucracy and, in the process, acquiring vast landholdings, these families developed a firmer power base than the landowning-scholars. Basically, they achieved their paramount position by linking their interests more closely with those of Istanbul than any other local force did in Damascus. Indeed, they adjusted most comfortably to the changing times.

The list of the most politically influential non-scholarly landowning families in 1900 numbers at least eleven: the 'Azm (including the Mu'ayyad al-'Azm), 'Abid, Yusuf (including the Shamdins), Mardam-Beg, Quwwatli, Sham'a, Barudi, Sukkar, Mahayni, Agribuz and Buzu families. In 1860 these families were dispersed throughout Damascus. The 'Azms had moved to Suq Saruja. The four Kurdish *aghawat* – Yusuf, Shamdin, Agribuz and Buzu – were residents of the Kurdish quarter (Hayy al-Akrad) on the northern extremes of al-Salhiyya. The wealthy grain-merchant *aghawat* – the 'Abids, Sukkars, and Mahaynis – all lived in the Maydan. The Mardam-Begs lived next to the central market place

35

(later Suq al-Hamidiyya), the Quwwatlis in Shaghur, the Sham'as in Bab al-Jabiyya (on the southwestern edge of the central market place), and the Barudis in al-Qanawat. Seven of these families—the 'Azm, 'Abid, Yusuf-Shamdin, Mardam-Beg, Quwwatli, Sham'a, and Barudi—deserve special attention for, in the last third of the nineteenth century, they came to constitute the most powerful political bloc in Damascus, and along with the five landowning-scholarly families ('Ajlani, Ghazzi, Kaylani, Hasibi and Jaza'iri) formed the effective political leadership of the city.

AL-'AZM

The 'Azm family was the only old face among this group of non-scholarly landowning families. With bases in Damascus and Hama, the family had become so large by the late eighteenth century that it split into two branches, the 'Azm and the Mu'ayyad al-'Azm, in both towns. In Damascus, the 'Azm branch seems to have been slightly more prominent than the Mu'ayyad branch; however, since both branches continued to intermarry distinctions of power and prestige were hazy.

During the events of 1860, the head of the Damascus 'Azms, 'Abdullah Bey, was a member of the *majlis*, and therefore exiled.[62] The 'Azms, however, quickly re-established their ties with Istanbul. Usually a family member could be found in the imperial capital in some high administrative post and sons, sent there for higher education, returned to the most important posts in the province. The 'Azms appear to have held more top provincial and imperial posts in the late nineteenth and early twentieth century than any other Damascus family. In the 1870s Muhammad 'Ali Pasha al-'Azm was an elected member of the Administrative Council of the Province, the most prestigious and influential council in local government.[63] At the same time five of his relatives were members of the District and Municipal Councils.[64] In the 1880s, al-'Azms sat on the *Awqaf* Council and the Court of Summary Justice and held two seats on the District Council.[65] The next decade saw al-'Azms on the Education Council, the Court of Appeals, the Chambers of Agriculture and Commerce, the People's and Municipal Councils, and the Commercial Court.[66]

The late 1880s marked the rise of Muhammad Fawzi al-'Azm, the son of Muhammad 'Ali Pasha, to family leadership and political paramountcy in Damascus. By 1892, he had become President of the Municipality, a post he retained until the early twentieth century when he was elected to the Administrative Council of the Province. He also served as Minister of the *Awqaf* in Istanbul and Director of Public Works for the Hijaz Railway.[67] In the early twentieth century he was the most influential politician in Damascus, and among the wealthiest. His son, Khalid, would follow him into politics in the next generation.

In the nineteenth century the Muhammad 'Ali line of the 'Azm family moved its residence from the 'Amara quarter to Suq Saruja, northwest of the central market place. There they built another luxurious palace which housed over seventy members of the extended family.[68] Their presence in Suq Saruja gave the quarter an aristocratic charm that attracted other wealthy families. After the enactment of the Land Code of 1858, the family registered its tax farms in Hama, the Ghuta and the Hawran as private property. With vast landholdings and valuable urban real estate in Hama and Damascus and a series of high administrative posts, the 'Azms acquired the reputation of the most socially prestigious family and one of the three most politically influential families in Damascus.[69]

Next to the 'Azms, the 'Abid and Yusuf families were the most adept at combining material wealth with administrative offices to secure political power. Both families followed a similar path. They initiated their rise to political power in the mid-nineteenth century, on the periphery of Damascus; the 'Abids in the Maydan and the Yusufs in al-Salhiyya. Both were of *agha* background and were connected to the city's grain and livestock trades. Both combined high posts in local administration and usurious capital in the city's hinterland to acquire vast landholdings. Both developed strong connections in Istanbul enabling them to preserve their power bases. Finally, when both families had accumulated sufficient wealth, posts and social status, they moved out of their popular quarters and joined the 'Azms in Suq Saruja.

AL-'ABID

The 'Abids claimed to have tribal origins as members of a tributary of the Mawali and they may also have been of Kurdish stock.[70] They appear to have settled in the Maydan in the early eighteenth century, building up strong connections in the grain and livestock trades. They eventually adopted the title of *agha*, though it is not known whether they received this title as commanders of local garrisons in the Maydan or because of their prominence as powerful grain merchants. The first family member to achieve prominence in the political arena was 'Umar Agha al-'Abid, a prosperous merchant of the Maydan wastani (middle Maydan),[71] who protected Christians in neighboring Bab Musalla and prevented the Maydan populace from joining mobs which entered Bab Tuma in July 1860.[72]

In the immediate aftermath of these events, the Ottoman government made a concentrated effort to promote new allies in Damascus as a counterweight to the power of the traditional political leadership. It also sought suitable agents to enact its reform program in the province. Suspicious of the religious notability, Istanbul turned to the only other source available in Damascus: those wealthy but less socially prominent families who had demonstrated independent influence in the city before and during the events of 1860, and middle-level functionaries and military officers who had served as agents of the *Tanzimat* in Damascus and elsewhere since the 1840s. The 'Abids fit into both these categories.

In 1860, 'Umar Agha was an elderly merchant with no position in the local administration. His son, 'Abd al-Qadir, appears to have joined his father in the family business, but his grandson, Hawlu (1824–95), chose to enter the Ottoman service sometime before 1860. In the 1860s and 1870s he served as *mutasarrif* (district governor) in Hama and Nablus.[73] Awarded the title of *pasha*, he returned to Damascus and was duly elected to the Administrative Council of the Province in 1878, eventually becoming its President in the early 1890s.[74] At different times he was President of the Court of Appeals and the Chamber of Agriculture.[75] Hawlu's two brothers also distinguished themselves as local officials. Muhammad Bey was elected to a seat on the District Council in the late 1870s and Mahmud Bey became President of the Municipal Council in the mid-1880s.[76]

Hawlu's two sons increased the family's political strength and prestige both at home and in Istanbul. Mustafa, who had been *qa'imaqam* (district commissioner under a *mutasarrif*) and *mutasarrif* of Mosul in the 1880s, returned to Damascus brandishing the title of *pasha* to replace his father on the Provincial Council in 1894.[77] However, the career of Ahmad 'Izzat was even more glorious than either his father's or his brother's. Educated in a Catholic mission school in Beirut, where he learned to speak French fluently,[78] he moved from post to post in the local judicial administration before making his way to Istanbul. There, as a judge on the Mixed Commercial Court, he caught the eye of Sultan 'Abd ul-Hamid and soon became his 'second secretary' and close confidant.[79] It was in this period, the 1890s, that the Sultan was actively promoting his pan-Islamic policy of consolidating the Ottoman heartlands after territorial losses in the European provinces. Two Arabs, 'Izzat Pasha and Abu'l Huda al-Sayyadi, a religious *shaykh* from the Aleppo province, exercised much influence on this policy. It was 'Izzat Pasha who promoted the Hijaz Railway scheme, geared to attract worldwide Islamic cooperation while serving to connect the Arab provinces more firmly with Istanbul.[80] While 'Izzat Pasha continued to play an influential role in Istanbul his son,

Muhammad 'Ali, began to rise quickly in the Ottoman civil service. Raised in an aristocratic milieu in Istanbul and educated at the Galataserail School and in Paris, he was named to the Ministry of Foreign Affairs in the early 1900s and was sent to Washington as Minister of the Ottoman Legation for a short term.[81] A quarter of a century later he was elected the first President of the Syrian Republic.

The material resource base of the 'Abids originally was rooted in their Maydan business enterprises. After accumulating sufficient capital, Hawlu Pasha put it to more profitable use by investing in Suez Canal Company shares. With his profits he purchased a number of fruit farms in the Ghuta and in Duma[82] which his son later expanded. More importantly, 'Izzat Pasha began to purchase real estate including a large hotel which he conveniently converted into a very prosperous family endowment.[83] He and his son also built up a series of valuable financial connections in the West, placing large amounts of capital in shareholding companies in Paris, London and New York.[84] By 1900, the 'Abids ranked among the three wealthiest families in Damascus. In less than four decades they had risen to the pinnacle of political power and prestige in Damascus and Istanbul. More than any other Damascus family they represented the new political leadership's identification with the ideology of 'Ottomanism.'

AL-YUSUF

The Yusuf family achieved social and political prominence in the second half of the nineteenth century, a derivative of interrelations with its chief rival in the Kurdish section of al-Salhiyya, the Shamdins. The Yusufs and Shamdins, competitors for the same Kurdish clientele in al-Salhiyya, decided to unify their respective power bases after mid-century. Sa'id Shamdin married his only daughter to Muhammad Pasha al-Yusuf. The couple produced one son, 'Abd al-Rahman, the principal heir to Shamdin Pasha's fortune.

The Yusufs appear to have arrived in Damascus at the turn of the nineteenth century from Diarbakir where they had been livestock merchants.[85] In the 1830s Ahmad Agha (d.1864) was an agent for the Amir Bashir al-Shihab of Mount Lebanon and received from him land in the plain of 'Anjar for his services. Later, in recognition of his courage and influence among the Kurds of Damascus and the tribes with which he traded, Ahmad Agha was appointed to the prestigious and lucrative post of *Amir al-Hajj* (Commander of the Pilgrimage), and district governor in Hawran.[86] Ahmad's son, Muhammad (d. 1896), was also to become *Amir al-Hajj*. Later he was appointed *mutasarrif* in Acre,

Hawran, Tripoli (Syria) and Hama respectively.[87] Finally, in the 1890s Muhammad, now a *pasha*, was elected to the Administrative Council of the Province in Damascus.[88]

The origins of the Shamdin family are obscure. A certain Kurdish tribal shaykh called Musa living in Acre had a son named Shamdin. It seems that sometime around the turn of the nineteenth century Shamdin Agha came to settle in the Salhiyya suburb of Damascus, quickly building up an independent power base there among immigrant Kurds by commanding a local garrison.[89] In the wake of the disbanding of the local garrisons in Damascus in 1859,[90] Shamdin Agha's son, Muhammad Sa'id, was appointed commander of one of the new garrisons, composed of Kurdish auxiliaries.[91] However, in 1860, Muhammad Sa'id was exiled to Mosul for failing to prevent Kurdish gangs from entering Bab Tuma to massacre Christians. He returned to Damascus shortly thereafter, after having earned the gratitude of the Sultan for restoring order to chaotic Mosul. As a reward he was appointed district governor of Hawran, replacing Ahmad (now Pasha) al-Yusuf, and eventually *Amir al-Hajj* in the late 1860s, replacing Muhammad Pasha al-Yusuf.[92]

Although the Yusufs do not appear to have acquired lands after 1860, Sa'id Shamdin Pasha used the capital that he had accumulated as *Amir al-Hajj* to purchase a series of farms and villages in the Ghuta, which he established as a valuable family endowment, and extensive property in the Hawran and in al-Qunaytra. By the 1890s, he was reputed to own more land than any other individual in the Syrian (Damascus) Province.[93]

'Abd al-Rahman al-Yusuf, the product of the marriage alliance between the Shamdins and the Yusufs, replaced his maternal grandfather as *Amir al-Hajj* in the 1890s and inherited Shamdin Pasha's landholdings and the bulk of his father's fortune between 1896 and 1901. At the turn of the century he not only was one of the wealthiest individuals in Damascus, but he also held one of the most important posts in the Empire, at a time when the Sultan's pan-Islamic policy was at the height of its effectiveness. Furthermore, 'Abd al-Rahman Pasha inherited the double network of Shamdin and Yusuf clientele in the Kurdish quarter.[94] However, both Sa'id Shamdin and Muhammad al-Yusuf had left al-Salhiyya to establish larger residences in Suq Saruja. There, in what came to be called 'Little Istanbul,' 'Abd al-Rahman Pasha began to weave a new fabric of social and political relations with the 'Azms and 'Abids, leaving his more distant Shamdin cousins, who continued to reside in al-Salhiyya, to watch over the Yusuf-Shamdin clientele.[95]

MARDAM-BEG

The Mardam-Begs claim to trace their origins to a certain La La Mustafa Pasha, an Albanian in the service of the Sultan's *harim* (harem) in the sixteenth century.[96] The family appears to have settled in Damascus sometime in the eighteenth century where it engaged in trade, though it only began to rise to power around the middle of the nineteenth century. Two brothers, 'Ali (1813–87) and 'Uthman (1819–96), who started their careers as low-ranking members of the local *shari'a* and commercial courts in the 1850s, went to Istanbul to revive what they claimed to be their ancestral *waqf*, which had long been unproductive. Granted permission to assume control over this inheritance, the brothers managed to turn their endowment into a profitable venture.[97] Then they reinvested their profits in valuable Damascus real estate and irrigated gardens in the Ghuta. At the same time they began to acquire high posts in the local administration which enabled them to expand their entrepreneurial activities. 'Ali served as a judge on the Commercial Court of Damascus in the late 1870s, and then was elected to the Administrative Council of the Province on which he served from 1878 to 1887.[98] These two posts provided him with valuable insights into land speculation and he constructed an extension to the central market place. By the end of his life rents collected from this new *suq* had made 'Ali one of the wealthiest real-estate barons in Damascus.[99] 'Uthman was appointed *mutasarrif* of Hawran and soon after, in 1878, he was elected to the District Council. At this time he probably began to purchase his Ghuta farms.[100] 'Ali's son, Hikmat, followed his father into government service, starting out as a judge on the Commercial Court in the early 1880s, and subsequently replacing his uncle on the District Council in the mid-eighties.[101]

The Mardam-Beg home was conveniently situated next to Suq al-Hamidiyya, where they could readily oversee the collection of their rents. Social and political upstarts in 1860, the Mardam-Begs were skillful entrepreneurs who used their political offices to expand their financial interests, and to climb to the upper ranks of the Damascus political élite by the end of the century.

AL-QUWWATLI

The Quwwatli family were Baghdad merchants who established themselves in the Shaghur quarter of Damascus in the eighteenth century.[102] By 1860, the family, and particularly Muhammad al-Quwwatli, had amassed a considerable fortune from long-distance trade and entre-

preneurial activities inside Damascus.[103] The Quwwatlis converted part
of their capital into landholdings sometime after 1860. Murad (d. 1908)
was probably the first Quwwatli to purchase large tracts of land. Whether
he bought lands before or after he was elected to the Administrative
Council of the Province in 1871[104] cannot be ascertained, but he certainly
must have used his position on the Council to increase any holdings he
had acquired beforehand. Murad also became a member of the Chambers
of Agriculture and Commerce and was re-elected to the Provincial
Council in the early 1890s.[105] Two of Murad's brothers, Hasan and
'Abd al-Ghani, also became large landowners in the Ghuta before 1900.
However, only Hasan held an important post; in the early 1890s, he was
President of the Chambers of Agriculture and Commerce. At the same
time he was considered one of the leading merchants in the city.[106]
One other Quwwatli, Ahmad, secured a high post in this period; he was
appointed President of the Agricultural Bank of the Province in 1894.[107]

The Quwwatli family did not give up its business enterprises as it
began to purchase land. Nor did it move to a more prestigious quarter.
It continued to reside in the popular Shaghur where it built up a diverse
network of clientele that served the family's political interests for three
successive generations.

By 1900, the Mardam-Beg and Quwwatli families ranked next to
the Suq Saruja aristocracy in terms of political power and social prestige.
Their smaller landholdings, and their fewer connections with the
Ottoman authorities, however, distinguished them from the 'Azms,
'Abids and Yusufs. But they had yet to reach the peak of their social and
political influence.

AL-SHAM'A

The origins of the Sham'a family remain obscure. They may have settled
in Damascus as early as the fifteenth century. By the eighteenth century
family members had entered the religious hierarchy though they never
achieved the status of religious notability.[108] By the nineteenth century
the Sham'as had become established merchants in Bab al-Jabiyya.[109] The
first noted political figure to emerge from this family was Ahmad Rafiq.
He was awarded the title of *pasha* for his services as a provincial
administrator in the 1870s, and he was elected to the Constituent
Assembly in Istanbul in 1876. After the suspension of the Assembly in
1878, he returned to Damascus and joined Hawlu Pasha al-'Abid and 'Ali
Mardam-Beg on the Provincial Council.[110] In the early 1880s, he served
on the *Awqaf* and Educational Councils. A decade later he was President
of the Provincial Council. In the 1890s his sons, Rushdi and Yusuf,

followed him into local government and rose to prominence in the early twentieth century.[111]

Ahmad Rafiq Pasha probably used his various offices to procure lands in the Ghuta after the 1870s. His sons may well have expanded his holdings afterwards. The Sham'a family continued to live in Bab al-Jabiyya and, like the Quwwatlis, maintained close links with the popular classes. Ahmad Rafiq Pasha was as important a political figure in Damascus as any 'Azm, 'Abid, Yusuf, Mardam-Beg, or Quwwatli in the last third of the nineteenth century. But unlike these other families who had two or more members in high posts at any given time, the Sham'a influence in Damascus was mainly rooted in one man and his offspring.

AL-BARUDI

In the last third of the nineteenth century the Barudis joined the small bloc of landowning-bureaucratic families who were to produce a disproportionate number of political and social leaders in Damascus for several generations to come. At the turn of the nineteenth century Hasan al-Barudi came from Egypt to serve 'Abdullah Pasha al-'Azm then *wali* of Damascus as his *ketkhuda* (steward). Hasan Agha was generously rewarded for his services.[112] A wealthy and influential man, not involved in the events of 1860, Hasan crowned his career with a seat on the Damascus District Council in 1870.[113] His son, Muhammad Bey, replaced him on this Council in the late 1870s and retained his seat until his death in 1889.[114]

Hasan Agha used the wealth he amassed during his tenure with 'Abdullah Pasha al-'Azm to purchase farms and villages in the Ghuta and in Duma from the Egyptian Governor-General of Damascus, Sharif Pasha, on his departure from Syria in 1840.[115] After 1860, these lands were registered and it seems that Muhammad Bey used their revenues to buy more farms in the 1870s and 1880s. He also built a large palace in al-Qanawat where he developed a powerful patronage system. His son, Mahmud, occasionally held government or elected office, but preferred to lead the life of a country squire in Duma. Mahmud's son, Fakhri, however, was already politically engaged by World War I.[116]

The main wing of the Damascus political leadership in 1900 was formed by the group of seven non-scholarly families, six of whom had only begun to construct their socioeconomic and political power bases just half a century earlier. This wing combined former local garrison chiefs, merchant-moneylenders, and up-and-coming officials who, after 1860, monopolized the highest posts in the local bureaucracy and amassed enormous wealth in agricultural land and urban real estate. Having no stake in the conservative religious institutions, these families readily served the Ottoman central government as agents of centralization, modernization and even secularization. They were thus entrusted with high offices which could be manipulated to their economic benefit. By 1900, these families formed an integral part of an Ottoman 'aristocracy of service' with a derived social status equal to that of the landowning-scholarly families.

The size of the political élite in 1900

At the turn of the twentieth century the effective political leadership of Damascus included the twelve families whose histories have been sketched above (as well as several others). These families can be divided into two subgroups: the landowning-bureaucrats and the landowning-scholars. The former was the more powerful bloc owing to its control of the highest posts in the civil bureaucracy, its closer identification with Istanbul, and its greater wealth. However, by this time the two subgroups had already begun to merge.

These twelve families were the cream of the political and social élite in Damascus, which consisted of approximately fifty other Muslim families. These twelve families can be distinguished from the rest by their greater wealth in land, and their control of the majority of high posts in the secular institutions of the Syrian Province. Though some families in the religious establishment, including the 'Attars, Hamzas, Mahasinis, Ustwanis and Muradis, administered charitable endowments and owned land,[117] they failed to amass fortunes comparable to those of the top twelve. And though they did place some members in the ascendant secular institutions, they remained tied to the moribund religious institutions. Still other families of scholarly origin, notably the Bakris, Ayyubis, Malkis, Halabis, 'Umaris and Maydanis who failed to acquire the highest posts in the religious hierarchy and therefore opted to compete for posts in the civil bureaucracy, had yet to secure the highest offices. They bided their time in building up their landholdings and business enterprises;[118] by 1900 they resembled the better-established landowning-bureaucratic families in terms of their resource bases and their political orientation towards Istanbul.

The remainder of the political élite, including the Rikabis, Haffars, Jallads, Sukkars, Mahaynis, Hakims, Tabba's, Rijlihs, Agribuz, Buzus, and 'Azmas, did not belong to the religious establishment and most were new on the political scene in 1860.[119] They tended to be influential as merchant-moneylenders involved in the Damascus grain trade and in industries, such as textiles, which had experienced a revival in the 1870s due to their 'ability to find new markets among Syria's urban and rural population as well as to recapture old ones previously lost to foreign competition.'[120] Some were also prosperous landowners and many hailed from the peripheral popular quarters of the town, especially the Maydan, Shaghur (Barrani), and the Kurdish area of al-Salhiyya. Members of these families competed for posts in the civil bureaucracy but few of them had secured any of the highest posts by 1900.[121] In the early twentieth century this group of families, and the group that included families like al-Bakri, were ranked just below the top twelve in social prestige and political power. Social interpenetration and certain key political events, however, would enable some of these families to join the ranks of the effective political leadership of the city in the early twentieth century.

The position of the minorities

The most influential Christian and Jewish families of Damascus, although leaders of their respective communities, cannot be considered part of the effective political leadership of the city.[122] Since they were the leaders of two minority communities, representing less than 20 percent of the population of Damascus in this period,[123] they could not hope to amass political influence equal to that of the leading Muslim families. Yet, the route taken by many Christian and Jewish families into the larger political élite was not unlike that taken by its Muslim members.

Ottoman modernization and centralization coming in the wake of the 1860 events included more rights for non-Muslims. The effects of their growing equality with Muslims, supported by their closer identification with deepening European financial and commercial interests, gave members of the Christian and Jewish bourgeoisie ample protection and social security to broaden their political bases in their communities. We must be careful, however, not to exaggerate this new feeling of security. Continued tensions between Muslims and the minorities could occasionally lead to outbreaks of violence especially against those Christians and Jews who were visibly prosperous. Such disturbances occurred in Damascus in the 1870s when many Muslims, including some of the town's leading notables, were experiencing severe economic difficulties as a result of a series of poor harvests and the decline of the Syrian desert trade with Baghdad owing to the opening of the Suez Canal.[124] Indeed, the seventies was a time when urban notables could still be found resisting Ottoman reform programs.

Both the Christian and Jewish communities won fairer representation in the local administration. Their respective leaders became increasingly active in government in the last third of the century, sitting on the two most important local councils, the Provincial and District Councils. They were also members of the Municipal Council and served as judges on the Commercial Court and the Courts of Appeal and Summary Justice.[125] They also sat on the Councils of Education and Property Taxation and the Chambers of Commerce and Agriculture. Offered both political and commercial protection under the wings of several European consulates, some Christian leaders served as dragomans (*turjuman*) and even consuls.[126]

Owing to the increase in security and freedom of action, these minority leaders were able to use their positions in the local administration and their financial and commercial connections with Europe to establish a solid base of wealth and influence. Their effective power was enhanced as they became the pre-eminent commercial class in Damascus. As merchants they handled the importation of luxury goods and European textiles and played a pivotal role in the gradual absorption of the provincial economy into that of Europe. As moneylenders-cum-bankers they controlled cash flow in the city and countryside and developed strong economic links with members of the Muslim absentee-landowning class by providing capital to finance their land purchases and housing projects.[127] In fact, two Christian families, the Qudsis and the Shamiyyas, combined administrative office with merchant capital to purchase large estates, with the result that by the end of the nineteenth century they had joined the club of great landowning families in Damascus.[128]

The behavior of the political and social leadership

In the Damascus power configuration, the local political leadership served as an intermediary between the society from which it came and the state. To be successful, an intermediary can neither risk its access to the central authority by outright opposition to that authority nor jeopardize the interests of its local clientele by being simply the instrument of the central authority.[129] In 1860, the notables failed to demonstrate decisive urban leadership when they obstructed the interests both of Istanbul and the local populace in Damascus. In the ensuing period (1860–1908), the behavior of the political leadership became less ambiguous. It openly identified with and defended the interests of the Ottoman state and more clearly defined its relationship with local society as one of outright control and domination.

In the last decades of the nineteenth century the political leadership in Damascus came to support the Ottoman central government in its efforts to reimpose calm and stability in the city and its environs, after a long period of turmoil and upheaval produced by the Egyptian occupation, the early years of the *Tanzimat*, and European commercial penetration. The Ottoman state's eagerness to gain a firmer grip on the Syrian Province and other Arabic-speaking regions of the Empire led to the introduction of centralizing and secularizing reforms in the areas of justice, education and finance, and in the army, the gendarmerie and the land-tenure system. These, in turn, enabled the leading families of Damascus (and other towns) to dominate local society in two related ways. By using their offices to acquire land they came to dominate the hinterland of Damascus. With title deeds in hand, these families ruthlessly exploited their peasants, extracting a large percentage of the agricultural surplus as rent. Without legal recourse or the possibility of resistance, since the judicial system was controlled by the landlords and the military might of the state was prepared to intervene on their behalf, peasants were obliged to comply.[130] The landowning families then used agricultural profits to buy posts. Through their posts they dispensed favors or benefits in the form of jobs, contracts, and access to and protection from government. Thus patronage networks were extended and diversified and a certain stability, unknown in Damascus for generations, reigned in the city and its province.

The behavior of the Damascus political leadership was also defined by the political and socioeconomic functions carried out by the family as a unit. The economic and social relations of the extended family (or clan) determined how wealth was preserved. In the years immediately after 1860, agricultural lands and urban real estate tended to be registered as private property in the name of the family as a unit and not in the name of any one member. Moreover, to protect landholdings from confiscation and division the family preferred to place a considerable portion in a family endowment (*waqf ahli*). Generally, the head of the family was charged with the task of administering this endowment.[131] Its profits served as the strongest economic link binding a wealthy family together. Family wealth was also preserved through marriages within the extended family. Marriages between first cousins were generally preferred when possible and some patriarchs were known to have prevented daughters from marrying at all if no male first cousins were available.[132] The members of an extended family often lived under one roof or in one compound.[133]

It was the aim of most of the landowning-bureaucratic families to place their members in as many posts as possible at any given time. Families like the 'Azms, 'Abids, Yusufs, and Mardam-Begs were especially successful at arranging a healthy spread of members in the various

government councils and institutions and in developing unofficial
hereditary rights over some offices. One common path to these ends was
bribery. For example, Muhammad Fawzi Pasha al-'Azm reportedly paid
the Ottoman *wali* one thousand Turkish gold pounds for his appointment
to the Presidency of the Damascus Municipal Council in the early 1890s.
An even more phenomenal sum, two thousand gold pounds, was
reportedly paid by 'Abd al-Rahman Pasha al-Yusuf to guarantee his own
succession as *Amir al-Hajj*. Purchasing such posts was not simply for
prestige. The President of the Municipal Council handed out contracts,
licenses and permits and created jobs for lesser bureaucrats. The *Amir
al-Hajj* organized the pilgrimage, protected it and had many trading
options during the season. Thus, both posts returned significant financial
dividends, but more importantly provided the means to gain and satisfy
clients.[134] Smaller bribes were often used to initiate sons into politics by
purchasing seats on various councils. In the highly competitive market
for offices in the Damascus province the enormous financial resources
of the great landowning families put them at a distinct advantage.

Political behavior involved the creation, strengthening and use of two
kinds of relationship: the family unit to its clients and the family to its
peers.

The landowning-bureaucratic family used its resource base in local
government and its material wealth to build clientele networks in its
quarter of residence and among specific ethnic groups or commercial
associations in the city and its countryside. Often, the large family home
in the quarter of residence served as the base of the family operation in
the city. The family promoted an informal style of association by
encouraging a plethora of socioeconomic groups, ranging from big
merchants and guild *shaykhs* to the destitute of the quarter, to seek
consultation, favors, loans or any other services. A special outer salon
was maintained for quasi-political and social purposes.[135] There a family
member could be found settling some personal conflict, offering assistance
to the needy or promising to use his influence to keep a government tax
collector from hounding a neighbor. It was expected that the beneficiaries
of family services would be prepared to offer the family support when
called upon.

Competition for patronage networks in Damascus was as fierce as
competition for high posts in the administration. Consequently, the
range of services a family had at its disposal was dependent on the
diversity of its political offices and contacts and the extent of its wealth.
To broaden the spectrum of their services even further, the landowning-
bureaucratic families began to break with tradition after mid-century by
cementing political and financial alliances through intermarriage.[136]

The first major alliance to be symbolized by marriage was that between the Shamdin and Yusuf clans. Shamdin Pasha married his only child to Muhammad Pasha al-Yusuf and the only male child of that marriage, 'Abd al-Rahman, inherited the combined Shamdin and Yusuf clientele and fortune. 'Abd al-Rahman Pasha al-Yusuf later married the daughter of Khalil Pasha al-'Azm and a long-term political alliance ensued.

Meanwhile, Hawlu Pasha al-'Abid had also married an al-'Azm girl. Two grandsons of this match married two sisters of 'Abd al-Rahman Pasha al-Yusuf. By the early twentieth century the 'Azms, 'Abids and Yusufs managed to consolidate their power base in Damascus society by linking their families together on a sociopolitical basis thus becoming a most powerful triumvirate.

However, the three families did not limit their marriage pool to Suq Saruja. Sami Pasha Mardam-Beg, the son of Hikmat, married an al-'Azm, and another of 'Abd al-Rahman al-Yusuf's sisters was married to Sami's cousin, 'Abdullah Mardam-Beg.

Another series of alliances by marriage resulted in the formation of a second social bloc consisting of the Quwwatli, Barude and Bakri families. Before the end of the nineteenth century Murad al-Quwwatli married the daughter of Muhammad al-Barudi while another al-Barudi daughter was wed to 'Ata al-Bakri. In the next generation these families continued to intermarry and also joined hands with the Yusufs and 'Azms to form a wider social and political network.

As the great landowning-bureaucratic families became increasingly interlinked they also took the opportunity to enhance their social status by contracting marriages with families from the religious aristocracy.[137] However, the landowning-bureaucratic families appear to have been just as interested in contracting marriages with up-and-coming merchant families. It should be remembered that although many industries in Damascus continued their decline under the impact of the European commercial invasion some sectors actually experienced a revival in the last third of the nineteenth century, especially the textile industry. A combination of factors, including a drop in the price of 'locally produced cotton silk and wool' as a result of the commercial depression of the 1870s and 'the abolition of the internal Ottoman customs tariff in 1874,' enabled textile weavers in Damascus and other Syrian towns 'to produce local goods which were cheap enough to find an expanding market among the poorer classes in the towns as well as among nomads and agriculturalists living in remote areas where European goods were less well known.'[138] Thus, it is not surprising to find that the wealthy textile manufacturing family of Jallad had joined hands with the 'Abids by the end of the century, or that the Dalati family, who dominated the renowned fruit-preserving and confectionary industry of Damascus and were important provisioners of the pilgrimage, intermarried with the Quwwatli, Barudi and Bakri families.[139] Rich merchants sought upward mobility through marriage with prominent political families. Families like the Jallads and Dalatis even began to purchase lands which expanded their material resource base and at the same time enhanced their value as attractive candidates for marriage with the more powerful and socially prominent landowning-bureaucratic families. In Damascus, as elsewhere in Syria, it was still difficult to draw sharp lines between families of landowners, merchant-moneylenders, and industrialists, for the same families could often be found situated in more than one branch of the local economy.

As more families were drawn into the Damascus élite by amassing wealth, offices and status through intermarriage, social differentiation became blurred. The religious aristocracy no longer monopolized the highest rungs of the social ladder. Although members of the religious establishment remained socially prominent, families like the 'Ajlanis, Hasibis and Ghazzis, who forsook religious power bases for secular power bases, maintained the greatest social prestige and political power in the hierarchy of religious families. But even these successful scholarly families did not adapt as well as the more recently established landowning-bureaucratic families to the new bases conferring political power after 1860.

Despite the similarity of means and goals and the increasing familial relatedness of the political élite, one last characteristic distinguished the top landowning-bureaucratic families. With the reassertion of Ottoman control and the modernization of communications and transport facilities, the cosmopolitan atmosphere of Istanbul began to attract members of the Damascus élite.[140] The sons of the great landowning-bureaucratic families led this movement to Istanbul. Encouraged by their farsighted fathers to master Turkish and to acquire an Ottoman professional education, they returned to Damascus with a clear advantage over local competitors for government posts. Turkish trappings were a definite asset, opening up a wider range of opportunities in government and rendering individuals and families more cosmopolitan in the eyes of their peers. An Ottoman education and marriage to daughters from refined and well-connected Turkish families became commonplace among landowning-bureaucratic families in Damascus. In the great salons of their palaces the Turkish language came to be politely spoken alongside Arabic. The Turkish fez and frock coat came to distinguish these new *effendis* from the religious dignitaries and from society in general. An Ottoman lifestyle in both the political and social realms was first assimilated by the great

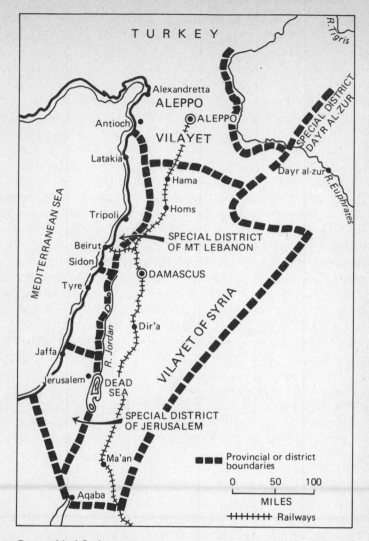

Map 2. Geographical Syria *c.* 1914.

landowning-bureaucratic families and then copied by the lesser members of their class. Political power and social status in Damascus had become closely defined by and identified with the state ideology of 'Ottomanism,' of an Ottoman nation principally of Turks and Arabs.

Although after 1860 the political game in Damascus was restricted to the interaction of a relatively small group of powerful families in possession of land and position in local government, the level of conflict among them was not minimized. In fact competition became more concentrated; it was endemic to Damascus political culture and the 'politics of notables.' The enlarged Ottoman military presence gradually reduced the political arena to the state bureaucracy; political options outside the bureaucracy were few. The level of conflict was heightened by a mounting number of qualified individuals seeking posts. By the end of the nineteenth century a new generation of notables graduated from Ottoman professional schools with the sole aim of entering the bureaucracy. Since the number of office-seekers was much higher than the number of offices, Istanbul could play individuals or factions against one another in an effort to ensure overall loyalty to the state.

In such a competitive political arena the landowning-bureaucratic families maintained a distinct advantage. As the chief representatives of Istanbul they used the ideological stick of 'Ottomanism' to beat opponent after opponent. Landowning-bureaucratic families, however, were not free of internal divisions. As the family increased in number, conflict over the management and distribution of the spoils of privilege surfaced. Division of the family patrimony was rarely equitable, creating distinct economic branches. Furthermore, not all eligible family members could be accommodated in high government posts. Signs of intra- and inter-family conflict and feuding between members in and out of office became more visible. Then, in 1908, a new shock wave rattled Damascus adding a new dimension to political factionalism and more clearly defining its foundation.

Chapter 3

Damascus notables and the rise of Arab nationalism before World War I

Following the 1860 events, but particularly after the commercial depression of the 1870s which had aggravated tensions between the Ottoman central authority and the local leadership in Damascus, the Syrian Province of the Ottoman Empire 'enjoyed a measure' of tranquility and prosperity absent in the first half of the century. Pacification throughout Greater Syria was carried out through the implementation of widespread modernization schemes. Roads, railways and telegraphs improved the transportation and communications network linking Syria to Iraq and Arabia, and to Istanbul. Rural security improved as beduin tribes were encouraged to settle in greater numbers. Agricultural production and rural population grew in many districts as the margins of cultivation were pushed eastward. Even some hardpressed industries began to enjoy a revival by finding increased demand in the towns and countryside. Regional and international commerce continued to expand. Modern elementary, secondary, technical and military schools, departments of justice, and a modernized gendarmerie were other derivatives of the consolidation and extension of reforms stemming from Istanbul during the reign of Sultan 'Abd ul-Hamid II.[1]

In Damascus and other Syrian towns, an ascendant landowning-bureaucratic class benefited from the series of modernizing reforms. This class came to identify with the ideology of Ottomanism and emerged as the agent of Ottoman centralization and modernization. The urban notables aligned with and defended the policies emanating from Istanbul fully cognizant that obstruction no longer served their interests. Even the autocracy and caprice of the Sultan could be ignored as long as the new balance of power in Damascus did not threaten this leadership's position. Indeed, the notables were content to accept directives from the imperial capital and did their utmost to harmonize their aims with those of the dominant power group in Istanbul, which now included members of the Damascus élite. It was under 'Abd ul-Hamid that these notables really began to come into their own within the Empire. With the loss of one Christian-populated Balkan province after another, the Sultan began to lay greater stress on the Islamic character of the Empire and in so doing pampered Arab notables in Damascus and other Syrian towns. He even brought some Arabs into his closest confidence. Indeed, by the early twentieth century, the Ottoman Empire looked much more like an Islamic state of Turks and Arabs, symbolized perhaps most vividly in the Muslim-inspired, funded and executed Hijaz Railway project completed in 1908. It was a state in which Damascene and other Syrian notables were still quite content to live.

There could be found at all times in Syria, of course, a level of opposition to the Sultan's authority and to the spread of European commercial and political influence in the Empire. In Beirut, for example, opposition came from Christians and Muslims. Christian intellectuals educated in western missionary schools, including the Syrian Protestant College and members of the Christian commercial bourgeoisie, became increasingly alarmed by the Sultan's pan-Islamic policies, which they perceived as threatening to their recently acquired security and prosperity. Christians were also joined by some members of the Muslim intelligentsia who focused their opposition on the Sultan's strict censorship laws and his anti-constitutionalism. Meanwhile other Muslims engaged in trade and petty-commodity production voiced their discontent with the state's failure to protect them from expanding European commercial competition. In Beirut, the Muslim notables tended to have stronger ties to the world of commerce than to government.

In Damascus this was not the case. Here notables had a much greater stake in the state system. Moreover, the Christian community was much smaller than that of Beirut and was less developed politically. As a consequence, opposition was even less crystallized. What opposition did exist in Damascus seems to have come from two sources. One included members of the Muslim religious establishment who were unable to diversify their power bases and thus remained ensconced in the decaying religious institutions. Although their influence in a socially conservative city like Damascus continued to be felt long after 1860, they were too impotent to oppose for long the forces of modernization and central-ization from inside local government or to win the approval or support of an increasingly secularized political élite. All these disaffected '*ulama*' could do was to focus their attention on the battle against secularization. They lodged fear in the minds of the unlettered and destitute in the city that without an immediate revival of purely Islamic doctrines and institu-tions, the European infidel and his local agents, the religious minorities, would destroy the Empire and defeat Islam in its Arab heartland. These religious experts manipulated an ideology of return to a pristine, unadulterated Islam, in the hope of upsetting or reversing the processes that had gradually pushed them towards the periphery of the power configuration in Damascus. By the late 1880s, however, 'Abd ul-Hamid had managed for the time being to temper this religiously inspired discontent. By propounding the same fears and beliefs through his pan-Islamic policies he skillfully pulled the rug of independent influence from under the feet of dissident religious leaders in Damascus and elsewhere in Syria. The Sultan's movement, which has been described as 'learn the sciences of war, establish more schools and develop the resources of the country, but in doing so adopt European ideas and techniques only where they agree with the spirit of Islam,'[2] left disaffected '*ulama*' with few issues around which to rally opposition and no recourse but to work as agents of a joint Ottoman–Islamic revival.

The other visible source of dissidence in Damascus came from secular (and some religious) dignitaries who seem to have lost position in the state system. Some were linked to a group of Turkish liberal reformers who focused their attention, often from exile, on the issues of restoring the Constitution, greater freedom of expression, and a decentralized administrative system. Eventually they were to channel their growing opposition to the Sultan into a secretly organized movement of Turks and Arabs. This movement was destined to bring an end to the era of political tranquility enjoyed for more than two decades in Syria.[3]

The Young Turk revolution and the Arabs

In 1906 a group of junior army officers stationed in Salonika formed a secret society which took the name, 'Committee of Union and Progress.' During the next two years other branches, composed of Turkish and Arab officers and civil servants, were organized in provincial centers throughout the Empire. The CUP members, primarily Turkish army officers, came from an ascendant middle class, were professionally trained in military schools and had little connection with Europe or knowledge of European culture and ideas. The CUP desired reform along internal lines to strengthen the Empire from within. Like a broader group of exiled Turkish liberals with which it was in contact, the CUP at this early stage in its development supported the ideology of Ottomanism, of a Turko-Arab nation and state. And it seized on constitutional demands to symbolize its opposition to Sultan 'Abd ul-Hamid's rule. In July 1908, the Committee successfully forced the Sultan to reinstate the Constitution, which he had suspended thirty years earlier.[4]

On the eve of the July coup the Damascus population was 'quiescent,' generally satisfied with Hamidian rule;[5] the leading local politicians were enjoying the fruits of thirty years of social stability and did not anticipate any tremors which might upset the established order. There did exist, however, a small loosely-knit group of Damascene intellectuals and functionaries who, in the two years before the coup, had been working to secure certain concessions for the Syrian provinces within an 'Ottoman framework.' Some individuals from this group had connections with or were recruits to the local CUP branch in Damascus, founded in early 1906, around the time that the Salonika branch took shape.[6] They also formed with other like-minded Damascenes a secret society inspired by the teachings of certain prominent religious reformers who sought to uncover and stress the great literary past of the Arabs. But before 1908 this society's political objectives were still undefined.

The reaction in Damascus to the July coup took several forms. When news confirming the reinstatement of the Constitution reached the city, demonstrations (*'aradat*) erupted supporting the CUP in various quarters. These demonstrations were not spontaneous; rather they were drummed up by CUP partisans in the city who took the occasion to openly display their dissatisfaction with the Hamidian régime.[8] The notables, however, were for the most part stunned by news of the coup and 'apprehensive' of the sudden manifestations that were beyond their control. Fearing the erosion of social stability and the rupture of political continuity some began to voice their opposition to the junior officers' show of force. Moreover, the idea of reviving the Constitution and holding elections did not appeal to Damascus political bosses who were generally satisfied with their positions of influence in the city. Elections might upset the delicate balance of power in Damascus and allow new challengers from within the political élite to test the strength of the political leadership's influence in society. The religious establishment also feared the consequences of the coup. Suspicious of the CUP's liberal views and its platform of equality for all citizens in the Empire, leading Damascus *'ulama'* began to come together against the new power behind the throne.[9]

In the months immediately following the coup the Damascus branch of the CUP pressured the *wali* to dismiss a number of high-ranking religious and secular notables in the provincial administration who were closely identified with the Hamidian régime. Among those officials who were either removed from office or resigned were the head of the Administrative Council of the Province, Muhammad Fawzi Pasha al-'Azm, the *Naqib al-Ashraf*, the Hanafi *Mufti*, an important judge on the *shari'a* court, and several district governors. Other families, for example the Bakri, lost their important ties to the central government when the CUP dismissed 'Abd ul-Hamid's close confidant, the Damascene 'Izzat Pasha al-'Abid.[10] The *'ulama'* of Damascus, in search of an issue around which to rally opposition, seized on the women's dress code. In late October 1908, an *'alim* closely connected to 'Abd ul-Hamid's Arab adviser on religious affairs led anti-CUP demonstrations in Damascus based on opposition to a more liberal dress code.[11] Though this opposition was inspired by the personal motives of some disaffected members of the religious establishment and focused on a minor issue, the *'ulama'* drew support from a wide range of locally influential personalities.

The antagonism generated by this conflict between CUP adherents and the *'ulama'* had direct bearing on the outcome of the parliamentary elections which followed soon after. Carried out in accordance with the Constitution of 1876, the elections were conducted in two stages, thus blunting the impact of popular resentment against the Committee which would have been more manifest in direct elections. In the Syrian provinces the CUP managed to win a number of nominal supporters from among urban and rural notables who had no real interest in major political issues or national questions. Politically apathetic, but fearing removal from office or exclusion from access to the CUP leadership, they chose to stand for elections as Unionist candidates. Only in Damascus did the CUP face a serious challenge. There an opposition party with religious undertones, led by several influential *'ulama'*, a few secular notables and supported by several thousand followers in the popular Muslim quarters of the city, had formed in the wake of anti-dress code manifestations.[12] Five parliamentary delegates to Istanbul were elected from Damascus: 'Abd al-Rahman Pasha al-Yusuf, Shaykh Muhammad al-'Ajlani, Shaykh Sulayman Jukhadar, Rushdi Bey al-Sham'a and Shafiq Bey Mu'ayyad al-'Azm.[13] Only Shafiq Bey was a declared opponent of the CUP before the election though the others were by no means pleased with CUP activities inside their city.[14] The Damascus notability had successfully defeated the CUP list at the polls by playing on religious sentiments and exaggerating CUP secularism, not by inspiring national considerations; clear distinctions of Arab and Turk had yet to surface.

Despite the electoral victory, the opposition party, the 'Muhammadan Union,' which was controlled by the higher *'ulama'* and linked to another Muslim association in Istanbul, continued to agitate against the CUP, demanding the full application of the *shari'a*.[15] When news of a counter-coup in April 1909 – engineered by the First Army Corps and supported by religious elements inside Istanbul – reached Damascus, the Muhammadan Union and its followers in popular quarters like the Maydan rejoiced wildly in the streets and set out to assassinate local Unionists. But the CUP's swift defeat of the countercoup, the removal of the Sultan and expanded supervisory efforts in the Damascus province temporarily put a damper on the activities of local opposition forces.[16]

'From Ottomanism to Arabism'

From the suppression of the countercoup in April 1909 till the outbreak of the First World War, serious political differences between the CUP and Syrian-Arab notables became more apparent, reflected in divergent interpretations of the ideology of Ottomanism. After ousting 'Abd ul-Hamid and replacing him with a more malleable Sultan, the Committee groped towards a definition of Ottomanism that seemed to stress a Turkish input. As the last European territories were lost, the Committee focused its attention on revitalizing and unifying what remained of the Empire – the Turkish and Arab provinces. But in the Arabic-speaking lands, and particularly in Damascus, the CUP's centralizing policy was construed as verging on 'Turkification' and thus as a distinct break with Hamidian policy. Turkish authorities replaced Syrian-Arab notables in key provincial posts and the Turkish language was imposed in schools and in administration. Arabic was relegated to a secondary position in administrative circles. The Unionist officers – young, professionally trained in military science, and from a small but aspiring middle class – inherently distrusted the Syrian-Arab notability. They saw these notables as an entrenched, unprofessional, untrustworthy provincial upper class and preferred to replace them with men closer to their own mold.

The Syrian-Arab interpretation of Ottomanism was also concerned with revitalizing and reunifying what remained of the Empire. But the extreme form of centralization proposed by the CUP was antithetical to the interests of provincial leaders. These notables had thrived best with the Hamidian blend of Ottomanism where Syrian-Arabs were allowed a larger measure of independent influence over their own territories. The Sultan's autocracy was not unpopular; the Syrian-Arab masses were loyal to their leaders and to Islam and generally these leaders were loyal to the Sultan. Moreover, 'Abd ul-Hamid surrounded himself with Syrian-Arabs: his spiritual adviser was from the Aleppo province, his political adviser from a prominent Damascus family. These and other Syrian-Arab officials in Istanbul and in the provinces channeled imperial favor to their clients. Some Syrian-Arab notables, then as always, were out of favor and out of power, and therefore in temporary opposition to the Sultan. It was not, however, an opposition based on a Syrian-Arab national identity as opposed to a Turkish identity.

Syrian-Arab notables – generally content with the measure of power they held under 'Abd ul-Hamid – were alarmed by the 1908 coup and even more shocked by the Sultan's deposition in 1909. His close Syrian advisers were dismissed and his bureaucracy was streamlined and pensioned off. Although there were Syrian members of the CUP, many resigned as the outlines of Unionist policy became clearer. Most joined a growing coalition of Syrian opposition forces. This opposition, however, even until the outbreak of the War, was primarily opposition to a particular ruling group in hopes of replacing it with another ruling group through which local power could be regained, all within the framework of the Empire. Much of the opposition in the provinces was couched in religious terms. The secularist CUP was denounced as an impious usurper of proper Muslim rule and thus of the established order. 'Arabism', a new ideological weapon developed by this opposition within the fold of Ottomanism to battle the Unionists, certainly figured in the call to return to pure Islamic life and institutions; it was not grounds for secession, however, but an ideological plea for attention and more power within the Empire.

No set of CUP reforms alienated the Syrian-Arab population more than the imposition of Turkish in government schools, the court system and in local administration. 'Small and large businessmen suddenly had to follow court proceedings in Turkish; school-children for the first time had to learn that language...and numerous citizens now had to deal with government functionaries in an alien tongue or worse, through an interpreter.'[17] Moreover the CUP's interest in eliminating redundancies in the bureaucracy and in replacing Arab officials with Turks, who were often ignorant of Arabic and of local customs, struck hard at the Syrian political élite. Resentment at being passed over in local appointments and at Arabic being replaced by Turkish helped secular notables and the religious establishment to coalesce into a force of opposition.[18] As pensioned ex-officials returned to their homes in Syria they added support to the growing feeling among the intelligentsia that Unionist centralization policies were actually a front for stepped-up 'Turkification' in the Empire.[19] As local religious leaders helplessly watched increased secularization spread over their domain and traditional preserves such as the Ministry of Justice and the *Awqaf* fall under strict CUP control,[20] they expressed their opposition in strong religious terms and, in the process, finally won the support of a greater number of discontented secular notables.

Damascus was the hotbed of pre-war Arabism. The Damascus brand of Arabism evolved in the early years of the twentieth century as a literary and cultural movement composed of young intellectuals connected to the circle of religious scholars around Shaykh Tahir al-Jaza'iri (b. 1851), a noted teacher and religious reformer.[21] This movement was directed by a loosely-knit organization called the Arab Renaissance Society (*jam'iyyat al-nahda al-'Arabiyya*). When Unionist policy was finally revealed after

1909, members of the Renaissance Society joined a coalition of disparate forces in opposition to the CUP, composed of journalists and writers, members of the religious establishment and a few ranking civilian dignitaries. This coalition began to express its opposition in the guise of Arabism. The common denominator underlying the opposition was a well-founded fear that Ottomanism, as the reigning ideology of Empire, was in the process of being rendered obsolete by Unionist centralizing reforms and thus the Syrian-Arab component in the Empire would be relegated to a tertiary political and administrative role in its operations. Two early Damascus supporters of the CUP expressed this fear quite sincerely after July 1909. Rafiq Bey al-'Azm, an Istanbul-educated notable and former government official, a writer and one of the leading lights in the early intellectual formulation of Arabism, felt that the CUP was interested in eroding the delicate balance of power inherent in Ottomanism at the expense of the Arabs.[22] 'Abd al-Rahman Shahbandar, a young Western-trained medical doctor, interpreted the CUP program as one geared to 'Turkify' the Arab component in the Empire.[23] But neither al-'Azm, Shahbandar, nor any other Damascus intellectual stressing Arabism promoted a separatist ideology of Arab nationalism as a viable alternative to the Unionist interpretation of Ottomanism. Rather, these personalities and others behind the emerging ideology of Arabism emphasized the need for a larger measure of political and administrative decentralization in the Arabic-speaking provinces.

Journalists played a leading role in fostering a Syrian public opinion in favor of Arabism after 1908. Ironically it was the CUP's lifting of Hamidian censorship laws which allowed greater freedom of expression in the Arabic-speaking provinces to be translated into Arabism. A growing number of newspapers and journals began to serve as a forum in which new political ideas could be expounded and disseminated. In Damascus, newspapers began to promote Arabism. The most influential, *al-Muqtabas*, was edited by Muhammad Kurd 'Ali, a clever journalist and man of letters from modest social origins, a former supporter of the CUP and member of the Arab Renaissance Society. Kurd 'Ali used his newspaper as a vehicle with which to encourage literate elements among the local populace to turn towards Arabism after 1909. Writers like Rafiq al-'Azm, who had originally attracted his friend, Kurd 'Ali, to the Damascus branch of the CUP, published articles in *al-Muqtabas* defending Arabism as a necessary component in reviving Ottomanism and the idea of Ottoman nationhood, as expressed during the Hamidian era. After 1912, a second newspaper, *al-Qabas*, appeared. It was edited by Shukri al-'Asali, an Istanbul-trained provincial governor and parliamentarian from a prominent landowning family of the

Maydan, and an early member of the Renaissance Society. *Al-Qabas* reflected a more radical and uncompromising interpretation of Arabism, including greater political autonomy for the Arabic-speaking provinces.[24]

Although the CUP had originally liberalized the censorship code, in the wake of the April 1909 countercoup it became far less keen on extending freedoms of speech and association. Meanwhile, as new journals in the Syrian provinces appeared, editors and writers developed greater expectations and applied pressure to win increased freedom of expression. The CUP press law, however, was not sufficiently flexible or liberal. Occasionally newspapers were suppressed or suspended and editors put on trial for printing articles stressing the political virtues of Arabism which the CUP found inimical to its own interests.[25] Single incidents promoted greater misunderstanding between Syrians and the Turkish Unionists, but their cumulative effect permitted latent hostilities to surface as outright conflict.

Syrian political grievances against various CUP measures could also be expressed in the Ottoman Parliament in Istanbul. Most Syrian-Arab deputies to Parliament, however, had been CUP nominees in 1908, and many remained uncritical of Unionist policies.[26] Fearing the wrath of the Unionists if contrary opinions were voiced, these deputies tended to vote for all Unionist-sponsored programs and legislation without considering the repercussions in their Syrian constituencies. Only a small, rather disorganized bloc of parliamentarians—the majority hailing from Damascus—dared openly to criticize the CUP and defend Arab rights within the Empire. This minority was unsuccessful in creating a larger unified Syrian-Arab bloc of delegates with either collective goals or a coherent platform; common political bonds between Syrian representatives from different regions were still rather flimsy.

In the series of parliamentary sessions held between 1909 and 1911 two Damascus deputies, Shafiq Mu'ayyad al 'Azm and Rushdi al-Sham'a, actively attacked the CUP. Their efforts were supported by a religious *shaykh* from Hama, 'Abd al-Hamid al-Zahrawi, who had been elected to the Chamber on the Unionist ticket but soon thereafter quarreled with his sponsor and switched his allegiance to the Damascus parliamentary opposition.[27] In this period attempts were made to establish a parliamentary party of 'liberal' Syrian-Arab delegates in order to strengthen the bonds of Ottoman unity by preserving rights of equality as outlined in the Constitution. But members of the *entente libérale* could not agree on a set of common principles and some returned to the Unionist camp.[28]

A by-election in 1911, after the death of Damascus deputy Muhammad al-'Ajlani, sent Shukri al-'Asali to Parliament. He was a forceful advocate of Arab rights and soon came to lead the Syrian 'liberal opposition' in Parliament. In a number of parliamentary sessions he vehemently attacked the CUP for showing weakness on the question of Zionist expansion in Palestine, where he had served as the governor of the Nazareth district.[29] He also condemned the CUP for avoiding Arabs when picking individuals for high administrative posts in the Empire.[30] Al-'Asali's political role in and out of Parliament helped to galvanize effective Syrian-Arab opposition to the CUP.[31] The outbreak of war in the province of Tripolitania in late 1911 and its subsequent loss to Italy added fuel to the fire of the 'liberal opposition' and even caused politically apathetic and conservative Syrian notables to question the capability of the CUP to defend the Empire against its European enemies.[32] Important sections of the Syrian population, already somewhat influenced in favor of Arabism, began to give more wholehearted support to that ideology by the outbreak of the Balkan Wars in 1912.[33]

The CUP called for new parliamentary elections in April 1912. In the Syrian provinces and elsewhere the elections were arranged so that Unionists won everywhere. The Damascus opposition, led by al-'Asali, Mu'ayyad al-'Azm and al-Sham'a, lost to a group of Unionist-backed moderates who followed the CUP line seemingly for no reason other than a desire to retain a position of influence in local society. Only 'Abd al-Rahman Pasha al-Yusuf was re-elected and he had carefully avoided political association with his former colleagues from Damascus who were the backbone of Syrian parliamentary opposition in previous years. Muhammad Fawzi Pasha al-'Azm, the most influential politician in Damascus – having patched up his differences with the Unionists – was elected, as were two prominent but politically quiescent *'ulama'*, 'Abd al-Muhsin al-Ustwani and Amin Tarazi.[34] The Ottoman Parliament would never again be a forum in which Arab demands could be cogently expressed.

Following its defeat in the 1912 parliamentary elections, the 'liberal opposition' shifted its political activities from Damascus and Istanbul to Cairo and Paris, and into more structured political organizations, some of which were clandestine. Owing to self-imposed or forced exile some of the leading intellectual lights of the Damascus-based opposition had already moved to British-occupied Cairo where they received the nominal protection of the Egyptian Khedive who had been entertaining designs on Syria and the Caliphate for some time.[35] Syrian dissidents from Damascus and other towns had previously been in contact with an active group of Syrian émigré-intellectuals led by Shaykh Rashid Rida, the noted theologian and disciple of Shaykh Muhammad 'Abduh. From

Cairo, Rida attacked the CUP and promoted the idea of an Arab monarch or Caliph.[36] By mid-1912, newly arrived personalities from among the Damascus opposition joined the Rida group in the safer confines of Cairo and began to denounce the Unionists through the widely circulated and politically influential Syrian-owned newspaper, *al-Muqattam*.

The sophisticated cultural and intellectual atmosphere of Cairo attracted Syrians from different cities and regions coming to discuss pertinent political issues affecting their respective communities. It was in Cairo that collective Syrian-Arab goals for the first time were formally articulated and common political bonds among representatives of an emerging Arab movement were formed. One practical outcome of this interaction was the creation of a political organization to guide the development of the infant Arab movement. In January 1913 the Ottoman Party of Administrative Decentralization (*Hizb al-lamarkaziyya al-idariyya al-'Uthmani*) was founded. Its Executive Committee, based in Cairo, included eight Muslims, five Christians and one Druze, all of whom were Syrians. Rafiq al-'Azm served as its President, his cousin, Haqqi, as its Secretary. Affiliated to the Decentralization Party was a defeated group of Syrian parliamentarians who had chosen to remain in Syria, including Shukri al-'Asali, Shafiq Mu'ayyad al-'Azm, Rushdi al-Sham'a and 'Abd al-Hamid al-Zahrawi.[37]

The program of the Decentralization Party was similar to that of an earlier Ottoman decentralization movement, the 'Liberal Union,' led by a group of Turkish bureaucrats and intellectuals, some of whom had been in exile during Sultan 'Abd ul-Hamid's reign, and who began to actively oppose the CUP after 1909.[38] Although it claimed to appeal to all Ottoman citizens, the Cairo Decentralization Party only attracted Syrians, and its branches were only found in Syrian towns. The Party was dominated by Muslims though efforts were made to encourage a secular attitude by giving a voice to Christian members. It called for greater administrative decentralization in the Arabic-speaking provinces, though certain members seriously considered a more radical plank demanding widespread political autonomy for Arabs. Although the Decentralization Party did not appeal to the Syrian masses, it did manage to gain significant support from more articulate and influential groups in Syrian cities. But it also faced serious opposition from Syrian notables, particularly in Damascus, who had managed to retain or regain their local power bases by collaborating with the CUP. Encouraged by the CUP to attack the Decentralization Party, Damascus Unionists like Muhammad Fawzi al-'Azm, 'Abd al-Rahman al-Yusuf, Ahmad al-Sham'a (member of the Municipal Council and father of Rushdi), Sami Mardam-Beg and Nasib al-Hamza accused the Decentralization Party founders of being political propagandists and agents of European powers.[39] Their accusations were not without foundation. The historical record indicates that before World War I British officials encouraged the idea of Arabism and some loose form of Syrian territorial unity as a potential safety valve to 'protect Egypt from Turkish or foreign invasion.' It also seems that some leaders of the Decentralization Party were interested in promoting the idea of British tutelage for the Arabs, as opposed to French protection, should the Empire be further dismembered.[40] From the vantage of Damascus politics, however, this condemnation was indicative of the growing power struggle within the local political élite and this conflict's expression in the ideological terms of pro-Unionist 'Ottomanism' versus anti-Unionist 'Arabism.'[41]

Conscious of mounting opposition, the CUP made some half-hearted attempts to alleviate discontent in Syrian towns. When in early 1913 the Turkish *wali* called for reforms in Damascus he encouraged a large group of notables to reach a consensus on the nature of reforms it wanted to see implemented. But this effort failed; the notables split along CUP and 'liberal opposition' lines, the former desiring material improvements and the latter, a more decentralized form of government.[42] Thus the growing ideological rift within the Damascus political élite became ever more apparent. As the demand for Arab 'rights' within the Empire grew, a small minority began to promote the notion of a secular Arab nationalism, claiming that Arabic-speaking Muslims, Christians and Jews were 'Arabs' before they were members of their respective religious communities.[43] In the months leading up to World War I the Arab movement developed rapidly.

Frustrated by its failure to win even a modicum of political concessions from the inflexible CUP, which had effectively seized control of most internal mechanisms of power in the Empire by 1913, the 'liberal opposition' turned to clandestine political activities to achieve its aims.

Secret societies were not new to the Syrian provinces; they had existed during 'Abd ul-Hamid's autocratic reign and again in the years following the 1908 coup. The Arab Renaissance Society had originally been a secret organization, but after the 1908 *coup* it functioned openly as a forum of cultural and political debate.[44] At the end of 1909 a new secret Syrian group was founded in Istanbul. The Qahtan Society (*al-jam'iyya al-Qahtaniyya*) included a number of Syrian army officers and active members of the Renaissance Society and seems to have stressed the idea of Arabism in reaction to the unveiling of Unionist 'Turkification' policy.[45] A second secret Syrian organization was established in Paris in 1909, the Young Arab Society (*jam'iyyat al-umma al-'Arabiyya al-fatat*). *Al-Fatat* eventually was to have considerable impact on the development of Arab nationalism, and many of its members were to be active in Syrian politics in the generation after World War I. Prior to 1914, its roster included Arabs studying in Paris and a group of young activists operating in Damascus and Beirut.[46] Members such as Jamil Mardam-Beg, Nasib and Fawzi al-Bakri, Fakhri al-Barudi and Muhibb al-Din al-Khatib came from illustrious Damascus families, some of which could count among their members a number of CUP supporters. Of all political organizations existing in or outside Syria before the War only *al-Fatat* seems to have stood for Arab independence from the Ottoman Empire. In the wake of the Committee's suppression of Syrian political organiz- ations, particularly the Damascus branch of the Decentralization Party and its cousin, the Beirut Reform Society (*jamʿiyyat al-umumiyya al-islahiyya fi Bayrut*), *al-Fatat* began to operate clandestinely in Damascus and Beirut circulating propaganda calling for the Syrian masses to revolt against their Turkish oppressors.[47] But, while its operations helped to disseminate the idea of Arabism in Syria, the popular upheaval *al-Fatat* desired had not materialized by the outbreak of the War.

With opposition inside Syria effectively curtailed by stringent CUP measures, the focus of Syrian agitation shifted to Paris. There the Syrians made a final effort to secure administrative decentralization within the framework of the Empire. Five Arab students, including one Damascene, Jamil Mardam-Beg, initiated an Arab Congress in June 1913. The participants, equally divided between Muslims and Christians, aimed to preserve the identity of the 'Arab nation' (*al-umma al-ʿArabiyya*) through increased reforms in the Arabic-speaking provinces. They posited the concept of 'Westernization' as the effective tool by which to revitalize the Arab provinces and the Empire at large in the face of an enfeebled and militarily impotent Ottoman state. Moreover, by holding the Congress in Paris the founders hoped to secure European sympathy for their demands. Realizing their own youth and lack of political reputation among the Arabs, the architects of the Congress established links with the Decentralization Party in Cairo in order to include prestigious politicians necessary to give the Congress an impact.[48]

The CUP waged a campaign of vilification in an effort to prevent the Congress from being held. It accused its initiators of not representing any legitimate interests in the Arab provinces and thus of having no legal right to speak on behalf of the Arab population. Simultaneously, opposition to the Congress was mustered in Syria, led by the influential Damascus notables, Muhammad Fawzi Pasha al-ʿAzm and ʿAbd al-Rahman Pasha al-Yusuf, who accused the Congress founders of being social upstarts with dangerous if not treasonable ambitions.[49] Despite these efforts, the Congress was held as scheduled. The Turkish authorities prevented individuals residing in Syria at the time from attending, however, and only one leading personality from the Decentralization Party played a significant role at its sessions. The Congress adopted a reform program similar to those of the Beirut Reform Society and the Ottoman Party of Administrative Decentralization. It called for decentralization within the framework of the Empire, not for Syrian independence; a program which received, at least temporarily, the backing of the French government.

A disturbed CUP then tried to dampen the effects of the Paris meeting by offering to negotiate a compromise agreement with the Syrian reformers behind closed doors. After some hard bargaining over the major points of contention the parties drew up a secret agreement that was to give the Arabic-speaking provinces a greater measure of political autonomy. But, to the dismay of the Syrians, the President of the Decentralization Party, Rafiq al-'Azm, carelessly revealed the outline of the settlement to the press against the wishes of the CUP. Ostensibly enraged, the CUP publicly denied the existence of any such agreement and relations between the opposing camps soured. In fact, the CUP had never intended to give in to a full-blown reform program in Syria, despite promises made to this effect. A significant military victory in the Balkans in the summer of 1913 gave the CUP the required confidence to back down on its promises, following which the Ottoman government presented the Syrians with a much less attractive, watered-down reform program in August.[50] The overwhelming reaction of Syrian 'Arabists' to the Unionist proposals was negative. Syrian sentiment was now pushed towards the brink of separatism.

Following the breakdown of negotiations in July 1913 the CUP made its most concerted attempt to sow dissension among the Syrian-Arab liberal reformers. Members of the stymied Beirut Reform Society, who had previously focused their attention solely on securing autonomy for the Beirut province while seeking British support in the face of rapidly expanding French political activities in the region, now resigned themselves to operating within a Unionist framework. One of the Reform Society's leading members, Salim 'Ali Salam, an influential Beirut notable, mended his fences and was elected on a CUP ticket to the Ottoman Parliament in April 1914.[51] The Unionist's biggest catch, however, was 'Abd al-Hamid al-Zahrawi, the President of the Paris Congress. Offered a seat in the prestigious Ottoman Senate, he broke with his allies, causing a fatal blow to the Decentralization Party leadership.[52] In Damascus the uncontested parliamentary elections of April sent four Muslim notables to Istanbul for the last time. All were

CUP sympathizers, led once again by Muhammad Fawzi Pasha al-'Azm; others included 'Ali Pasha al-Jaza'iri who was elected Vice-President of the Chamber, 'Awni Bey al-Qudamani, a high-ranking army officer, and Badi' Bey Mu'ayyad al-'Azm, the Istanbul-educated cousin both of Muhammad Fawzi Pasha and Shafiq Mu'ayyad al-'Azm of the Decentralization Party. Representing the city's minorities was Faris al-Khuri, a Christian lawyer and intellectual, who had previously served as Dragoman at the British Consulate in Damascus and who was cautiously sympathetic to the 'liberal opposition.'[53] Thus by the time the Ottoman Empire entered the First World War on the side of the Central Powers, in November 1914, the Unionist government had cunningly out-maneuvered and divided the nascent Syrian-Arab movement.

The social origins of Arab nationalism

The origins of both Ottomanism and Arabism are linked to the broad changes that took place in the Ottoman Middle East in the second half of the nineteenth century. A modernized system of administration and law, new patterns of trade and production, faster means of communication, and the steady expansion of Europe, were to have profound effects on all communities and classes in the region, but perhaps most visibly on the upper classes, both Turkish and Arab.

More specifically, the origins of Ottomanism and Arabism can be traced to a reaction at this time to the failure of the ruling élite in Istanbul to defend Islamic civilization against Western economic, cultural and political penetration.[54] As intellectual currents both were primarily negative in the sense of being defensive reflexes raised to buffer the pain of humiliation and defeat. But Ottomanism, which acquired ideological content before Arabism,[55] remained the reigning political ideology of the Empire until the end of the First World War. Arabism, in its ideological context, sprang from the bosom of Ottomanism only when the latter ideology was refashioned by an ascendant group of young Turkish army officers and bureaucrats to consolidate its power base in the Ottoman territories. Until 1914, the aims of Arabism did not differ radically from those of Ottomanism. Indeed, the majority of adherents to Arabism, who constituted a political minority in the Arab provinces, sought neither the separation of the Arab territories from the Empire nor the creation of a distinct Arab nation with defined territorial boundaries. Rather their demands more accurately reflected the interests of a growing number of politically active members of an urban absentee landowning and bureaucratic class that had failed to achieve power and influence commensurate with their expectations. And these expectations still belonged within the framework of Empire.

The new opposition shaped the ideology of Arabism into a political weapon to be used against two very different opponents, one an external enemy and the other an internal rival. The CUP was defined as the enemy which had either stripped the Arabist opposition of its traditional power base in local society or had denied it the opportunity to build such a base. The internal rival was composed of a powerful group of politically-active elements from the same class as the 'Arabists' but who were more successful in the highly competitive struggle for both office-based property in the local or central administration and for material resource bases. Although the Arabist opposition distinguished between enemy and rival it also realized that the latter maintained itself through collusion with the enemy. Thus Arabism was a challenge to both.

Prior to 1914, Arabism was a Syrian-inspired and Syrian-dominated ideology. Syrians, whether political activists operating in Syrian towns, or in Istanbul, or exiled intellectuals sitting in Cairo and Paris, directed the nascent 'Arab movement.'[56] Furthermore, Syrian localist and personal ambitions and conflicts were as much involved in the development of the ideology and its dissemination as were the cultural and political expressions which lent it content.

Damascus was the major center of Arabism in Syria during the period 1908–14. Damascenes played a disproportionate role with respect to other Syrians in promoting the ideology of Arabism and in directing the Arab movement, even though many were forced to seek refuge outside their city and outside the effective borders of the Ottoman Empire in order to continue their agitation for Arab rights within the Empire.[57] But Damascus was also the most formidable seat of resistance to Arabism and the Arab movement in Syria. Thus the nature of ideological confrontation between an ascendant Arabism and a dominant Ottomanism can best be elucidated in the political struggle of Damascenes. In Damascus, several objective factors helped to distinguish Arabists from their Ottomanist counterparts. These concerned their respective relationships to local administration, age, educational background, profession and position in the social hierarchy.

The most glaring distinction between Arabists and Ottomanists concerned the holding of administrative office. Most Damascus Arabists who were of the right age and had the proper qualifications to hold either high or middle-level government posts failed to retain them after 1908 when the CUP began to replace Syrians with Turks in the provincial and central administration. One example of how a member of the local élite converted to Arabism can be illustrated by briefly tracing the career of

Haqqi al-'Azm. Born into an illustrious Damascene family in 1864, and educated at the Lazarist missionary school in Damascus and later at the military college in Istanbul where he learned Turkish, Haqqi began his career as a government clerk during the late Hamidian era. In 1910 he was appointed Inspector-General to the Ministry of the *Awqaf*, a prestigious post in Istanbul. However, when the CUP seized control of this Ministry in 1911, Haqqi Bey was pensioned off and replaced by a Turk. In the 1912 parliamentary elections he opposed the Unionists by running on the 'liberal opposition' ticket, [58] but was soundly defeated along with his Arabist colleagues. Embittered, he moved to Cairo where he joined his cousin, Rafiq, in founding the Ottoman Party of Administrative Decentralization. Three other leading figures in the opposition group of Arabists—Shafiq Mu'ayyad al-'Azm, Rushdi al-Sham'a and Shukri al-'Asali—were also Istanbul-trained, spoke Turkish and held high administrative posts before the CUP crackdown.[59] They lost their jobs not for attacking Ottomanism *per se*, but for attacking the Unionist brand of Ottomanism. All three were delegates from Damascus to the Ottoman Parliament before 1912. But when the CUP prevented them from regaining their seats in the next elections and from holding any other administrative posts they reacted by turning to more concerted political activities against both the Unionists and their collaborators within the Damascus political élite who had managed to hold on to their posts.

There was also a much larger group of younger élite members who had either expected to succeed their prominent fathers or uncles in the upper echelons of the local bureaucracy or who were qualified by Hamidian standards to assume middle-level posts, but were unable to do so because of the vagaries of Unionist policy. A number of these young notables had been sent by their families to exclusive Ottoman professional schools in Istanbul in preparation for government service. On returning home, however, they found their possibilities greatly diminished. The CUP had ousted some landowning-bureaucratic families like the 'Abids and Bakris from positions of local power owing to their close connection to the Hamidian régime;[60] it had also streamlined the provincial bureaucracy and filled many of the remaining posts with Turks. Their expectations crushed, these frustrated and idle young men whiled away hours in coffee houses[61] reading newspapers and discussing their various grievances. Many became associated with the slightly older group of disaffected notables constituting the 'liberal opposition' and under its influence began to voice similar political views in terms of Arabism. Several young, educated but unemployed Damascenes formed a local branch of *al-Fatat* and through increased underground political activities in the months leading up to the 1914 War developed a more radical and divergent interpretation of Arabism that called for the separation of the Arabic-speaking provinces from the Empire.

The age structure of the 'liberal opposition' did not differ noticeably from that of pro-Ottomanist politicians. Arabists like Shafiq Mu'ayyad al-'Azm, Shukri al-'Asali, Rushdi Sham'a and Haqqi al-'Azm belonged to the same generation as that of non-Arabist politicians like Muhammad Fawzi al-'Azm, 'Abd al-Rahman al-Yusuf, Muhammad al-'Ajlani and Sami Mardam-Beg. Although among the 'overt' Arabists, men like 'Abd al-Rahman Shahbandar, Muhammad Kurd 'Ali and Rafiq al-'Azm could be characterized as part of a second generation of Arabists, the group of pro-Ottomanist politicians in Damascus also had second-generation support. However, the age structure of the clandestine group of Arabists, primarily members of *al-Fatat*, formed a distinct second generation in contrast to both the 'liberal opposition' and the Ottomanists. Young Damascene activists in *al-Fatat* like Fawzi, Nasib and Sami al-Bakri, Jamil Mardam-Beg, Fakhri al-Barudi, Muhibb al-Din al-Khatib and Ahmad Qadri ranged from their late teens to their mid-twenties between 1908 and 1914, making them on the average approximately twenty years younger than the overt groups of competitors within the local political élite.[62] Their youthfulness, idleness and inexperience in traditional Ottoman methods of political bargaining and compromise were reflected in their mode of political behavior and their more violent opposition to the local group of pro-Ottomanist notables and to the CUP itself. Thus the ideological confrontation between Arabism and Ottomanism, though primarily reflecting the nature of intra-class and intra-élite conflict in Damascus, at least in part also reflected inter-generational conflict.

Educational backgrounds tended only slightly to differentiate Damascus Arabists from their Ottomanist rivals. Within the older generation of politicians, both Arabists and Ottomanists appear to have acquired the same level and form of education, an advanced Ottoman state education, which included professional training in Turkish. Furthermore almost all personalities from both factions had served in various capacities within the local or central bureaucracy during the Hamidian era. There did exist, however, a small minority of slightly younger Arabists, mostly from less established families, who were not products of the Ottoman state educational system. Some, like Muhammad Kurd 'Ali, received a traditional Islamic education at the feet of private tutors from among a discontented body of 'reformist' religious scholars. Others, like 'Abd al-Rahman Shahbandar, were sent to regional foreign missionary schools and not to Istanbul for higher education.[63]

This slightly higher incidence of 'traditional religious' and 'advanced

Western' education among the older generation of Arabists as compared to the more strictly Ottoman-educated pro-Unionist group of politicians reflected two divergent intellectual trends within Arabism—one religious, the other secular. On one hand we find that a number of religious scholars were among the first leaders of the anti-Unionist opposition bloc, men who represented the 'traditionalist' strain within the Arab movement. Fearing the Western threat to Islamic civilization and embittered by the decline of religious institutions over the previous two generations, which rapidly accelerated under the impact of stringent Unionist secularization and 'Turkification' policies, these religious leaders preferred to emphasize the Arab contribution to Islam and the negative features of four hundred years of Turkish rule. On the other hand, we find Western-educated opponents of the CUP framing their cure in terms of the need for a thorough revitalization of the Empire through the systematic application of Western technology and modes of thought. While the 'traditional Islamic' and 'modern Western' trends characterized the development of both Syrian Arabism and Ottomanism, by 1914 they were more clearly pronounced in the ideological content of Syrian Arabism. Among the younger generation of Arabists who operated clandestinely before the War, the modern Western trend had a distinctly anti-Turkish flavor. Several members of the younger group graduated at about the same time from the one secondary school in Damascus which served the city's élite. Maktab 'Anbar, as it was called, contained a circle of young teachers and students who had begun to promote the idea of Arabism in and out of the classroom before the coup of 1908. Some teachers were even known to have discouraged their students from studying their Turkish lessons.[64] Moreover some members of this informal circle were connected to the group of religious scholars around Shaykh Tahir al-Jaza'iri and the Arab Renaissance Society. While a number of graduates of Maktab 'Anbar went on to Istanbul to receive advanced professional training in Turkish, a significant proportion stopped at the secondary level or, significantly, opted to go to Europe for a higher education. Not surprisingly, young men like Jamil Mardam-Beg and Ahmad Qadri, among the first Syrian Muslim students to go to Europe prior to 1914 for their higher education, came to identify with the concept of 'secular Westernization' as the effective tool by which to reinvigorate the Empire.[65]

Regarding occupation, the older generation of Arabists differed from their Ottomanist contemporaries in two important ways. First, a high percentage of pro-Ottomans occupied government positions throughout the period 1908–1914, while government employment among the Arabists was much less frequent in the same period.[66] Several Arabists had held high posts at the end of the Hamidian reign but either voluntarily left government service or were sacked by the CUP after 1908. Secondly, the Arabists were actively engaged in intellectual pursuits while Ottomanists generally steered clear of such activities. Journalism and the liberal professions (doctors, lawyers and engineers) were the most common occupations among the Arabists. Doubtless this was because Arabists needed to have a livelihood and could only secure one outside government. For instance, Shukri al-'Asali was a former district governor and parliamentarian turned journalist; Rafiq al-'Azm was a well-known writer; Muhammad Kurd 'Ali edited the most influential Damascus newspaper of the day; and 'Abd al-Rahman Shahbandar was an American-trained physician and lectured on sociology. The Arabists played a conspicuous role in promoting the nascent Arab movement in the fields of journalism and letters. Conversely local Ottomanists in Damascus favored using their government positions and not their pens to defend Ottomanism.

Among the second generation of Arabists there was a high incidence of individuals trained for the liberal professions, particularly law, which served as a stepping-stone into government service, and as military officers.[67] However, in this period most professionally trained Arabists were either too young to have advanced far in government service or were unsuccessful in the highly competitive market for administrative office. Although Damascus military officers played an insignificant role in the pre-1914 Arab movement, from an ideological perspective two factors may have fostered their Arabist tendencies. First, like the Unionist military officers, they were professionally trained, from a small but aspiring middle class, and inherently suspicious of the local unprofessional notability. This conflict had been exacerbated by the landowning-bureaucratic class which for several generations had discouraged its members from entering military service. Able to use their influence with the State to win exemptions from conscription for their sons, urban notables came to view military careers as more suitable for those classes further down the social scale. Secondly, from what little biographical information exists on these officers it seems that as a group they were of lower social rank than their pro-Ottomanist counterparts.[68]

Finally the class origins and social status of the group of pre-1914 Damascus 'Arabists' played a role in differentiating it from its Ottomanist rivals. Socioeconomic distinctions were reflected in the nature of intra-élite conflict. The older generation of Arabists was composed of individuals from powerful landowning-bureaucratic families as well as several personalities from less prominent families. Rafiq, Haqqi and Shafiq Mu'ayyad al-'Azm, and Rushdi al-Sham'a, by virtue of their surnames, belonged to the cream of Damascus society. Shukri al-'Asali came from a slightly less prominent and more recently established landowning-bureaucratic family of the Maydan quarter.[69] However, Muhammad Kurd 'Ali and 'Abd al-Rahman Shahbandar were from distinctly lower social origins—one the son of a small landowner and the other from a middling merchant family – and by World War I had not acquired the social status of their Arabist comrades.[70] The second generation of Arabists was also composed of young men from prominent Damascus families like the Mardam-Begs, Bakris, Barudis and Khatibs as well as members of families which were considered by the aristocracy to be social climbers. On the other hand, proclaimed and active Damascus Ottomanists were invariably members of the political élite and of the local upper class.

Socioeconomic distinctions, however, were even more pronounced at the level of intra-familial competition for administrative posts. As aristocratic families expanded in number over a few generations distinct branches developed. 'Some of their branches actually suffered a relative decline' in wealth, influence and the ability to obtain public office. 'It was not uncommon for men of the same large family to be on opposite sides politically.'[71] For instance, Rafiq and Haqqi al-'Azm, both Arabists, came from the poorer and less politically influential branches of the aristocratic al-'Azm family, while Muhammad Fawzi Pasha al-'Azm, an avowed Ottomanist and CUP supporter, headed the leading branch (As'ad) of the family, and was far and away the wealthiest and most influential al-'Azm in Damascus.[72] 'Uthman and Jamil Mardam-Beg had both become Arabists prior to 1914 while their first cousin, Sami Pasha Mardam-Beg, remained an active Ottomanist. Although their respective grandfathers, 'Uthman and 'Ali, had established the Mardam-Begs as one of the wealthiest and most influential Damascus landowning-bureaucratic families in the last third of the nineteenth century, by the third generation of prominent Mardam-Begs, the 'Ali branch was considerably wealthier and also held higher public offices than the 'Uthman branch.

Two factors appear to have caused these intra-familial distinctions in the Mardam-Beg family. First, the 'Ali branch was able to secure a steadier and larger flow of revenues from the *suq* it had built than the 'Uthman branch was able to derive from its irrigated Ghuta farms. Secondly, Sami Pasha's father, Hikmat, was a high government official who managed to create a line of bureaucratic succession for his sons. Hikmat's brother, 'Abd al-Qadir, a prominent notable, died prematurely, leaving his sons to fend for themselves within the highly competitive arena for administrative posts. 'Abd al-Qadir's eldest son, 'Uthman, was unsuccessful in securing a top office. Before his own premature death

'Uthman had become an active member of the Arab Renaissance Society. He had also managed to inculcate in his younger brother, Jamil, strong anti-Turkish sentiments, including an aversion to the Turkish language even though their mother was a Turk. Instead of encouraging him to go to Istanbul to complete his education, 'Uthman steered Jamil to Europe, where as a student in Paris he joined *al-Fatat* after 1909.[73] Meanwhile Sami Pasha Mardam-Beg joined his al-'Azm in-laws in the local bloc of staunch pro-Ottomanist and Unionist supporters.[74]

Thus the group of Damascus Arabists which constituted the mainstay of the pre-1914 Arab movement possessed certain characteristics differentiating it from the group of local Ottomanists. Above all, Arabists were individuals who had failed to secure public office and had therefore less of a stake in the Ottoman state. But they also tended to be slightly younger than the Ottomanist group, from more diverse educational backgrounds, more actively engaged in intellectual pursuits, and from less wealthy and influential branches of local aristocratic families or from families which were not socially prominent. These distinctions, however, were not sufficiently pronounced to clearly differentiate 'Arabists' from 'Ottomanists' along class lines. Class conflict was not the foundation of political rivalry in Damascus or for that matter in other Syrian towns. Rather, conflict was mainly confined to the politically active elements in one particular class that rested at the top of the social hierarchy in Damascus. However, this class—the landowning-bureaucratic class—had its own internal differentiating characteristics which centered on families and family branches whose economic and political interests were either on the rise or on the downgrade. And though intra-class conflict as defined by struggles for public office and scarce resources was witnessed in the late nineteenth century, it was only after 1908 and the CUP Revolt that this conflict was suddenly sharpened and shifted onto a new foundation with added dimensions, defined in terms of two opposing ideologies, Arabism and Ottomanism. In the case of Arabism, it was not translated from an idea into a viable political instrument until just before the 1914 War. And though it was in ascendance, managing to attract and convert influential elements in Damascus in this period, it nevertheless remained a humble minority position in Damascus and elsewhere, unable to erode the loyalty of the dominant faction of the local political élite in Syria to Ottomanism.[75]

Chapter 4

Notables, nationalists and Faysal's Arab government in Damascus, 1918–20

Most members of the Syrian political élite opted to identify with Arabism only after European and Sharifian troops occupied the Syrian provinces of the Ottoman Empire in 1918.[1] For these men the occupation signified the final defeat of the Empire. Consequently its prevailing ideology, Ottomanism, no longer served their interests. Their switch to Arabism was a convenient one, designed both to fill an ideological void and to protect their standing in local society. With no other viable option left, they embraced Arabism hoping to mold it in their own image and thereby to continue practicing politics from a position of strength.

In the case of the older generation of Damascus notables, who had collaborated closely with the CUP until the Turkish defeat, shifting allegiance to Arabism was particularly difficult. The extermination, exile or quasi-conversion of their chief Arabist political rivals before and during the War, some of whom were relatives, created a considerable amount of bad blood. The draconian measures adopted by the CUP aroused the anger and hatred of many young Arab nationalists and turned several prominent older notables against the Turks and their allies in Damascus before the end of the War. But since the Arabists were accused of intriguing with the declared wartime enemies of the Ottoman state– France and Britain–the accusation of treason against Islam and the Empire could be used against them. As long as the CUP was in control, and the Empire still alive, anger and discontent with the Unionist notables, who had been unable to save their own, remained subdued.

The CUP met with little resistance in Syria as it set out to eliminate the last vestiges of opposition to its 'Turkification' policy. Jamal Pasha, the Ottoman governor in Syria, considered several of the pre-1914 Arabists to be no more than self-seeking individuals.[2] He defined the aims of men like Muhammad Kurd 'Ali and Shaykh 'Abd al-Hamid al-Zahrawi as financial or office-seeking. He was able to turn Kurd 'Ali's pen to Unionist panegyric with cash handouts. Al-Zahrawi was temporarily silenced with a seat in the prestigious Ottoman Senate. Other Arabists like Dr 'Abd al-Rahman Shahbandar were simply threatened into acquiescence, and eventually had to go into exile.[3] However, the internal leadership of the Ottoman Party of Administrative Decentralization had to be dealt with by more repressive measures. In early 1915 the Turkish authorities began to arrest those Arabists who had not chosen exile. Treasonable evidence in the form of confiscated diplomatic correspondence between members of the Decentralization Party and French and British agents in Syria and Egypt was revealed. The CUP interpreted this correspondence as proof that the leaders of the 'Arab movement' aimed to sever the Arabic-speaking provinces from the Empire and to encourage European territorial designs. Among the leaders arrested for intriguing with French authorities were Shafiq Mu'ayyad al-'Azm, Shukri al-'Asali, Rushdi al-Sham'a, the Amir 'Umar al-Jaza'iri, and 'Abd al-Hamid al-Zahrawi. By mid-1916 all had been sentenced to death and duly executed.[4] The group of Syrian émigrés and exiles in Cairo led by Rafiq and Haqqi al-'Azm and the religious reformer, Shaykh Rashid Rida, who had been directing the political activities of the Decentralization Party since 1913, were accused of supporting a British project to detach the Arab provinces from the Empire and to place them under the suzerainty of an Arab Caliphate by preparing an Arab rebellion. They were sentenced to death *in absentia* along with approximately fifty other Syrian and Lebanese colleagues residing in Cairo.[5]

That a growing number of Syrian Arabists were actually keen on fomenting a rebellion against the Turkish authorities and on territorial secession from the Empire by 1916 seems clear. Within Syria, however, there was little possibility of sparking a revolt. Those remaining Arabists constituted a small and feeble minority in Syria and possessed no internal organization, military or otherwise, by which to lead a revolt. By 1916 the Turks had ruthlessly suppressed Arabist political activities in Syria. Although Syrian-Arabist leaders in Cairo continued their agitation for Arab rights and autonomy, and several entertained the idea of rebellion through close contact with high-ranking British officials, what little political influence they could still muster in Syria was never sufficient to encourage rebellion there. When an Arab revolt did erupt in mid-1916, it was in the Hijaz, led by non-Syrian Arabs with somewhat different motives and ambitions from those of the group of Syrian Arabists. The contribution of Syrians to the revolt was marginal. The Arab movement had temporarily moved outside of Syria and out of the hands of Syrians.

The impact of the Arab Revolt of 1916

The Arab Revolt of 1916 had its origins in the ambitions of the Sharif of Mecca.[6] From January 1909 until the outbreak of revolt in June 1916,

Sharif Husayn resisted attempts by the CUP to limit his influence and authority in the Hijaz. The Unionist policy of establishing a more strictly centralized government was anathema to Husayn's primary goals of preserving the autonomous status of the Hijaz under his authority and of guaranteeing his immediate family's succession to the Amirate. But because the protection of the pilgrimage and of the Holy Cities remained high on the Ottoman government's list of priorities, its aims and those of the Sharif 'coincided' over the problem of pacifying regional tribes which were a major obstacle to the implementation of Ottoman policy in the Hijaz. Thus while the CUP threatened Husayn's position with one hand it offered him 'material assistance' to check the ambition of his internal rivals with the other.[7]

Sharif Husayn subscribed to the traditionalist interpretation of Ottomanism. He looked upon Ottomanism as the necessary ideological weapon by which to battle both secular and atheistic Turkish modernization and the emerging schismatic Arab movement. Not surprisingly, he expressed his brand of Ottomanism in religious terms, calling for a revival of pure Islamic life and institutions. As Ernest Dawn suggests, 'the ideological position which he professed was in harmony with his political interests; therefore he, like most of his contemporary coreligionists, could be sincerely firm in his conviction that a truly Moslem Ottoman State was the best hope of defending Islam from the political and intellectual encroachments of Christian Europe.'[8]

Sharif Husayn was also a pragmatic politician. He fully understood his dependency on the Ottoman government in his struggle to thwart the designs of rival tribal chieftains professing a more radical and often more appealing brand of religious fundamentalism. But, as the CUP government was intent on certain policies inimical to Husayn's interests, namely the extension of the Hijaz Railway (and thus direct Ottoman control) to Mecca, he could not reconcile his personal interests with those of the State. The War offered Husayn the chance to fulfill his ambitions. It came in a series of vaguely worded British promises, embedded in what has come to be known as the Husayn–McMahon Correspondence, made to the Sharif in 1915 and 1916, which offered to guarantee his right to rule Arabia and possibly other Arabic-speaking territories if he consented to commit his forces to the Allied war effort.[9] After making one final but unsuccessful attempt to patch up his differences with the CUP, Husayn reluctantly chose the British option. Though the revolt in the Hijaz was given 'Arab nationalist' ideological content by more sophisticated Syrians to the north and in Cairo, the Sharif had more limited aims.[10] From the ideological perspective he conceived of his action as an attempt to resurrect traditionalist 'Ottomanism' and to revive Islam, and more practically, as the best way to defeat hostile tribal neighbors in Arabia. Nevertheless, to acquire legal sanction for his revolt, he was obliged to '...adopt the goal of the nationalist societies and to seek kingship over the Arab nation in order to acquire a defensible claim to supremacy over his dangerous neighbors.'[11]

The ideology of Arabism, and the Syrian-Arab movement it spawned, played a relatively insignificant role in the origin of the Arab Revolt, although the Revolt itself was the most significant step in the growth of Arab nationalism before 1918. The Syrian reaction to the Revolt was mixed. Prewar Arabists in Damascus and other Syrian towns were naturally excited by news of armed rebellion against their Turkish oppressors, but were in no position to contribute physically to the Revolt. Other Syrian activists exiled in Cairo, like Rafiq and Haqqi al-'Azm, had already established contacts with both the Hashemites and the British.[12] But although a significant proportion of the Sharif's Northern Army, commanded by his third son, Faysal, included Syrian officers and enlisted men,[13] the majority enlisted after being taken prisoners of war. Only a minority were deserters from the Ottoman armies who had joined the Arab movement when news of the Hijaz Revolt had spread. The Arab armies contained a much higher proportion of Hijazis and Iraqis than Syrians; though the younger generation of Syrians in the Arab nationalist *al-Fatat* did contribute to the war effort, Syrians were generally unwilling to rise against the Turks. The political leadership in the Syrian towns either continued to identify with the ideology of Ottomanism, and thus with Empire, or they opted not to take a stand until the outcome of the War was known. Many retained their administrative posts throughout the War and viewed the rebellion to the south with alarm and disdain, and even as treason. And though Sharif Husayn made his call to revolt in the strongest religious terms, the strength of Islam as the supreme integrating force of Empire drowned out the call to holy war by Arab tribes which were considered culturally inferior, socially backward and only nominally pious. Moreover, certain high-ranking and influential political leaders distrusted Hashemite political ambitions or were not on friendly terms with Sharif Husayn and his sons.[14]

The political configuration of Faysal's Arab state

On the eve of capitulation in the fall of 1918, Damascus was loosely controlled by a group of local notables, many of whom were staunch opponents of the Hashemites. As news of one Ottoman military mis-adventure after another reached the town, these political bosses reached a consensus that Turkish support for their positions of local power and influence was no longer reliable. Moreover, as British and French troops and their Arab allies marched on Damascus, local political leaders were alarmed at the prospect of outright Hashemite domination buttressed by an army of occupation. With Damascus in social turmoil, its economy disrupted by the ravages of war, and its political future uncertain, these local leaders discovered a need to moderate their anti-Sharifian and pro-Ottoman views in order to present themselves as the single local political force on which the foreign occupiers could depend to restore order. To survive, the local landed and bureaucratic class would have to reinforce its traditional political role as the intermediary between society and a new authority. Its political representatives fully realized that the Arab movement headed by the Hashemite family was that new authority. Thus one prerequisite for self-preservation was to switch their loyalty from Ottomanism to Arabism—an ascendant ideology and movement many of these notables had concertedly tried to eradicate during the previous decade. Switching allegiance for some, however, proved to be a most uncomfortable task.

On 1 October 1918, Damascus was ceremoniously surrendered to the Commander of the Third Australian Light Horse Regiment by a committee of local notables headed by Amir Sa'id al-Jaza'iri and his brother, Amir 'Abd al-Qadir. The Jaza'iris, grandsons of the Algerian resistance leader, claimed to have been entrusted with the functions of civil government by the Turkish governor prior to his departure the previous day. They also had proclaimed the independence of Syria and their own right to govern Damascus in the name of Sharif Husayn.[15] But when the British political agent, T. E. Lawrence, arrived in Damascus later in the day he dismissed the Jaza'iri brothers and appointed Shukri al-Ayyubi, a former high-ranking Ottoman army officer, member of another Damascene notable family and close confidant of Amir Faysal, as Acting Military Governor.[16] Lawrence rejected the claims of the Jaza'iris, who represented the dominant faction of the Damascene political leadership, because he 'feared their French connection' and the potential influence they might have on Faysal ibn al-Husayn.[17] This rebuff caused the ambitious Jaza'iris to go to the streets with their armed Algerian retainers and bands of town thugs, calling for holy war on the grounds that Faysal and his supporters were British stooges. On the following day, however, the Jaza'iri forces were soundly defeated and temporary calm was restored in the city, but only after Amir 'Abd al-Qadir had been killed and the general populace had suffered many casualties.[18]

The October skirmish marked the beginning of Amir Faysal's turbulent 22-month reign in Damascus. It expressed the deep-seated hostility of leading Damascene notables to the Hashemites. But their defeat also taught these notables the painful lesson that to preserve local influence some compromise with Faysal would have to be reached. They somehow had to convince the Amir that as an established force of social control they were in the best position to restore the type of lasting stability both he and the notables needed to support their respective ambitions. If chaos, instability and widespread violence continued unchecked, Faysal would soon be forced to relinquish control to ambitious groups of young militants riding the crest of an Arab nationalist victory.

But throughout most of Faysal's short-lived rule in Syria (October 1918–July 1920) local notables in Damascus were constantly rebuked, insulted, ignored or pushed aside by those elements closest to the Amir: his armed Hijazi troops, Iraqi and Syrian military officers who had deserted to him during the War, and an increasingly influential group of young civilian nationalists composed of Syrians and Palestinians who had been nurtured on clandestine politics before and during the War. These outsiders made concerted efforts to keep city notables and other men of local standing away from Faysal. Damascus notables were conspicuously absent from government, often passed over for Palestinians and Iraqis.[19]

To the dismay of the old political guard, Faysal was a 'captive of his supporters' as much as he was a captive of the 'national principle.'[20] He was in the unenviable position of having to establish a viable and independent Arab state with Damascus as its capital; he realized that to justify his family's revolt against the Caliphate in Istanbul and the subsequent separation of the Arabic-speaking provinces from the Ottoman Empire he had to guarantee that these severed territories would not succumb to European encroachment. His personal ambitions, the threat of European-imposed mandates on the Arab territories and the pressures of a burgeoning Arab nationalist movement led by some of his closest confidants and supporters forced the Amir to adopt a brand of nationalism that he thought could be used as an effective bargaining instrument to wrest concessions from the European powers as well as to satisfy his more militant and idealistic comrades.

Faysal was both puzzled by and lacked confidence in the notables. He had expected that they would immediately rush to his side, express their views on independence and offer him sound advice rooted in long political experience. He could not comprehend why most influential Damascene notables were not dedicated nationalists seeking a leadership role in the nationalist movement. He felt that if the 'renowned' notability (*wujaha*') did not move to the forefront of the Arab nationalist movement, then it was no longer faithful to its own traditional political role in society.[21] Faysal failed to realize that the Damascene notability distrusted him almost as much as they did his nationalist followers. Excluded from their traditional positions of authority, notables were unwilling to cooperate directly with forces bent on eroding their power.

The most prominent Damascene notables, men like Muhammad Fawzi al-'Azm, 'Abd al-Rahman al-Yusuf, Sami Mardam-Beg, 'Ata al-'Ajlani, Muhammad 'Arif al-Quwwatli, Muhammad 'Ali al-'Abid and Badi' Mu'ayyad al-'Azm, had only one aim at heart, to sue at any cost for peace and tranquility in Damascus so that they could re-establish themselves in their traditional place as an 'aristocracy of service.' With the Arab Revolt, the collapse of the Ottoman Empire and the ensuing period of instability under Faysal they came to fear for the first time that they might not survive the coming years with their power bases intact. Once Ottomanism had been rendered obsolete it really did not matter what replaced the Ottoman system of authority as long as they preserved their socioeconomic and political place in Damascus. In fact most notables remained unaffected by Arabism.[22] But with Ottomanism dead they had few qualms about paying Arabism at least nominal respect. They could not tolerate, however, the political forces directing the Arab nationalist movement, that so threatened their influence. For the first time they found themselves cast in the minority role of an opposition group in their own city. Many notables began to seek support and protection from the French liaison officer in Damascus,[23] waiting for Faysal to sink deeper into the nationalist quicksand. They hoped that he then would be forced to call upon them to serve as a countervailing force to the militant groups which were pushing the Amir to strike a very uncomfortable political stance.

Faysal was not a leader of Atatürk's caliber and his effort to build a strong centralized Arab government in Damascus anchored on the 'national principle' was doomed to failure from the outset. In the economic sphere, the country had been devastated by war. Agricultural production and distribution had been severely disrupted. During Faysal's short tenure Syria continued to suffer from famine due to hoarding, profiteering and corruption. Local industrial production, which had been in decline since the mid-nineteenth century, rapidly shrank during the War and in its aftermath.[24] The monetary and banking system was in a state of almost complete collapse. Hindered by gold hoarding the value of the Turkish pound fell by nearly 50 percent during the first two months of the Amir's reign; soon the British were to replace it by the Egyptian gold pound.[25] Syria's communications network had also been disrupted during the War. Railways no longer operated regularly and the road system was sorely deficient. The division of Greater Syria into three administrative districts with the French and British controlling the coastal regions threatened to choke the landlocked Arab state. The interior towns forming the backbone of Faysal's principality (Damascus, Homs, Hama, Aleppo) felt increasingly cut off from the eastern Mediterranean ports, especially Tripoli, Beirut and Haifa, putting the infant Arab state at a pronounced economic disadvantage.[26]

Social problems and conflicts were equally severe in the postwar period. Though agricultural production gradually increased after the wartime devastation, Damascus and Aleppo were beset with thousands of rural immigrants who had fled their famine-stricken districts.[27] Aleppo also suffered from the influx of thousands of Armenian refugees escaping Turkish oppression. Armenians now competed with natives in an already depressed labor market. Tension between the two communities exploded in a masscre of Armenians in February 1919. Meanwhile, Damascus had been inundated by Hijazi and Syrian tribesmen who formed the rank and file of Faysal's army. As the army became stationary, idleness and discontent led to the formation of armed bands which roamed the city and neighboring countryside creating fear and chaos. Added to these newcomers were the non-Damascene military officers and civilians; many were recent converts to the Arab movement who rushed to Damascus in search of posts in the new government. Local hostility to the waves of outsiders was conspicuous and tensions reached alarming proportions as natives and new immigrants clashed.

The fragility of government: nationalist pressures

The Faysal administration was only new in terms of its personnel. The Amir, absorbed by diplomatic negotiations in Europe, found no time to initiate a thorough reformation of the Ottoman governmental apparatus. Instead he decided to operate through the existent administrative apparatus rooted in a labyrinth of Ottoman law codes.[28] Faysal used the bureaucracy to repay numerous wartime debts to his followers and confidants with government jobs. In order to accommodate the demands of a plethora of pressure groups within the Arab movement he was forced to expand the bureaucracy. Many Damascene notables and middle-level functionaries in the Ottoman mold soon found themselves out of office and out of favor as young nationalist lieutenants, clerks and intellectuals were appointed to key administrative posts, in the process bringing their friends and wartime comrades into government at the lower echelons. From the sidelines the local urban notability angrily watched these newcomers to government, many of whom were outsiders with no administrative experience, levy taxes, conscript men and purchase arms.

Moreover, the newcomers enjoyed the right to administer a monthly British subsidy of £150,000 at their own discretion; financial scandals, nepotism and chaos quickly swept through the central administration.[29] Although some sectors of the new administration did begin to show signs of increased efficiency, all departments suffered from a scarcity of funds. Consequently few benefits filtered down to the local populace of Damascus or to other towns and districts since the individuals now in power were not dependent on local interests and affiliations.[30]

Faysal's aim to establish a strong centralized government was also hindered by his inability to directly oversee its administrative operations. Leaving the task of day-to-day government to his factionalized group of supporters, he focused his attention on combatting French designs in Syria. From the outset the Amir failed to muster the requisite support from his British patrons to counter French ambitions in the Syrian interior. Britain, while formally turning Syria over to her Arab allies, eventually agreed to withdraw her troops from Damascus and eastern Syria in response to France's move to secure a more complete implementation of the Sykes–Picot wartime agreement (1916) delineating future British and French territorial spheres of influence in the Arab provinces of the Empire. Before the British withdrew their army of occupation, French military forces had already been reinforced in Lebanon and western Syria.[31]

Threatened by the growing possibility of French aggression and with only the skeleton of an Arab fighting force at his command, a vulnerable Faysal turned to diplomatic negotiations in the hope of preserving his power base in Syria. But he was also bound by the demands of his more fervent nationalist supporters not to enter into any discussion or undertake any agreements that would lead to Arab territory falling under a European mandate or any other type of foreign control.[32]

The internal pressures on Faysal came out clearly when he made his first major move to win British diplomatic backing against French designs on the interior. In January 1919, he signed an agreement with Chaim Weizmann, the Zionist political leader, permitting increased Jewish 'infiltration' into Palestine in return for Zionist support for his Arab state in Syria. Faysal did not support, however, the idea of an independent Jewish 'national home' in Palestine and specifically wanted Jewish immigration to take place under British and not international cover. The Amir had calculated that the Palestine question was not a crucial issue; therefore a compromise would bolster his position when turning to deal with France.[33] But Faysal had miscalculated the Palestinian reaction. Among Palestinian Arabs—Muslims and Christians—there existed a unified opposition to the Zionist movement that had solidified after 1908 and had manifested itself locally in wide-spread ill-feeling against the Jews, and officially in the Ottoman Parliament.[34] Palestinian Arabs had in general been unmoved by the Hashemite Revolt in 1916; they chose to stick by Istanbul and the Empire until the Allied occupation in 1918, and few Palestinian notables considered Faysal their representative.[35]

At the time of the Faysal–Weizmann negotiations there emerged in Damascus a political organization with a cultural front composed of militant Palestinian and Syrian-Arab nationalists, but whose leadership was entirely Palestinian. The Arab Club (*al-Nadi al-'Arabi*) was set up expressly to conduct anti-Zionist activities and to pressure Faysal into opposing the Zionist movement. Several members of the Club's executive committee occupied key posts in Faysal's administration, including that of Chief of Police in Damascus and the Commander of the Gendarmerie.[36] Though Faysal signed the agreement with Weizmann, the Arab Club's anti-Zionist propaganda and the influential role of Palestinians in government foiled the Amir's plan to use the Zionists to secure British backing in his future dealings with France.

The Palestinian reaction to Faysal's political maneuvers revealed divisions in the nationalist leadership around the Amir and in his fledgling government. It reflected the political reality that power did not rest in the central administration but rather in extra-governmental groups and parties composed of nationalist elements with diverse yet overlapping aims and interests.

The most influential political organization during the short-lived Arab régime in Damascus was *al-Fatat*. This society continued to operate clandestinely as it had before and during the War, though after the capture of Damascus its leadership was 'reconstituted' to include certain prominent Sharifian officers such as the Iraqi, Yasin al-Hashimi, and the military governor of Damascus, 'Ali Rida al-Rikabi, as well as younger civilians who had been among its earliest members such as Jamil Mardam-Beg, Nasib al-Bakri, Ahmad Qadri and Shukri al-Quwwatli.[37] *Al-Fatat* gave unqualified support to Faysal until the end of 1919, and no major policy decisions could be taken in this period without prior consultation with the party's leadership.[38] While *al-Fatat* chose to remain small, secret and tightly-knit, it decided in December 1918 to create a large frontal organization, The Party of Arab Independence (*Hizb al-istiqlal al-'Arabi*), to serve as its mouthpiece in Syria. The *Istiqlal* Party was headquartered in Damascus, with branches throughout Syria, and maintained an open registration policy.[39] The leadership of this party, which stood for the 'liberation of all Arab countries from foreign domination,' included young Syrian and Palestinian political activists like Shukri al-Quwwatli and 'Izzat al-Darwaza; its rank and file were predominantly Syrian.[40]

The other political organization that exercised considerable influence on Syrian political life was the *jam'iyyat al-'Ahd* (The Society of the Covenant). *Al-'Ahd* was a secret society founded in October 1913 by a group of disaffected Ottoman military officers from Iraq and Syria. At the time *al-'Ahd* desired political autonomy for the Arab provinces of the Empire and the formation of a dual monarchy along the lines of the Austro-Hungarian Empire.[41] After the war *al-'Ahd* remained limited to army officers but split along geographical lines (Iraqi–Syrian) with the Iraqi element holding the greater share of power.[42] Moreover, though several of the Iraqi officers in *al-'Ahd* held ministerial rank in Faysal's government, the party focused most of its attention on affairs in Iraq.[43]

The leaderships of the three nationalist extra-governmental organizations, the Arab Club, *al-Fatat* including the *Istiqlal* Party, and *al-'Ahd*, dominated local political life during Faysal's reign in Syria. Though they maintained a unified political front based on complete Arab independence before the European powers, their respective political ambitions betrayed localist and regional tendencies that had begun to overshadow pan-Arab sentiments. The Arab Club was the first organization to begin withdrawing its support for Faysal. Its Palestinian leadership felt that the Amir and other Arab nationalist leaders, particularly the Iraqi officers in *al-'Ahd*, were not paying sufficient attention to the Palestine question. The radical nationalist posture assumed by the Arab Club executive shed light on the outlines of an emerging independent Palestinian national movement as distinct from the larger and less well-articulated Arab national movement.[44] *Al-Fatat* and its frontal organization, the *Istiqlal* Party, though more willing to back Faysal's policies, were also sympathetic to the complaints of the Arab Club leadership. Indeed, young Damascene nationalists like Jamil Mardam-Beg, Shukri al-Quwwatli and Ahmad Qadri belonged to the leaderships of *al-Fatat* and/or the *Istiqlal* Party while remaining active members of the Arab Club.[45]

The greatest regional division was that between Greater Syria and Iraq. Palestine was part of Greater Syria while Mesopotamia and the Lower Euphrates had always been treated as frontier provinces by the Ottomans. Under the Empire, Damascus and its hinterland maintained strong trading links with Palestine supported by a well-integrated communications network, while Syrian and Palestinian economic ties with more distant Iraq had noticeably weakened during the nineteenth century, owing to the decline of the Syrian desert trade. Furthermore, with the growth of Arabism after 1908, loose political bonds between Syrians and Palestinians were established, first at the Ottoman Parliament in Istanbul where Syrian delegates like Shukri al-'Asali had supported the attempts of Palestinian Arabs to halt Zionist immigration into Palestine, and later in Cairo where Syrian and Palestinian leaders had taken refuge in order to continue their agitation for Arab rights and political autonomy in the provinces. Palestinian and Iraqi nationalists seemed to be united solely in their opposition to the European powers. Internal cooperation between the Arab Club and the Iraqi-dominated *al-'Ahd* was never strong.[46] Competition between *al-'Ahd* and *al-Fatat* for influence with Faysal caused strained relations between the two organizations.[47] Political contacts between Palestinian and Syrian nationalists and Iraqis were a more recent development, occurring when they first met in Damascus at the end of the War. Finally the majority of Palestinian and Syrian nationalist leaders were civilians often from prominent urban notable families while the Iraqis were predominantly army officers from more obscure social backgrounds.[48]

Elections to the Syrian Congress

By mid-1919, Faysal found himself in a dangerous predicament. Not only was the Syrian economy in a state of near collapse but his government was divided and chaotic. His supporters who controlled the extra-governmental nationalist organizations were the centers of influence in Syria, though they too were far from united. Their localist aims and ambitions and their more radical brand of nationalism obstructed the Amir's efforts to present himself to Europe as the uncontested ruler of a smoothly functioning independent Arab state and as a moderate nationalist. In addition, the local Damascus notability, which still retained a considerable measure of independent influence over the local populace, was in search of external support that could help it vault back into political control in Damascus. Meanwhile French political agents in Damascus and Beirut, also in search of local collaborators who could challenge Faysal's claims to Syria, had already begun to promote an alliance with leading members of the disaffected notability.

In response to the growing political malaise in Syria Faysal called for an elected Congress to be convened in Damascus, which he hoped would have the dual effect of channeling the political activities of the nationalist organizations into more productive support for his régime and of establishing a representative body with a united front to back his independence program before the Powers.[49] Elections were conducted on the Ottoman two-tier system in the territory under Faysal's control; in the areas under foreign control–the coastal regions of Lebanon and Palestine–the notables and 'leaders of opinion' elected their deputies directly.[50]

In Damascus elections to the Syrian Congress were a heated contest. The traditional political leadership of the city, a powerful group of landowning-notables headed by Muhammad Fawzi al-'Azm and 'Abd al-Rahman al-Yusuf, took the opportunity to demonstrate their influence in Damascus as well as their dislike of Faysal and the nationalists. Both al-'Azm and al-Yusuf had been bitter enemies of Sharif Husayn and his offspring, and the vanguard of conservative opposition to the Syrian-Arab movement for over a decade. Muhammad Fawzi Pasha had bickered with the ambitious Husayn and his son, Faysal, in Istanbul before 1908 and later opposed their Revolt, accusing the Hashemites of being traitors to Islam and the Ottoman Empire.[51] 'Abd al-Rahman Pasha became an avowed enemy of the Sharif when in early 1909, as *Amir al-Hajj*, he announced in Mecca that the pilgrimage would return to Syria by sea because the traditional land route was prone to attack by hostile tribes. Sharif Husayn felt that al-Yusuf, a CUP sympathizer, chose an alternative route to challenge him, on behalf of the Unionists, in his principal function as Sharif, 'that of guaranteeing the security of the pilgrimage.' In reaction Husayn forced the pilgrimage party to return by land under the command of his own brother. An enraged al-Yusuf returned alone by sea, and without the valuable merchandise he had acquired on the pilgrimage.[52] The old guard's dislike and distrust of the local Damascus faction of nationalists led by Jamil Mardam-Beg, Shukri al-Quwwatli, Ahmad Qadri and the Bakri family came out clearly during the elections. These young activists, fearing the strong local support the old guard could muster, sent Mardam-Beg to try to persuade Muhammad Fawzi al-'Azm to throw in his lot with the Damascene nationalists by running on their ticket. Al-'Azm immediately rejected this proposition as an insult to his integrity.[53] The outcome of the Congress elections confirmed the worst fears of the nationalists. The conservative list won a resounding victory. Only two nationalists, Fawzi al-Bakri and Fa'iz al-Shihabi, secured places on the sixteen-man Damascus delegation to the Congress.[54]

The Syrian Congress was first convened in Damascus on 6 June, 1919. In attendance were 89 representatives from towns, rural districts and the beduin tribes in Syria, Lebanon and Palestine. Over 40 percent of the delegates came from the four interior towns of the Syrian-Arab state: Damascus, Aleppo, Hama and Homs. Like those deputies elected to the Congress from Damascus, the overwhelming majority from the three other interior towns were members of locally powerful landowning-bureaucratic families. Among the sixteen representatives from Aleppo and its hinterland were a Jabiri, a Mudarris, a Qudsi, a Kikhiyya, a Kayyali, a Hananu, a Rifa'i, a Hiraki, a Nayyal and a Mar'ashli. From Hama came a Barazi, a Kaylani and a Barudi; and from Homs, two Atasis and a Raslan.[55] Indeed, local landowning interests were even better represented by these three delegations than by the one from Damascus. However, the political orientation of the delegations from Aleppo,

Hama and Homs differed significantly from that of the Damascus delegation. Before the Allied occupation of Syria in 1918, political rivalries in the three towns north of Damascus were not as sharply expressed in terms of the competing ideologies of Ottomanism and Arabism. Syrian-Arabism and its concomitant Arab movement had been a Damascus-based ideological and political development that had a less pronounced impact on politics in the three other interior towns. With few exceptions the great landowning-bureaucratic families of Aleppo, Hama and Homs remained avowed Ottomanists in the service of the Empire until its collapse. Moreover, political relations between the two Syrian provincial capitals of Damascus and Aleppo had not been particularly strong prior to 1918. Both cities were administered separately under the Empire. And though the trade route linking them was important, Aleppo and Damascus were situated on different commercial axes with their most valuable economic markets located in opposite directions. The imposition of Faysal's Arab state, with Damascus as its capital, however, forced political leaders in Aleppo to join the Arab nationalist bandwagon to ensure that their personal interests and those of their constituents were not overlooked in Damascus.[56]

Although the locally-based nationalist leadership in Damascus headed by Mardam-Beg, Quwwatli and Qadri failed to defeat the Damascus conservatives at the polls, the Congress was nonetheless dominated by representatives of *al-Fatat* and the *Istiqlal* Party. The Damascus old guard's appeal to moderation and stability was drowned out by the louder demands of nationalist delegates calling for absolute and uncompromising independence. Faysal had hoped that the formation of this representative body would not only lead to greater support for his policies but also to greater moderation in Syrian political life by harnessing the more radical nationalist activities of the extra-governmental societies. The extreme nationalist tenor of the Congress, however, proved more embarrassing to the Amir than supportive.[57] In early August 1919, Faysal set up a Council of Directors to replace the military administration that had existed since the capture of Damascus. The Council was composed of Faysal's closest confidants, headed by the Damascene ex-Ottoman army officer and military governor of Damascus, 'Ali Rida al-Rikabi, and included the Iraqi officer, Yasin al-Hashimi.[58] The Amir's aim in creating the Council was to 'take steam out of the Syrian Congress,' without having to disband it, and to revitalize the weak internal administration of the country.[59]

Failure of diplomacy

By early autumn 1919 the Syrian Congress had indeed become silent and inactive, but not so much owing to the Council of Directors as to the fact that the Amir was off in Europe on a second round of shuttle diplomacy between London and Paris. The Congress leadership continued to support Faysal in the hope that he would still be able to persuade the European powers to grant complete independence to the Arabs. But, with French troops surrounding the Syrian-Arab state and no sign of a favorable agreement in sight, nationalist leaders grew increasingly skeptical about the outcome of the Amir's bargaining. Too many promises had been broken and too little support for their goals had been forthcoming from Europe. Skepticism turned to fear and outrage in late October as British troops withdrew from the Syrian interior.[60] Anti-Sharifian demonstrations broke out in Damascus followed by the creation of a Committee of National Defense, composed of Damascene quarter bosses and the local leadership of *al-Fatat*, in reaction to unconfirmed reports filtering back to Syria that Faysal had reached an unfavorable compromise with the French Premier, Clemenceau. Nationalist agitation directed against the Amir continued to mount in the final two months of 1919.[61]

Indeed the French interpretation of the Sykes–Picot Agreement of 1916 prevailed over that of the British. Lloyd George agreed to Clemenceau's demand for a complete withdrawal of the British army of occupation from the Syrian interior. Faysal had failed to play the British against the French and was forced to acquiesce to the painful demands of the latter. At the beginning of 1920 an agreement between Faysal and Clemenceau was reached in Paris. The Amir had secured the following terms: Arab rule in inland Syria would be assured but Faysal would recognize a separate and French Mandated Lebanon; the Druzes would be autonomous within Syria and the Biqa' would be a neutral zone; Syrian diplomatic representation abroad would be a French responsibility; and the French would have priority in providing assistance to Syria.[62]

Faysal returned to Damascus in January to face the antagonism of his nationalist followers. The *al-Fatat* executive, recently reconstituted to include the most ardent Syrian and Palestinian nationalists, rejected the Amir's agreement with Clemenceau.[63] Left with no external and little internal political leverage, Faysal had no alternative but to turn to the only source of local power and influence in Syria he had yet to tap, the conservative core of Damascus notables. Faysal had purposely ignored this group since its early refusal to cooperate with the Sharifian officers and radical nationalists. This conservative opposition, removed from the seat of political power for an uncomfortably long period and fearful of even more calamitous results if the nationalists pushed the Amir into war with France, was ripe for wooing. Faysal began by patching up his family's personal differences with its long-time enemy, 'Abd al-Rahman Pasha al-Yusuf (Muhammad Fawzi Pasha al-'Azm had died in November, 1919). By the end of January he managed to get al-Yusuf and other Syrian notables from the four interior towns to form a new political party which included among its leaders such disaffected landowners and ex-Ottoman officials as Sami Pasha Mardam-Beg, Muhammad 'Arif al-Quwwatli, Muhammad 'Ali Pasha al-Qudamani, Badi' Bey Mu'ayyad al-'Azm, 'Ata al-'Ajlani, 'Ata al-Ayyubi, 'Ala al-Din al-Durubi and several nationalist turncoats.[64] The National Party (*al-Hizb al-watani*), as it was called, soon emerged with a program demanding full Syrian independence within its natural boundaries (Syria, Lebanon and Palestine), and a constitutional monarchy headed by Faysal.[65] But this program was merely window-dressing to dispel the fears and anger of radical nationalists and to attract a larger coterie of supporters. Pragmatic politicians, the leadership of the National Party realized that Syria was in no position to resist the French. Quietly they sought a compromise with France along the lines of the Faysal–Clemenceau Agreement (which had not been signed), in the meantime strengthening their contacts with French political agents in the region in the case of a military invasion.[66] The National Party was not committed to independence. Furthermore it was willing to recognize a Jewish 'national home' in Palestine.[67]

To check the tide of the Syrian conservative opposition and to force Faysal to back down on his agreement with the French, nationalist leaders reconvened the Syrian Congress in early March 1920. A vicious attack on the Amir's compromise with Clemenceau was leveled by a Damascene religious shaykh, Kamil al-Qassab, an al-Azhar graduate and prewar Arabist who had joined the Arab Revolt at its inception, and in late 1919 founded the Committee of National Defense with the sole purpose of military recruitment to resist the French.[68] The Congress, presided over by Hashim al-Atasi, a respected notable of Homs, demanded the absolute independence of Greater Syria, the withdrawal of all foreign armies, and the complete rejection of Zionism and the idea of a Jewish 'national home' in Palestine. To take steam out of the National Party's earlier call for a monarchy, the Congress proclaimed Faysal King of Syria. In return Faysal was obliged to dissolve the Council of Directors and a nationalist cabinet was formed with 'Ali Rida al-Rikabi as its chief minister, manipulated behind the scenes by the leadership of *al-Fatat*.[69]

During the following two months King Faysal tried to postpone coming over to the side of his more uncompromising supporters. He attempted to appease French territorial ambitions in the Syrian interior by offering to send military assistance to the French army which was fighting the Turks in the north and Syrian rebel bands in the Aleppo and Latakia regions aided by Kamalist officers, propaganda and weapons.[70] But the April declaration at San Remo giving the Syrian Mandate to France all but realized French intentions. In response to this declaration the nationalists forced the King to sack Rida al-Rikabi, who they believed was not determined to fight France. On 7 May, the King appointed Hashim al-Atasi Prime Minister and he formed a cabinet composed of the most radical Syrian nationalist and anti-French spokesmen including 'Abd al-Rahman Shahbandar and Yusuf al-'Azma, a German-trained ex-Ottoman army officer.[71] In the final analysis the King indeed proved to be a 'captive' of his nationalist supporters, succumbing to their pressures.[72] The Arab Kingdom was prepared to fight till the end.

Final days

When the French caught wind of the radical nationalists' success in bringing Faysal around to their point of view they prepared to move on Damascus. General Gouraud, commander of France's Army of the Levant, first concluded an armistice with Mustafa Kamal, securing himself on the Turkish front, and then sent troops to crush rebel bands inside Lebanon which, since the end of 1919, had been harassing Christian districts in the north and south considered sympathetic to France.[73] On 14 July Gouraud dispatched an ultimatum to Faysal demanding the demobilization of his army, recognition of the French Mandate, and the 'dismissal of the extremists' among his supporters. The King was given four days to accept. His government vacillated between endorsement and rejection,[74] while his military brass made it known that armed resistance was tantamount to suicide.[75] Despite grave reservations Faysal gave his acceptance, 'but only in principle.' An outraged Syrian Congress reconvened only to be dissolved by the government. Military demobilization was already underway. When news of the King's capitulation reached the general populace angry and violent mobs took to the streets of Damascus in protest. Faysal, his own residence under attack, ordered his gendarmerie to restore order. In the process over one hundred people were killed. To add to the King's discomfort Gouraud demanded 'a more definite acceptance of his terms,' extending the deadline until 21 July. Faysal accepted on the day before its expiration hoping that Damascus would be spared a French occupation.[76] But the French army was already advancing.[77] On the morning of 24 July, a motley Sharifian army, supplemented by elements from the popular quarters, and led by the Minister of War, Yusuf al-'Azma, clashed with the advancing French army at Khan Maysalun to the west of Damascus. The battle was over by the early afternoon; Arab forces had been defeated and dispersed.[78] On the following day the French army entered Damascus without encountering resistance.

Faysal had already left for the outskirts of town the previous evening. There he received some signs of encouragement from followers in Damascus that he still might be recognized as Head of State by General Gouraud.[79] In one final effort to appease the French he appointed a caretaker government of conservatives headed by 'Ala al-Din al-Durubi of Homs, an influential landowner. Al-Durubi, a leading member of the National Party with pronounced French sympathies, formed a cabinet of like-minded Damascus notables including 'Abd al-Rahman al-Yusuf, Badi' Mu'ayyad al-'Azm and 'Ata al-Ayyubi.[80] But though the French were not dissatisfied with the new cabinet, they never had any intentions of relinquishing to Faysal what they had captured. After his brief return to Damascus they requested Faysal to leave Syria on 27 July. He moved by train first to Dir'a and then on to Haifa where ironically he was 'greeted' by the British High Commissioner of Palestine 'with official honours.'[81]

In the meantime many of Faysal's nationalist followers had made themselves scarce. Some fled to Palestine, others to Egypt and Iraq. Thirty-two leaders were immediately condemned to death by the French military authorities, though most had managed to escape to safer confines.[82] The nationalist rank-and-file, mostly Damascenes, were not so fortunate. Hundreds were rounded up by French security and thrown into prisons or summarily executed.

By the end of July 1920 the hope of Arab independence had been shattered. The Arab nationalist movement seemed to be on its deathbed, its leadership dispersed.[83] The Arab Kingdom in Syria had been laid to rest. Damascus—the heart of Arabism—was under the strict supervision of France, and in her service was the core of conservative urban notables who had managed to weather the chaos and upheaval of the previous two years.

Conclusion

Prior to the events of 1860, the political configuration in Damascus included both a traditional sociopolitical leadership competing directly with the Ottoman central authority for control of Ottoman-imposed institutions, and disparate power groups, socially differentiated from the traditional leadership, whose power base was rooted in control of certain autonomous organizations such as local garrisons and the grain trade.

The events of 1860 gave the Ottoman government an opportunity to alter the local political configuration to facilitate its program of centralization and modernization. Already the earliest institutions established by the *Tanzimat* (after 1841) had begun to break down the local paramilitary power base of leaders outside the traditional leadership; these individuals and some of their followers were, at the same time, offered a new power base within the local bureaucracy. Then a decisive Ottoman intervention to check the traditional leadership's attempt to shift the local balance of power in its own favor occurred in 1860. The 'honorable citizens' were punished for failing to prevent or control the militant outburst of the populace and the erosion of their local power was drastically illustrated and their lack of zeal in implementing Ottoman policies severely acknowledged. The events of 1860 permitted the Ottoman government to forge a new and more useful political élite by expanding the local bureaucracy and supporting upcoming families not previously a part of the traditional leadership.

During the next fifty years the Ottoman government managed to remold the Damascus power structure in three important ways. First, with a stronger provincial administration controlled more efficiently by Istanbul, the exercise of local political power became a function of position in the bureaucracy. Consequently, maintaining and expanding wealth and influence depended on securing high administrative office. Instead of being a tool to wield against the state, possession of independent power became a means of access to it. Exclusion from the bureaucracy generally meant loss of independent influence and therefore loss of access to those with authority. Secondly, since the Ottoman government was

93

the sole distributor of offices, it became necessary to identify with the interests of Istanbul to acquire a post. Thirdly, the creation of powerful secular institutions meant that greater influence was derived from office in these institutions rather than from the traditional religious institutions. Thus, after 1860, the political leadership of Damascus underwent a significant metamorphosis owing to the diversification of its power base and the change in its political orientation.

As for the urban families that produced the political leadership in Damascus and other Syrian towns, they quickly took advantage of their direct access to government to further enrich themselves. They used their influence in the local bureaucracy to manipulate state laws to gain legal rights to private property, the demand for which was created by the recent agrarian commercialization in Syria. Office-based property and land accumulation combined to define the contours of the new class that came to rest at the head of local society. Furthermore, this combination made the class virtually unassailable from below, for nearly a century.

The measure of political power in Damascus was a combination of two interconnected sets of relationships. The first concerned the family unit's ability to attract a clientele by constructing a series of vertical linkages through society binding individuals and groups to the family. The second pertained to the family unit's ability to make key alliances with other family units, in the process binding clientele networks together. After 1860, the success a Damascus family had in combining both sets of relationships to achieve significant political power was determined by its ability to secure offices. Offices could in turn be manipulated to build and enlarge a family's material resource base. Offices and wealth together created a pool of benefits or services with which a family could attract clients and make alliances with equals.

The political field in Damascus was restricted to the interaction of powerful family units. Most political groupings, cliques, factions or blocs were the personal vehicles of the family unit or an alliance of families. These groupings cut vertically through society and hindered the recognition of horizontal interests. Even the guilds at times operated as personal vehicles of powerful family interests. In Damascus, though the planting of capitalist relations helped to initiate the process of modern class formation, class conflict had yet to become of primary importance. Rather, society remained 'ordered according to relations of personal dependence.'[1] These relations were rooted in the vertical linkages that bound clients to family units. In addition, relations of personal dependence imposed few constraints on the formation or dissolution of alliances between upper-class families. Finally, since patronage networks were socially and economically heterogeneous, preventing clients from

94

organizing themselves in any meaningful horizontally bound groups with defined interests and collective goals, no alternative forces arose to challenge the social and political leadership of the landowning-bureaucratic families, at least not before World War I.

Although patronage systems cut across class lines, diminishing the potential for class conflict, the landowning-bureaucratic class eventually revealed its own lines of socioeconomic differentiation which led to intra-class conflict. As relations among the network of families became more complex and the size of the extended family grew, the competition for scarce resources intensified. Some families were more successful than others at procuring posts and land. Some became embroiled in conflicts over inheritance leading to the formation of different economic branches: there were rich 'Azms and then there were their poorer cousins. Intra-class conflict, however, only took on a distinctive political coloring after the CUP Revolt of 1908. The forces of stepped-up Ottoman centralization and 'Turkification' jeopardized the material well-being and careers of a large enough fraction of the landowning-bureaucratic class in Damascus to elicit a political reaction. Politically active members of the class whose economic interests may already have been on the downgrade or who were dismissed from their government offices or who were denied entry into government, despite their proper qualifications, found sufficient reason to seize an emerging idea, Arabism, and fashion it into a political movement of opposition. These Arabists focused their grievances on both the Young Turks and those members of their class who managed to survive the upheaval with their interests and positions intact and who thus had reason to support the new régime and the new *status quo*.

The structural changes that swept the Ottoman Empire in the nineteenth century—in administration and law, in commerce and industry, in communications, in the movement of goods, people and ideas and, above all, in the Empire's relations with Europe—were bound to produce a serious disturbance in men's minds. Different communities produced different responses to their changing circumstances. However, one kind of response seemed to predominate over all others: this was the growth of national consciousness which first infected the Christian minorities in the Balkans and was then communicated in an eastward direction to the Turkish- and Arabic-speaking regions.

Secular Arabism, as expressed in terms of the primacy of the Arabs, their language and their contribution to civilization, was first planted by some Syrian Christians involved in an Arabic literary revival (*nahda*) in the last half of the nineteenth century. These Christian intellectuals, who were linked both to Western missionaries and to an ascendant indigenous

Syrian Christian commercial bourgeoisie, saw in a secular cultural identity a way to avert the stress on Islam and on being a Muslim, which received renewed emphasis in the last decades of the century under Sultan 'Abd ul-Hamid. As minorities who were culturally Arab, these Syrian Christians sought a way to become recognized as equals with Muslims once and for all, with equal rights to security and opportunity. Thus, we find them trying to attract Arab Muslims to the idea of secular Arabism, by emphasizing their common Arab culture and past. And, as was the case of other Ottoman minorities before them, Syrian Christians began to promote the idea of nationalism at a time when their interests were rising, that is after they had already begun to enjoy the fruits of increased security and prosperity under the umbrella of Ottoman reforms and deepening commercial and moral ties to the European Powers.[2]

But if Christian Arabs in the Syrian provinces played a disproportionate role in the formulation of the idea of a secular Arabism, as some historians suggest, they were to play only a minor role in the physical growth of the Arab nationalist movement in its earliest stages before World War I. Furthermore, these Christians were not alone in their efforts to promote a new loyalty to Arabism at the expense of older loyalties to religious community or Ottomanism. Indeed, at about the same time we find a group of Muslim religious reformers of Syrian origin also beginning to promote their own particular version of Arabism. These reformers, however, were more concerned with why Islamic civilization had failed to defend itself against an expanding West. They blamed corrupt and incompetent Turkish rule for Islam's degradation and weakness. But to justify their rejection of the present and immediate past, they did what traditional reformers everywhere did; they began to emphasize a distant past when the Arabs had dominated a greater, more dynamic Islam, to which they contributed its Prophet, language and geographical birthplace. Before the War, however, only a handful of religious experts had gone as far as ' ... to denigrate the Ottoman Turkish contribution to Islam and finally to make the step from praising the Arab's role in Islam to glorifying the virtues of all Arabs, both Muslim and Christian, which transcended Islam.'[3]

A more important contribution to the emergence of an Arab political movement than either that of Christian secularists or Islamic modernists came from members of the absentee landowning class in Syria's cities. These men received their introduction to the ideas of nationalism in Istanbul where they attended Ottoman professional schools in preparation for careers in the Ottoman civil service and, to a lesser extent in the case of Syrians, in the army. Since these young men were being drawn into the state system it is only natural that the ideas they first embraced focused on an Ottoman nationalism, the ideology of the Empire's ruling élite. All the more so, since by the late nineteenth century Ottomanism in practice really only applied to the two major Muslim ethnolinguistic groups in the Empire, the Arabs and the Turks, as the Balkan provinces were in open revolt against Ottoman rule.

While most of the Syrian Arabs trained in Istanbul for Ottoman service were concerned with what needed to be done to keep the Empire afloat, and some even were critical of the ruling establishment's policies in Istanbul, very few found reason to express their discontent in terms of their 'Arabness.' Indeed, it was only after the Young Turk 'revolution' of 1908 that some of these urban notables and officials of the state began to feel increasingly estranged from the 'inner circle' of the Ottoman élite, which had always been mainly Turkish.[4] As some notables were excluded from the Ottoman system of rule and denied access to the central authority, they found a need to restate the ideas they had picked up in Istanbul in terms better suited to their changed circumstances. Their search for these new terms did not take long, since already available to them were two versions of Arabism, one articulated by Syrian Christians and the other by Syrian Muslim reformers.

So it was the Ottomanized urban élites of Syria who were most instrumental in activating the idea of Arabism and translating it into a loosely structured political movement before World War I. And though Arabism had yet to replace either Ottomanism or pan-Islamism, as Albert Hourani suggests, its appearance at this time '...indicates that for some at least of the Arabic-speaking Ottomans neither the traditional idea of authority nor the other ideologies could provide a guide to social action.'[5]

Aside from the fact that the Arab movement prior to 1914 was a Syrian political concoction and strictly an urban-élitist phenomenon, we also know that within the boundaries of Syrian cities and élites, the movement remained a minority political position. Moreover, it was mainly in Damascus[6] that the Arab movement had its most profound political impact and it was also in that city that its most articulate political opposition was to be found. The important point to underscore, however, is that before World War I the mainstream of the Arab movement sought neither the separation of the Arabic-speaking provinces from the Ottoman Empire nor the creation of a distinct Arab nation with defined cultural and territorial boundaries. Rather the movement desired more modest changes, in particular greater measures of administrative decentralization and political autonomy for the provinces. Its goals, elaborated within the ideological context of Arabism, reflected the interests of a certain fraction of the urban absentee landowning class that had failed to achieve political power commensurate with its expectations. In this period the Arab movement did not achieve its goals.

The Arab Revolt of 1916, which was sponsored by the British and originated outside Syria, constituted a second stage in the development of Arab nationalism. Although it was given ideological justification by Syrians, they scarcely contributed to the actual Revolt. It was not until late 1918, when the Arab provinces had been liberated from the Ottoman Empire, rendering Ottomanism obsolete, and an Arab government had been set up in the Syrian interior, that the fulcrum of 'Arabist' political activities shifted back to Damascus and Arab nationalism was galvanized into a full-blown movement.

Arab nationalism assumed its place as the reigning ideology in Syria and other Arab countries after World War I. However, it was not until the eve of World War II that a 'serious attempt was made to define the meaning of Arab nationalism and what constitutes the Arab nation.'[7] In the meantime, Arab nationalism continued to embody the two competing trends that had characterized it in the prewar period, one religious and the other secular.

The religious content in Arab nationalism stressed the primacy of the Arabs within Islam. Arab nationalism was posited as an 'indispensable' intermediary 'step towards the revival of Islam.' Not surprisingly, intellectuals who tried to mold Arab nationalism into an ideological tool by which to secure Arab political and cultural domination of Islam were most often clerics reared and trained in a traditional Islamic cultural milieu in preparation for employment in religious institutions. But not only had religious institutions been in a state of decline for nearly half a century—a decline that had rapidly accelerated after 1908 under the impact of Unionist centralization and secularization policy—they had also lost considerable autonomy in the Arab provinces of the Empire. CUP centralization policy put the religious institutions more firmly under the thumb of the state. Thus Arab religious leaders tried to use Arab nationalism as a double-edged sword: one edge would permit Arabs to cut their way back to their traditional position of leadership and influence among Muslims; the other would cut out a 'truly Islamic State' based on purely religious solidarity,[8] one in which the political influence of Arab religious experts would be paramount.

Arab nationalism was also imbued with secularist content by a young group of political activists mostly from Syria and Palestine. The overwhelming majority of these men were educated in Ottoman professional schools, but in some cases at the Syrian Protestant College in Beirut or in Europe, and were nurtured in the 'secularist atmosphere of Young

Turk politics and secret societies.'[9] The composition of this group included civilians from aristocratic as well as middle-class families, military officers and a sprinkling of Christians mostly from the Orthodox rite. Unlike their counterparts, the religious scholars, the secular nationalists were far less concerned with expressing their ideas and beliefs in systematic writings. Rather they were preoccupied with molding Arab nationalism into a movement through practical political action. Their secular training and intellectual orientations allowed them to accept more readily the need for modernization and adaptation to Western institutions without offering a systematic justification in strong religious terms. Pragmatic politicians, however, some were willing to go along with Arab religious leaders at the time of the Arab Revolt in branding the oppressive Young Turks as atheistic and impious rulers who sought to break up the unity of Islam. But this was merely a tactical maneuver at a moment of weakness and uncertainty when an extreme political action required strong justification. When they reached political maturity during the Faysal years in Damascus and assumed high positions in the Arab government as well as the leadership of the extra-governmental nationalist organizations they came to display their secular nationalist character more openly.

The secular nationalists regarded the idea of an Arab-led pan-Islamic movement and the creation of an Islamic state based on purely religious solidarity as indefensible.[10] Though they toyed with the re-establishment of an Arab Caliphate before and during the war, they came to reject this idea in the immediate postwar period in favor of setting up a modern independent Arab state, but not an absolutist one. A constitutional monarchy in which nationalist leaders could directly exercise influence over the King and steer the course of national development was at first preferred, though gradually republicanism was to supersede monarchism. Although their definition of Arab nationalism and what constitutes the Arab nation lacked clarity, secular nationalists openly opposed the idea of religious solidarity as the binding substance of the nation. Rather they conceived of an Arab nation cemented together by one common language, culture and history. They never denied the importance of Islam as an integral foundation of the nation; but they interpreted it in terms of its culture and civilization and not as the Divine Law.[11] They adopted the view that Islam provided the cement of the Arab nation. Islam enshrined and elevated the language of the nation, it strengthened and broadened Arab culture, and, in its original manifestation, served to delineate the nation's territorial boundaries. Indeed, if Islam was interpreted in this way, then loyalty to the nation would logically supersede loyalty to Islam as the Divine Law. The higher religious doctrines of Islam could govern

Arab Muslims in their daily lives but they could never appeal to Arab Christians and Jews. Furthermore, Islam was too outmoded to serve as the supreme governing principle of the modern nation and state.

In 1920 the Syrian-Palestinian leadership of the General Syrian Congress meeting in Damascus issued a statement of principles which unofficially expressed both the ideals and the pragmatism of secular Arab nationalists. Claiming to have the 'authorization' of Arab Muslims, Christians and Jews, the Congress leadership called for the absolute independence of geographical Syria within its natural frontiers. Syria's form of government was to be a 'democratic civil constitutional Monarchy on broad decentralization principles safeguarding the rights of minorities.' Jewish immigration and the idea of a Jewish 'national home' in Palestine as well as the separation of Palestine and Lebanon from Syria were rejected. Iraq was to be independent but with no economic 'barriers' between it and Syria.[12] Less than a year after this declaration the Arab Kingdom fell and its territory as well as that of Lebanon came under French rule. Meanwhile, Britain had assumed control of Palestine and Iraq. But for the coming twenty-five years the principles proclaimed at the Syrian Congress formed the broad outline of a program for Arab nationalists in these divided territories.[13]

Syrian nationalists from Damascus, Homs, Hama and Aleppo, many of whom were members of influential landowning-bureaucratic families in their respective towns, roughly the same age, educated in Ottoman professional schools and influenced by similar life experiences, were instrumental in framing the statement of principles issued by the Syrian Congress. Linked by common political aims and now accustomed to working together in nationalist societies and in government, they had already begun to build a loose alliance by the time France occupied Syria in the summer of 1920. Under French rule this alliance was transformed into a broader coalition of nationalist forces which city-based nationalist leaders molded into a political vehicle in which to return to power in Syria. The Syrian national independence movement continued to be based in Damascus and, like parallel independence movements in neighboring Arab countries, it continued to strive in principle for Arab unity and independence. Its character and development, however, became increasingly provincial after 1920, circumscribed on one level by the specific socioeconomic problems that faced a truncated Syria governed by France and on another by the nature and behavior of its leadership, members of Syria's urban upper class whose background, personal style, methods of organization and mechanisms of political action betrayed its Ottoman heritage.[14]

Notes

Introduction

1 Although I do not intend to examine in systematic fashion why Damascus, and not Aleppo—a city with a comparable population and even greater commercial importance in the Ottoman Empire—played such a critical role in the birth of Arab nationalism, there seem to have been several factors which combined to place Damascus more squarely in the Arab nationalist limelight by World War I. (1) Damascus was a more important religious and political center than Aleppo because of its role as the gathering place for Muslims coming from the North and East to make the annual pilgrimage to Mecca. (2) Damascus maintained its strongest commercial ties to the Arabic-speaking territories to its South and East while Aleppo's strongest commercial ties were to its Turkish-speaking hinterland to the North and Northeast. (3) Damascus contained a more homogeneous Arab-Muslim population than did Aleppo with its significant Arab-Christian, Turkish and Kurdish populations. (4) Damascus supported political and commercial élites which were predominantly Arab and Muslim (though Christians were active in commerce), whereas Aleppo supported a political élite composed of a mix of Arabs, Turks and Kurds, and a commercial élite with a significant Christian component. Indeed, the only town in Syria to rival Damascus in its contribution to the development of Arab nationalism was Beirut; but Beirut's contribution was more to the birth of the idea than to the physical growth of the nationalist movement. As for cities outside Syria that contributed heavily to the rise of Arab nationalism before World War I, only Cairo merits mention, both in its capacity as a great intellectual center and haven or refuge for Syrian émigré-intellectuals and political activists.

2 I acknowledge here my debt to the theories of Max Weber on the relationship between ideology, bureaucracy and politics. More specifically, I have been deeply influenced by the Weberian framework of analysis employed by C. Ernest Dawn in his *From Ottomanism to Arabism* (Urbana, 1973).

3 On the relations of city and countryside, and government and society, in the Islamic Middle East, see the following studies: Jean Sauvaget, *Alep. Essai sur le développement d'une grande ville syrienne des origines au milieu du XIXe siècle*, 2 vols. (Paris, 1941); Jacques Weulersse, *Paysans de Syrie et du Proche-Orient* (Paris, 1946); Ira M. Lapidus, *Muslim Cities in the Later*

Middle Ages (Cambridge, Massachusetts, 1967); Albert Hourani *The Emergence of the Modern Middle East* (London, 1981); A. H. Hourani and S. M. Stern (eds.), *The Islamic City* (Oxford, 1970); André Raymond, *Artisans et commerçants au Caire au XVIIIe siècle*, 2 vols. (Damascus, 1973–74); Roger Owen, *The Middle East in the World Economy 1800–1914* (London, 1981); Janet L. Abu-Lughod, *Cairo: 1001 Years of the City Victorious* (Princeton, 1971).

4 Albert Hourani, 'Ottoman Reform and the Politics of Notables,' in W. R. Polk and R. L. Chambers (eds.), *Beginnings of Modernization in the Middle East* (Chicago, 1968), pp. 41–68.

5 A. H. Hourani, 'The Islamic City in the Light of Recent Research,' in A. H. Hourani and S. M. Stern (eds.), *The Islamic City*, p.19.

6 Albert Hourani, 'Revolution in the Arab Middle East,' in P. J. Vatikiotis (ed.), *Revolution in the Middle East and Other Case Studies* (London, 1972), p.67.

7 Although the configuration of politics in Damascus in the nineteenth century included Ottoman state officials, urban notables, and European consuls, in this study I shall be primarily concerned with the interaction of the notables and the Ottoman state. No picture of political life, in this period, however, would be complete without an analysis of the role of European consulates. As Albert Hourani has suggested, European consulates in Damascus, Aleppo, Beirut and elsewhere in Syria at times acted as notables, that is as intermediaries and 'political organizers' between state and society. Because consulates had access to government, the urban population would at times seek their intervention. 'Ottoman Reform,' pp. 64–8. It would be safe to suggest, however, that the European consular role in Damascus politics, while not insignificant, was clearly of less importance than it was in Beirut where European commercial and cultural interests were far more extensive.

8 Hanna Batatu, 'Class Analysis and Iraqi Society,' *Arab Studies Quarterly* 1 (Summer 1979), p. 231. Batatu, of course, is drawing on Karl Marx's conception of class.

9 *Ibid.*, p. 233.

10 *Ibid.*, p. 234.

11 *Ibid.*, p. 234.

12 *Ibid.*, p. 238. For an elaboration of this argument, also see Hanna Batatu, *The Old Social Classes and the Revolutionary Movements of Iraq* (Princeton, 1978), especially Book 1. I have adopted this argument in my 'The Politics of Nationalism: Syria and the French Mandate, 1920–1936' (Ph.D. diss., Harvard University, 1980).

13 See Batatu, 'Class Analysis,' pp. 231–7.

14 See my 'Politics of Nationalism,' Vol. 3, Appendix 3, Tables 3-E, 3-G, 3-H, pp. 1164, 1166, 1167.

15 See my 'The Tribal Shaykh, French Tribal Policy and the Nationalist Movement in Syria between Two World Wars,' *Middle Eastern Studies* 18 (April 1982), pp. 180–93.

16 Jean-Paul Pascual, 'La Syrie à l'époque ottomane (le XIXᵉ siècle),' in André Raymond (ed.), *La Syrie d'aujourd'hui* (Paris, 1980), pp. 49–50; Owen, *The Middle East*, pp. 171–3, 261–4; Theodore R. Swedenburg, 'The Development of Capitalism in Greater Syria, 1830–1914: an Historico-Geographical Approach' (MA diss., University of Texas at Austin, 1980), pp. 49–63.

1 The political configuration of Damascus in 1860

1 K. S. Salibi, 'The 1860 Upheaval in Damascus as Seen by al-Sayyid Muhammad Abu'l Su'ud al-Hasibi, Notable and Later *Naqib al-Ashraf* of the City,' in W. R. Polk and R. L. Chambers (eds.), *Beginnings of Modernization in the Middle East: The Nineteenth Century* (Chicago, 1968), p. 197. Salibi claims that 5,500 people were killed on the first day. Also see Fritz Steppat, 'Some Arabic Manuscript Sources on the Syrian Crisis of 1860,' in J. Berque and D. Chevallier (eds.), *Les Arabes par leurs archives* (Paris, 1976), p. 189.

2 Salibi, 'The 1860 Upheaval,' p. 201. A number of Christian families were resettled in homes requisitioned in Muslim quarters, particularly in al-Qanawat.

3 Elias N. Saad, 'The Damascus Crisis of 1860 in Light of "Kitab al-Ahzan," an Unpublished Eye-Witness Account' (MA diss., American University of Beirut, 1974), pp. 88–9, 92. This anonymous account by a Damascus Christian offers some idea of the wealth of certain leading personalities in Bab Tuma who were members of the compensation committee. For example, Sarkis Dibbanah claimed 800,000 piastres in compensation and was awarded 425,000. Antun Shami, the most prominent Christian on the committee, had his home completely restored by 1866; it was recognized as the most beautiful home in Damascus at the time.

4 Saad, 'The Damascus Crisis,' pp. 71–6. Names of the most prominent notables hanged by Fu'ad Pasha are: Mahmud al-Rikabi, Muhammad al-Qatana, Salih al-Ayyubi, Hasan al-Bahnasi, Mustafa Bey al-Hawasili. The Ottoman *wali* at the time of the events, Ahmad Pasha, was shot in Istanbul after his recall. Among those exiled, however, were even more prominent notables of the *majlis*: Sa'id al-Kaylani, Shaykh 'Abdullah Halabi, Tahir al-'Imadi, Ahmad al-'Ajlani, Shaykh 'Umar al-Ghazzi, Ahmad al-Hasibi, and 'Abdullah Bey al-'Azm.

5 *Ibid.*, p. 44; Nu'man al-Qasatli, *Kitab al-rawda al-ghana' fi Dimashq al-fayha'* (Beirut, 1879).

6 Salibi, 'The 1860 Upheaval,' p. 197.

7 Saad, 'The Damascus Crisis,' pp. 71–5; Salibi, 'The 1860 Upheaval,' p. 196; Muhammad Adib al-Husni, *Kitab muntakhabat al-tawarikh li-Dimashq* (Damascus, 1928), Vol. 2, pp. 850–1.

8 Salibi, 'The 1860 Upheaval,' p. 189.

9 Karl Barbir, *Ottoman Rule in Damascus, 1708–1758* (Princeton, 1980), pp. 72–3. The standard published history of Damascus political life in the

eighteenth century remains Abdul-Karim Rafeq, *The Province of Damascus, 1723–1783* (Beirut, 1966).

10 Albert Hourani, 'Ottoman Reform and the Politics of Notables,' p. 52; Barbir, *Ottoman Rule*, pp. 72–3. Through meticulous empirical work based largely on materials in the Ottoman State Archives in Istanbul, Barbir provides an important revisionist interpretation of the complex question of the so-called eighteenth-century Ottoman 'decline.' He argues that 'during the first half of the eighteenth century the central government contained the notables' political ambitions in the province of Damascus. This containment was an important part of the Ottoman policy that reorganized the provincial governorship and the pilgrimage. Seen in this light, the long-accepted, artificial distinction between periods of "strong" and "weak" Ottoman rule – between the age of Süleyman the Magnificent and the centuries that followed – becomes inadequate.'

11 The most perceptive analysis of the phenomenon of urban notables in the Arabic-speaking lands of the Ottoman Empire remains Hourani, 'Ottoman Reform,' pp. 41–64. Also see his 'Revolution in the Arab Middle East,' in P. J. Vatikiotis (ed.), *Revolution in the Middle East and Other Case Studies* (London, 1972), pp. 65–72 and 'The Ottoman Background of the Modern Middle East,' in Hourani, *The Emergence of the Modern Middle East* (London, 1981), pp. 1–18. Although he agrees that the term 'notables' is unsatisfactory as a political concept, he also agrees that there is no better alternative. For an informed discussion of Hourani's definition of notables and those of other scholars see Barbir, *Ottoman Rule*, pp. 67–74. For a brief account of the meaning of the Arabic term *a'yan*, see Harold Bowen, 'A'yan,' *Encyclopedia of Islam*, new edition, Vol. 1, p. 778. For an example of the phenomenon of urban notables in Syria in an earlier period, see Ira M. Lapidus, *Muslim Cities in the Later Middle Ages* (Cambridge, Mass., 1967).

12 Hourani, 'The Ottoman Background,' p. 11; John Voll, 'Old "Ulama" Families and Ottoman Influence in Eighteenth-Century Damascus,' *American Journal of Arabic Studies* 3 (1975), pp. 50–1. I have deliberately chosen to include the *ashraf* (or at least the leading *ashraf*) in the broad category of the religious establishment. In a recent article Linda Schatkowski Schilcher has suggested that we should clearly distinguish between an '*ulama*' category and an *ashraf* category of notables in Damascus. She characterizes the '*ulama*' as belonging to a group of families all residing in the center city who were intimately involved in the intellectual life of the city, including *sufism*. They all had incomes from landholdings in the Damascus area and/or trade and they often received salaries for administering the religious institutions. They were all wealthy. While such a description is fundamentally sound it is also true that many of these characteristics of the '*ulama*' are also attributable to the leading *ashraf* of Damascus in the eighteenth and nineteenth centuries. Families like the 'Ajlanis, Hamzas, Kaylanis and Muradis were also residents of the center city and were active contributors to the 'religious and learned life of the city'

as teachers or *sufis*. They often patronized religious institutions and drew large incomes from landholdings or tax farms in the Damascus area and/or from trade. It is true that families belonging to the *ashraf* received certain privileges by virtue of their membership in the family of the Prophet; however, the leading *ashraf* in Damascus were very often members of the religious establishment, that is, they were '*ulama*'. Indeed, if we look at the one religious post in Damascus that conferred great socioreligious prestige and was at the same time not the preserve of a single family, we find that at least 11 (and perhaps 13) of the 15 '*ulama*' who held the post of Hanafi *Mufti* between the 1740s and the early 1850s were *bona fide* members of the *ashraf*. Naturally all members of the *ashraf* were not '*ulama*' but it is remarkable how often the head of a family of *ashraf* was a member of the '*ulama*'. Thus, for the purposes of my argument, separating the '*ulama*' from the leading *ashraf* is not particularly helpful. It is more helpful to distinguish the religious establishment ('*ulama*' and *ashraf*) from the *aghawat* (a category Dr Schilcher recognizes) and a group of secular dignitaries who were merchants and tax farmers with no base in the religious establishment but who often lived in the center city (and whom Dr Schilcher apparently does not recognize). See her 'Ba'd muthahir ahwal al-a'yan bi-Dimashq fi awakhir al-qarn-al-thamin 'ashar wa awa'il al-tasi' 'ashar,' in *Al-Mu'tamar al-dawli al-thani li-ta'rikh Bilad al-Sham* (Damascus, 1980), Vol. 1, pp. 326–56 and my 'Tabi'at al-sulta al-siyasiyya wa tuwazzi'ha fi Dimashq 1860–1908,' in *Ibid.*, pp. 437–84. Both articles are translations of the original English versions.

13 H. A. R. Gibb and Harold Bowen, *Islamic Society and the West* (London, 1950 and 1957), Vol. 1, Pts. i, ii; Albert Hourani, 'The Changing Face of the Fertile Crescent in the Eighteenth Century,' *Studia Islamica* 8 (1957), pp. 89–122.

14 Voll, 'Old "Ulama" Families,' p. 52. The *khatib* delivered his sermon (*khutba*) at Friday noon prayers when government officials and local dignitaries were present.

15 *Ibid.*, p. 52.

16 Muhammad al-Amin al-Muhibbi, *Khulasat al-athar fi a'yan al-qarn al-hadi 'ashar* (Cairo, 1867), Vol. 3, p. 408; Muhammad Khalil al-Muradi, *Silk al-durar fi a'yan al-qarn al-thani 'ashar* (Cairo, 1883), Vol. 1, p. 250.

17 Shaykh Muhammad Jamil al-Shatti, *A'yan Dimashq fi al-qarn al-thalith 'ashar wa nisf al-qarn al-rabi' 'ashar, 1201–1350 A.H.*, 2nd ed. (Beirut, 1972), p. 116. Interestingly, competition between Mahasinis and Khatibs continued in the Mandate period, but here it was between a moderately pro-French Mahasini and a nationalist Khatib. Both politicians were lawyers.

18 Voll, 'Old "Ulama" Families,' p. 54. The biographical dictionaries suggest that until the end of the eighteenth century the Shafi'i *Mufti*, of Damascus was as important a personality as the Hanafi *Mufti* and Shafi'i '*ulama*', in general, were among the leading intellectual figures in Damascus. Schilcher, 'Ba'd muthahir,' p. 353.

19 Khayr al-Din al-Zirikli, *Al-A'lam; qamus tarajim li-ashhar al-rijal wa nisa'*

min al-'Arab wa al-musta'ribin wa al-mustashriqin (Cairo, 1954–59), Vol. 5, p. 169.

20 Gabriel Baer, 'Village and City in Egypt and Syria – 1500–1914,' paper presented to the *Conference on the Economic History of the Near East* (Princeton, June 1974), p. 47.

21 Al-Shatti, *A'yan Dimashq*, p. 102; al-Zirikli, *Al-A'lam*, Vol. 6, p. 352; Shaykh 'Abd al-Razzaq al-Bitar, *Hilyat al-bashar fi ta'rikh al-qarn al-thalith 'ashar* (Damascus, 1961–63), Vol. 1, p. 318 and Vol. 3, pp. 1467–76.

22 Al-Husni, *Kitab muntakhabat*, Vol. 2, p. 592; al-Muradi, *Silk al-durar*, Vol. 2, p. 294: al-Shatti, *A'yan Dimashq*, p. 102. A Kaylani held the post in the early eighteenth century and a Muradi in the late eighteenth century.

23 Baer, 'Village and City,' p. 47.

24 Al-Husni, *Kitab muntakhabat*, Vol. 2, pp. 809–10.

25 Voll, 'Old "Ulama" Families,' p. 56.

26 Al-Muradi, *Silk al-durar*, Vol. 1, p. 3 and Vol. 3, p. 216; On the Naqshabandiyya see Albert Hourani, 'Sufism and Modern Islam: Mawlana Khalid and the Naqshabandi Order,' in Hourani, *The Emergence of the Modern Middle East* (London, 1981), pp. 75–89.

27 Salibi, 'The 1860 Upheaval,' p. 187.

28 Al-Husni, *Kitab muntakhabat*, Vol. 2, p. 828.

29 Salibi, 'The 1860 Upheaval,' pp. 185–6.

30 Moshe Ma'oz, 'The 'Ulama' and the Process of Modernization in Syria During the Mid-Nineteenth century,' *Asian and African Studies* 7 (1971), pp. 77–8.

31 Voll, 'Old "Ulama" Families,' p. 59. Voll uses this term to describe the switch from localism to identification with Istanbul.

32 The reforms enacted by Sultans Salim III and Mahmud II before 1830 never reached Syria.

33 Ma'oz, 'The 'Ulama',' pp. 80–1; Moshe Ma'oz, *Ottoman Reform in Syria and Palestine 1840–1861: The Impact of the Tanzimat on Politics and Society* (Oxford, 1968), pp. 90–8; Theodore R. Swedenburg, 'The Development of Capitalism in Greater Syria, 1830–1914' (MA diss., University of Texas at Austin, 1980), pp. 35–7.

34 Swedenburg, *op. cit.*, pp. 35–7; Roger Owen, *The Middle East in the World Economy 1800–1914* (London, 1981), pp. 76–8. Just before the Egyptian occupation of Damascus, the British established a consulate in Damascus for the first time but had to wait until the occupation to station a consul there.

35 Ma'oz, 'The 'Ulama',' 84. The *iltizam* system was abolished in 1839 but was soon revived in 1842 because the government was not receiving the revenues it had hoped for. The *malikane* system continued to exist up until 1860. Ma'oz, *Ottoman Reform in Syria*, pp. 79–80.

36 Ma'oz, 'The 'Ulama',' p. 83. Those *'ulama'* who belonged to the *ashraf* were automatically exempted from military service before the Eygptian occupation. See Schilcher, 'Ba'd muthahir,' pp. 327–31; Ma'oz, *Ottoman Reform in Syria*, pp. 182–5.

37 Ma'oz, *Ottoman Reform in Syria*, pp. 182–5.
38 Rafeq, *The Province*, p. 92; For a good summary of the debate on the al-'Azm family's origins see Barbir, *Ottoman Rule*, pp. 56–64.
39 Rafeq, *The Province*, pp. 205, 238, *et passim*.
40 *Ibid.*, pp. 161–9; Schilcher, 'Ba'd muthahir,' pp. 338–42; Barbir, *Ottoman Rule*, pp. 89–97.
41 Rafeq, *The Province*, p. 318. Actually, 'Abdullah, son of the last noted al-'Azm *wali* (Muhammad, d. 1783), was appointed governor of Damascus three times around the turn of the nineteenth century. Also see al-Husni, *Kitab*, Vol. 2, p. 847.
42 See Swedenburg, 'The Development of Capitalism in Greater Syria, 1830–1914,' pp. 25–8. Syrian Christians handled the littoral trade with Egypt as well.
43 *Ibid.*, p. 25; Pascual, 'La Syrie à l'époque ottomane,' p. 38.
44 In the province of Damascus, the *iltizam* did not completely replace the system of rural administration, i.e., the *timar* or fief which the state awarded to a cavalryman (*sipahi*). In return, the cavalryman performed the twin functions of ensuring the cultivation of the land and of maintaining local security and fighting the Empire's wars (using the taxes he collected from the land to finance his endeavors). For a brief but informed discussion of Ottoman land administration before the nineteenth century see Owen, *The Middle East*, pp. 10–21.
45 Kemal H. Karpat, 'The Land Regime, Social Structure, and Modernization in the Ottoman Empire,' in W. R. Polk and R. L. Chambers (eds.), *Beginnings of Modernization in the Middle East*; Gibb and Bowen, *Islamic Society*, Vol. 1, Pts. i, ii; Ma'oz, *Ottoman Reform in Syria*; Baer, 'Village and City.'
46 For example, the Rikabi family were wealthy merchants and tax farmers who had intermarried with the Hasibis. See p. 9.
47 Hourani, 'Ottoman Reform,' p. 48; Rafeq, *The Province*, p. 25; Barbir, *Ottoman Rule*, pp. 89–97.
48 Hourani, 'Ottoman Reform,' p. 48.
49 Abdul-Karim Rafeq, 'The Local Forces in Syria in the Seventeenth and Eighteenth Centuries,' in V. J. Parry and M. E. Yapp (eds.), *War, Technology and Society in the Middle East* (London, 1975), pp. 277–307; Rafeq, *The Province*, p. 122; Barbir, *Ottoman Rule*, p. 90.
50 For example, see Ahmad al-Budayri, *Hawadith Dimashq al-yawmiyya, 1154–1176 A.H.* (Cairo, 1959) and al-Muradi, *Silk al-durar*, Vol. 2.
51 K. Dettmann, *Damaskus: Eine orientalische Stadt zwischen Tradition und Moderne* (Nürnberg, 1967), p. 212; René Danger, 'L'Urbanisme en Syrie: la ville de Damas,' *Urbanisme (Revue mensuelle)* (1937), pp. 123–64; Anne-Marie Bianquis, 'Damas et la Ghouta,' in André Raymond (ed.), *La Syrie d'aujourd'hui* (Paris, 1980), pp. 372–8. Al-Salhiyya was a suburb with the characteristics of a large village.
52 For example, the Sukkar and al-Mahayni families of the Maydan. On the acquisition of tax farms in return for policing areas for the Ottoman state, see Schilcher, 'Ba'd muthahir,' pp. 335–7; Barbir, *Ottoman Rule*, pp. 120–1;

L. Schatkowski Schilcher, 'The Hauran Conflict of the 1860s: A Chapter in the Rural History of Modern Syria,' *International Journal of Middle Eastern Studies* 13 (May 1981), pp. 159–79.

53 Al-Muradi, *Silk al-durar*, Vol. 2, p. 261.

54 Baer, 'Village and City,' p. 47; Rafeq, *The Province*, pp. 186–7; Rafeq, 'The Local Forces,' pp. 306–7.

55 Baer, 'Village and City,' p. 47.

56 Salibi, 'The 1860 Upheaval,' p. 189. Clearly the acquisition of hereditary tax farms began in the previous century but became more commonplace for *aghawat* in the early nineteenth century. See al-Husni, *Kitab*, Vol. 2, pp. 859, 883.

57 Conversation with Hasan al-Hakim (Damascus, 12 March 1976). For example, the Mahayni *aghawat* intermarried with the Hakim family, a civilian family with a large family *waqf*, and with the Bitar family, the leading religious family of the Maydan. These three families resided in the Maydan fawqani or upper Maydan.

58 Salibi, 'The 1860 Upheaval,' p. 189.

59 See K. S. Salibi, *The Modern History of Lebanon* (New York, 1965).

60 Ma'oz, *Ottoman Reform in Syria*, p. 83.

61 The growing physical and psychological security enjoyed by Syrian Christians in Damascus and other towns, especially by the upper classes, manifested itself in several ways. Christians now had the freedom to dress (and to ride) as they wished. They constructed new churches, monasteries and schools and held large religious processions more regularly. See Swedenburg, 'The Development of Capitalism in Greater Syria, 1830–1914,' p. 47.

62 Hourani, 'Ottoman Reform.'

63 I. M. Smilianskaya, 'The Disintegration of Feudal Relations in Syria and Lebanon in the Middle of the Nineteenth Century,' in Charles Issawi (ed.), *The Economic History of the Middle East 1800–1914* (Chicago, 1966), pp. 227–47; Owen, *The Middle East*, p. 169.

64 Ma'oz, *Ottoman Reform in Syria*, p. 235.

65 Saad, 'The Damascus Crisis,' p. 31.

66 *Ibid.*, pp. 56, 70–1; the father of Shaykh 'Abd al-Razzaq al-Bitar (author of *Hilyat al-bashar*), himself a noted religious figure, also protected the Christians of the Maydan; Ma'oz, *Ottoman Reform in Syria*, p. 234. For instance, al-'Abid and Nuri were established grain merchants while the two Mahaynis were recently recruited *aghawat* of new local garrisons established on the eve of the 1860 crisis. The emergence of Maydan patrons was assisted and encouraged by events in early 1859, when the *wali* had arrested and exiled forty *aghawat* of local garrisons after disorders in the Maydan. After disbanding these garrisons, he organized new forces of auxiliaries throughout the city. This action limited the number of competitors for control of the Maydan to a few *aghawat* who had already converted to civilian occupations (like 'Umar Agha al-'Abid and Sa'id Agha Nuri) and chiefs of these forces (like the Mahayni *aghawat*).

67 Owen writes that after the disturbances 'it was Maidani merchants who were active in advancing capital to a new group of weavers, mostly Muslims, anxious to revive the local textile industry, and it may be that this was one of the reasons why the city's productive capacity was so quick to return to its pre-riot volume.' *The Middle East*, p. 170.

68 Salibi, 'The 1860 Upheaval,' pp. 189–90. Al-Hasibi condemns the 'rabble' but also members of the army and police (probably referring to the *aghawat* who had recently become part of the state apparatus) for showing 'disrespect' to their social superiors, the *'ulama'* and civilian dignitaries.

2 The consolidation of leadership in Damascus after 1860

1 Gabriel Baer, 'Village and City,' pp. 47–8. The acquisition of property on a large scale by the leading families of Damascus was much more prevalent in the Ghuta and Biqa' than it was in the Hawran where small peasant proprietorship was the norm. Several leading families of the Maydan did acquire, however, large estates in the Hawran at this time, while many others dominated the peasantry through the extension of usurious capital. See Pascual, 'La Syrie à l'époque ottomane,' p. 47.

2 Ya'kov Firestone, 'Production and Trade in an Islamic Context: Sharika Contracts in the Transitional Economy of Northern Samaria, 1853–1943,' *International Journal of Middle Eastern Studies* 6 (1975), Pt i, p. 192.

3 See Norman Lewis, 'The Frontier of Settlement in Syria, 1800–1950,' *International Affairs* 31 (1955), pp. 48–60; Salim Tamari, 'Factionalism and Class Formation in Recent Palestinian History,' in Roger Owen (ed.) *Studies in the Economic and Social History of Palestine in the Nineteenth and Twentieth Centuries* (Carbondale and Edwardsville, 1982), pp. 177–202.

4 On the commercial depression of the 1870s see Owen, *The Middle East*, pp. 171–2.

5 See Doreen Warriner, *Land Reform and Development in the Middle East*, 2nd ed. (London, 1962), pp. 68–9. Land reforms and other types of reform applied throughout the Ottoman Empire had parallels in many parts of Asia and Latin America in the latter half of the nineteenth century. See Joel Migdal, 'Urbanization and Political Change: The Impact of Foreign Rule,' *Comparative Studies in Society and History* 19 (July 1977), p. 331.

6 Jacques Weulersse, 'Régime agraire et vie agricole en Syrie,' *Bulletin de l'Association de Géographes français*, No. 113 (April 1938), p. 58; Paul J. Klat, 'The Origins of Landownership in Syria,' *Middle East Economic Papers* (1958), p. 62.

7 Gabriel Baer, 'The Evolution of Private Landownership in Egypt and the Fertile Crescent,' in Charles Issawi (ed.), *The Economic History of the Middle East 1800–1914* (Chicago, 1966), pp. 83–4; Jacques Weulersse, *Paysans de Syrie et du Proche-Orient* (Paris, 1946), pp. 95–6; Robert Montagne, 'Le Pouvoir des chefs et les élites en Orient,' *Centre de Hautes Études Administratives sur l'Afrique et l'Asie Modernes*, No. 17 (12 May 1938), pp. 3–4. Hereafter *CHEAM*.

8 Eliahu Epstein, 'Notes from a Paper on the Present Conditions in the Hauran,' *Journal of the Royal Central Asian Society*, 23 (1936), pp. 598–9, 601. Peasant indebtedness was particularly widespread in the Hawran.

9 See George Young, *Corps de droit ottoman* (Oxford, 1905–06), Vol. 6, for the articles of the Land Code of 1858.

10 One source in 1907 estimated that only 20 to 30 percent of the lands in Syria (probably the Syrian Province) was in peasant hands. See Owen, *The Middle East*, p. 255.

11 Hourani, 'The Ottoman Background,' pp. 15–16; Ma'oz, *Ottoman Reform in Syria*, p. 241.

12 For example, the Ghazzis and the Ayyubis sent some sons to Istanbul, while they encouraged other sons to enter the religious professions.

13 Ma'oz, *Ottoman Reform in Syria*, p. 242. One author claims that the sons of the Muslim élite of Damascus did not begin to send sons to mission schools until the turn of the twentieth century. Pascual, 'La Syrie à l'époque ottomane,' p. 50.

14 Analyses of this literary revival and role of Western missionaries are many. The classic account is found in George Antonius, *The Arab Awakening* (London, 1938). The most profound account remains Albert Hourani's *Arabic Thought in the Liberal Age, 1798–1939* (London, 1962). Also see Robert M. Haddad, *Syrian Christians in Muslim Society* (Princeton, 1970). The major critic of the Western missionary role and the contribution of Syrian Christians argues that the Arab language was not dead in the nineteenth century and that language reform was inspired more by Egyptians and Syrians, many of whom were Muslim, than by Western missionaries. See A. L. Tibawi, 'Some Misconceptions about the Nahda,' *Middle East Forum*, 47 (Autumn & Winter 1971), pp. 15–22. A most convincing interpretation has recently been suggested on the subject of the *nahda* by a young American scholar who happens to have been raised in the American Protestant community of Beirut a century after the *nahda* began. He writes: 'Nonetheless, many figures of the *nahda* were associated with missionaries and the rising native commercial interests engaged in trade with the West. The *nahda* then was not so much a missionary-inspired resuscitation of a "dead" language, as the reworking, modification, and streamlining of the Arabic language by native Syrians (with missionary ties) to make it serviceable for the introduction of Western ideas, particularly positivist science, into the area.' Theodore R. Swedenburg, 'The Development of Capitalism in Greater Syria, 1830–1914: An Historico-Geographical Approach' (MA diss., University of Texas at Austin, 1980), pp. 42–3.

15 Ma'oz, *Ottoman Reform in Syria*, pp. 154–5.

16 *Ibid.*, p. 155.

17 For an informed discussion of the division of Syrian provinces into administrative districts and subdistricts after 1864, and for the general administration of the region, see 'Abd al-'Aziz Muhammad 'Awad, *Al-Idara al-'Uthmaniyya fi wilayat Suriyya 1864–1914* (Cairo, 1969), pp. 65–72; Muhammad Kurd 'Ali, *Khitat al-Sham* (Damascus, 1928), Vol. 3, pp. 38–40.

A good analysis of the character of reforms instituted in the late 1870s under the reform-minded Ottoman governor, Midhat Pasha, is Shimon Shamir's 'The Modernization of Syria: Problems and Solutions in the Period of Abdülhamid,' in W. R. Polk and R. L. Chambers (eds.), *Beginnings of Modernization in the Middle East* (Chicago, 1968), pp. 351–81. Also see Najib Saliba, 'Wilayat Suriyya, 1876–1909' (Ph.D. diss., University of Michigan, 1971); and 'The Achievements of Midhat Pasha as Governor of the Province of Syria,' *International Journal of Middle Eastern Studies* 9 (1978), pp. 307–23.

18 This is based on a careful reading of the *Salname* for this period. See, for example, *Salname: Suriye vilayeti* 1313 AH/1894–95 AD, p. 71. All references to the *Salname* in this chapter are to the Syrian Province, whose capital was Damascus.

19 *Salname*, 1302/1884–85, pp. 58–9.

20 Smilianskaya, 'The Disintegration of Feudal Relations,' pp. 227–47. On the population of Damascus in late Ottoman times see Stanford J. Shaw, 'The Ottoman Census System and Population, 1831–1914,' *International Journal of Middle Eastern Studies* 10 (1978), pp. 325–8; Muhammad Sa'id Kalla, 'The Role of Foreign Trade in the Economic Development of Syria 1831–1914' (Ph.D. diss., American University, 1969), pp. 284–5; Owen, *The Middle East*, pp. 244–5; René Danger, 'L'Urbanisme en Syrie: la ville de Damas,' *Urbanisme (Revue mensuelle)* (1937), p. 137. The population of the city of Damascus in 1885 has been placed at 150,000.

21 Weulersse, *Paysans*, p. 119.

22 Al-Husni, *Kitab muntakhabat*, Vol. 2, p. 350; al-Shatti, *A'yan Dimashq*, p. 116. For example, the Khatib family replaced the Mahasini family in 1869 as preachers (*khatibs*) of the Umayyad Mosque.

23 The development of this phenomenon can be traced in the *Salname*: 1288/1871–1312/1894–95, and through the various biographical dictionaries cited in the Bibliography and Notes. Two religious families that began to seek employment in the secular institutions were the Ayyubis and Bakris.

24 It is unlikely that we shall ever be able to provide accurate data on landownership in Ottoman Syria because nearly all the local land registers were destroyed or disappeared (perhaps the Turks took them back to Istanbul) during World War I. My decision to include the families that I do among the very biggest landowners of Damascus is based on the following sources: the inheritance records of the *mahakim al-shari'a* of the Syrian Province: interviews with descendants of some of these families; and information supplied to me by Ramez Tomeh, whose research into the relationship between landownership and political power in Damascus has assisted me greatly.

25 Al-Husni, *Kitab muntakhabat*, Vol. 2, pp. 809–10; Saad, 'The Damascus Crisis,' pp. 71–6.

26 *Salname*, 1288/1871–72, p. 72.

27 Al-Husni, *Kitab muntakhabat*, Vol. 2, pp. 809–10; Voll, 'Old "Ulama" Families,' p. 51.

28 Yusif Ibish, 'Elias Qudsi's Sketch of the Guilds of Damascus in the Nineteenth Century,' *Middle East Economic Papers* (1967), pp. 43–4.

29 *Salname*, 1309–10/1892–93, pp. 107, 111.

30 Al-Bitar, *Hilyat al-bashar*, Vol. 1, p. 440; Capt. C. D. Brunton, 'Who's Who in Damascus, 1918–19,' *Brunton File*, Middle East Centre, St Antony's College, Oxford.

31 *Salname*, 1309–10/1892–3, p. 109; 1308–9/1890–91, p. 53; 1313/1894–95, p. 58; Brunton, 'Who's Who,' p. 3. Sadiq al-'Ajlani was a member of the Court of Appeals in 1890, and Muhammad 'Ali al-'Ajlani, was a member of the Education Council in 1894.

32 Baer, 'Village and City,' p. 47.

33 Ibish, 'Elias Qudsi's Sketch,' p. 43.

34 *Ibid.*, p. 43.

35 Al-Husni, *Kitab muntakhabat*, Vol. 2, p. 551; al-Zirikli, *al-A'lam*, Vol. 1, p. 153.

36 Saad, 'The Damascus Crisis,' 71–6; al-Shatti, *A'yan Dimashq*, p. 439; *Salname*, 1288/1871–72, p. 83; 1302/1884–85, pp. 58–9.

37 *Salname*, 1296/1878–79, p. 142; 1309–10/1892–93, p. 112; 1312/1894–95, p. 80.

38 *Ibid.*, 1312/1894–95, p. 80.

39 *Ibid.*, 1302/1884–85, p. 62; 1309–10/1892–93, p. 127.

40 Al-Shatti, *A'yan Dimashq*, p. 439.

41 Al-Zirikli, *Al-A'lam*, Vol. 4, pp. 171–2.

42 Najm al-Din al-Ghazzi, *Al-Kawakib al-sa'ira bi-a'yan al-mi'a al-'ashira* ed. Jibra'il Jabbur (Beirut, 1945–59), Vol. 1, p. 250; al-Muradi, *Silk al-durar*, Vol. 3, pp. 46–47.

43 Voll, 'Old "Ulama" Families,' 55; al-Shatti, *A'yan Dimashq*, pp. 148–9.

44 Sa'id's grandfather was born in Damascus and became a leading member of the Qadiriyya *sufi* order as well as a member of the Administrative Council in the early nineteenth century. Al-Bitar, *Hilyat al-bashar*, Vol. 3, pp. 1338–9; Saad, 'The Damascus Crisis of 1860,' 71–6.

45 *Salname*, 1288/1871–72, p. 83; 1296/1878–79, p. 144.

46 *Ibid.*, 1302/1884–85, pp. 58–9; 1308–09/1890–91, pp. 62, 66; 1309–10/1892–93, pp. 120, 127; 1312/1894–95, pp. 76–8.

47 Al-Shatti, *A'yan Dimashq*, p. 438.

48 Al-Bitar, *Hilyat al-bashar*, Vol. 3, pp. 1338–9. Al-Bitar claims that the Kaylanis of Damascus were not landowners but evidence from the *Salname* and later yearbooks of the Mandate period prove him wrong.

49 *L'indicateur Libano-syrien*, 5th ed. (Beirut, 1928–29), pp. 370–1.

50 There is some doubt as to when the Hasibis were officially recognized as *ashraf*, but the fact that Ahmad was a full-fledged member of the *majlis* in 1860, suggests that the family was at that time a recognized member of the religious aristocracy.

51 Saad, 'The Damascus Crisis,' 71–6; Salibi, 'The 1860 Upheaval,' p. 201.

52 *Salname*, 1296/1878–79, p. 144; 1309–10/1892–93, p. 124; 1308–09/1890–91, p. 66; 1312/1894–95, p. 91; al-Bitar, *Hilyat al-bashar*, Vol. 1,

p. 100; al-Shatti, *A'yan Dimashq*, pp. 441, 444; Brunton, 'Who's Who,' p. 2. Abu'l Su'ud was stripped of the post of *Naqib* by the Committee of Union and Progress in 1908. His sons 'Ali and Ahmad, resumed the post between 1918 and 1936, through the initial assistance of their relative, 'Ali Rida Pasha al-Rikabi in 1918. Al-Rikabi was, at the time, the chief of Faysal's Syrian government.

53 Al-Judayda lies northwest of Damascus at the present Syrian-Lebanese border. At the time, many Damascenes owned lands in this region and further west in the Biqa' Valley. However, it seems unlikely that the Ottoman land grants to the Hasibi family were in the form of *iqta'* as al-Husni claims. They were probably held as *malikanes* or *iltizams*; Salibi, 'The 1860 Upheaval,' p. 192; al-Husni, *Kitab muntakhabat*, Vol. 2, pp. 828–9; Ma'oz, *Ottoman Reform in Syria*, pp. 78–81.

54 Al-Shatti, *A'yan Dimashq*, pp. 176–9; *L'indicateur Libano-Syrien* (Beirut, 1923), pp. 375–6.

55 Al-Bitar, *Hilyat al-bashar*, Vol. 3, p. 1423.

56 For one interpretation of 'Abd al-Qadir's motives in 1860, see Hourani, 'Ottoman Reform,' p. 67.

57 The *Salname* published between 1871 and 1895 do not mention any members of the Jaza'iri family holding posts in either the religious or the secular institutions in the Damascus province. The biographical dictionaries confirm this.

58 Al-Shatti, *A'yan Dimashq*, pp. 176–9; al-Husni, *Kitab muntakhabat*, Vol. 2, p. 799.

59 The 'Attars were an old religious family of Aleppo who arrived in Damascus in the late eighteenth century. Some family members became Hanafis but most remained Shafi'is. After 1860, al-'Attar shaykhs were found on the District Council, the Municipal Court, the Commercial Court and the Court of Appeals. They also sat on the *Awqaf* Council and the *shari'a* courts. Shaykh Najib was head of the family in the last third of the century. Al-Husni, *Kitab muntakhabat*, Vol. 2, pp. 841, 842; al-Bitar, *Hilyat al-bashar*, Vol. 1, p. 239; al-Shatti, *A'yan Dimashq*, pp. 13, 338, 378, 407–411, 439; *Salname*, 1288/1871–72; 1296/1878–79; 1302/1884–85; 1309–10/1892–93. The Hamzas, after losing the *Naqib al-Ashraf* chair to the 'Ajlanis, dominated the post of Hanafi *Mufti* after 1860. They were also on the Councils of the Province (permanent members), the District, and Education, as well as on the *shari'a* courts. Shaykh Mahmud was *Mufti* and head of the family after 1860. Al-Bitar, *Hilyat*, Vol. 3, pp. 1467–76; al-Shatti, *A'yan*, pp. 341–2, 429, 442; al-Husni, *Kitab*, Vol. 2, pp. 810–13; *Salname*, 1288/1871–72; 1296/1878–79; 1302/1884–85; 1309–10/1892–93. The Mahasinis lost their control of the office of *Khatib* to the Khatib family in 1869, but continued to hold high posts in the religious institutions, particularly as judges on the *shari'a* courts. Al-Shatti, *A'yan*, p. 444; al-Husni, *Kitab*, Vol. 2, p. 839; *Salname*, 1288/1871–72; 1296/1878–79; 1308–09/1890–91. The Ustwanis came from Palestine in the thirteenth century as Hanbali *'ulama'*, but became Hanafis in the eighteenth century. They held a series of high

---

religious posts connected to the Directorate of the *Awqaf* and *Fatwa* Department. They were also magistrates on the *shariʻa* courts. After 1860 they could be found in the Bureau of Taxation. They were renowned as religious scholars. Al-Husni, *Kitab*, Vol. 2, pp. 585, 837–38. Al-Shatti, *Aʻyan*, pp. 120, 440, 442. *Salname*, 1288/1871–72; 1302/1884–85; 1309–10/1892–93. After 1860 the Muradis were on the District Council, judges on the *shariʻa* courts, and leading religious scholars. By the end of the century they appear to have sold most of their Ghuta lands, originally tax farms, to the Yusuf family. Al-Shatti, *Aʻyan*, p. 440; *Salname*, 1288/1871–72; 1302/1884–85; 1309–10/1892–93. One other family, the Bitars, deserve mention. Because of their wealth, power and influence in the Maydan as the quarter's leading religious family, they may well have had comparable power to that of the landowning-bureaucratic families. They were also well-known biographers and scholars; after 1860, they were on the *shariʻa* and Commercial Courts and in the Bureau of Taxation. *Salname*, 1296/1878–79; 1308–09/1890–91.

60 The Ayyubis claimed to be from the *Ansar* (partisans) of the Prophet, but they only achieved prominence in the religious establishment in the early nineteenth century. Unable to secure any prestigious religious posts, the family shifted its identity in the direction of Istanbul, even sending some of its sons there for professional and military education. Members became secular court judges and the Ayyubis were the only scholarly family, not owning lands or large business enterprises, to have secured a seat on the Municipal Council before 1900. Al-Husni, *Kitab*, Vol. 2, pp. 833–5; *Salname*, 1302/1884–85. The Malkis could not cut the competition for high religious posts and therefore focused their attention on posts in the civil bureaucracy. Having gained important seats on the Municipal Council and in the secular court system they managed to purchase lands in the Ghuta, and shortly thereafter came to join a select group of landowners in the Chamber of Agriculture. *Salname*, 1308–09/1890–91, p. 56. The Halabis made their name in religious circles through the teachings of Shaykh ʻAbdullah, a noted preacher at the Umayyad Mosque in the 1850s. They also became prosperous wool and silk merchants and in the process turned away from the religious institutions to posts on the Municipal Council. Maʼoz, *Ottoman Reform in Syria*, p. 235; *Salname*, 1309–10/1892–93, p. 127; *L'Indicateur Libano-syrien* (Beirut, 1928–29), p. 381. The ʻUmaris had the status of *ashraf* and scholars while always maintaining strong links with local industry. Unable to secure high posts in the religious hierarchy after 1860, they harnessed their resources and built the largest glass factory in Damascus. Later they also built the largest tanning factory in the city. Al-Husni, *Kitab*, Vol. 2, pp. 539, 882–4; al-Bitar, *Hilyat*, Vol. 2, p. 663; al-Shatti, *Aʻyan*, pp. 315, 440; *Salname*, 1312/1894–95, p. 94. The Maydanis were an old *ʻulama* family dating from the sixteenth century in Damascus. Like the ʻUmaris they maintained strong links to merchant trades. While holding posts within both religious and civilian institutions, they became one of the most noted grain-merchant families in Damascus in the last third

of the nineteenth century. This enterprise probably enabled the family purchase of its lands in the Ghuta. Al-Ghazzi, *Al-Kawakib*, Vol. 1, p. 72; al-Muradi, *Silk al-durar*, Vol. 1, pp. 11–12; al-Bitar, *Hilyat*, Vol. 1, pp. 327–8; al-Shatti, *A'yan*, pp. 407–8.

61 France: Ministère de la Défense, *Service Historique de l'Armée* (Vincennes), 7N 2141 (Arabie 1917–18–19) 'La famille de Bakri,' Akaba, 20 June 1918; al-Husni, *Kitab muntakhabat*, Vol. 2, pp. 819–22; al-Shatti, *A'yan Dimashq*, p. 341; *Salname*, 1312/1894–95, pp. 77–8. The two villages were al-Qabun, due north of Damascus, and Jarmana (populated by Druze peasants) southeast of Damascus. See Map, 'Environs of Damascus,' in Karl Baedeker (ed.), *Palestine and Syria. Handbook for Travellers*, 5th ed. (Leipzig, 1898).

62 Saad, 'The Damascus Crisis,' 71–6. His son, 'Ali, was also exiled.

63 *Salname*, 1288/1871–72, p. 72; al-Husni, *Kitab muntakhabat*, Vol. 2, p. 847.

64 *Salname*, 1288/1871–72, pp. 80, 83; 1296/1878–79, p. 847.

65 *Ibid.*, 1302/1884–85, pp. 59, 63, 92.

66 *Ibid.*, 1308–09/1890–91, pp. 62, 66, 68; 1309–10/1892–93, pp. 93, 107, 111, 120, 127; 1312/1894–95, pp. 76, 94, 179.

67 *Ibid.*, 1309–10/1892–93, p. 127; 1312/1894–95, p. 94; al-Husni, *Kitab muntakhabat*, Vol. 2, p. 847; Khalid al-'Azm, *Mudhakkirat Khalid al-'Azm* (Beirut, 1973), Vol. 1, pp. 153–5.

68 Kazem Daghestani, *Étude sociologique sur la famille musulmane contemporaine en Syrie* (Paris, 1932), p. 184.

69 The 'Azm branch in Hama was also one of the three most influential families in that town. They were wealthy landowners and high-ranking officials in the local administration of that central-Syrian town. They were joined by the Kaylani (also with a branch in Damascus) and Barazi (of Kurdish origin) families. See [J. Gaulmier], 'Note sur la propriété foncière dans la Syrie centrale,' *L'Asie française* No. 309 (April 1933), pp. 130–7.

70 Al-Shatti *A'yan Dimashq*, p. 364. The 'Abids claimed to be from the Masharifa Tribe. The Mawali was found in central Syria.

71 The inhabitants of the Maydan divide their quarter into at least three subquarters: Maydan fawqani or sultani (upper Maydan, the southernmost area of the quarter); Maydan wastani (middle Maydan) of which Bab Musalla is a subdivision; and Maydan tahtani (lower Maydan) or the northernmost area, including al-Suwayqa. These divisions are not always clearly demarcated in everyone's mind, but they do serve to delineate areas in this long quarter extending over $1\frac{1}{2}$ miles from top to toe. Conversation with Hasan al-Hakim (Damascus, 12 March 1976).

72 Saad, 'The Damascus Crisis,' 56, 70–1.

73 Al-Shatti, *A'yan Dimashq*, p. 364.

74 *Salname*, 1296/1878–79, p. 103; 1309–10/1892–93, p. 102.

75 *Ibid.*, 1302/1884–85, pp. 58–9.

76 *Ibid.*, 1296/1878–79, p. 140; 1302/1884–85, p. 94.

77 Al-Shatti, *A'yan Dimashq*, p. 364; *Salname*, 1312/1884–85, p. 71.

78 FO 371/548, file 29285. 'General Report on Turkey for the year 1906,' by Fitzmaurice.

79 A. L. Tibawi, *A Modern History of Syria including Lebanon and Palestine* (London, 1969), p. 183; al-Shatti, *A'yan Dimashq*, p. 364. One cynical version of how 'Izzat al-'Abid won the confidence of Sultan 'Abd ul-Hamid comes from the British Foreign Office. In the provinces 'Izzat 'entered the Judicial branch of the Government service, becoming Public Prosecutor in one of the Syrian tribunals, when Djevdet Pasha, then Minister of Justice about 1887, being attracted by his evident cleverness, brought him to Constantinople as President of the Mixed Chamber of the Commercial Court. Here he distinguished himself, mainly by his exceptional venality, and gave rise to such universal dissatisfaction that he had to be removed, and was relegated to the Council of State. Izzet, however was much too resourceful a person to remain for any great length of time in obscurity. Having obtained an entrance to the palace through the instrumentality of the First Chamberlain, Hadj Ali Bey, a stupid man dazzled by his superficial brilliancy, he very soon succeeded in acquiring a powerful influence over the Sultan by working upon his vanity and upon his personal fears. He has made many gross mistakes and has frequently been on the verge of disgrace, but his extraordinary astuteness and intimate comprehension of his master's character have invariably sufficed to save him from a fall,' FO 371/548, file 29285. 'General Report on Turkey for the year 1906' by Fitzmaurice.

80 Tibawi, *A Modern History of Syria*, p. 183. According to the British, ''Izzat's 'best stroke of business was probably the invention of the Hedjaz Railway scheme. Whether the original suggestion was his own or Von der Goltz Pasha's, it was Izzet who brought home to the Sultan's understanding how such an undertaking might serve to strengthen his position as Khalif, by consolidating his hold upon the sacred places of Islam, and enhance his prestige by firing the imagination of Mussulmans throughout the world. The success of this project has probably surpassed his own expectations; and, until the railhead has been advanced at least to Medina, Izzet's position is fairly safe. He is, however, too cunning to rely blindly even on that. The bulk of his enormous fortune that he must undoubtedly have amassed is safely invested in Europe, and every possible preparation made for a rapid flight in case of necessity,' FO 371/548, file 29285.

81 Al-Shatti, *A'yan Dimashq*, p. 364.

82 Conversation with Wajiha al-Yusuf (Beirut, 15 August 1975).

83 Syria, Markaz al-watha'iq al-ta'rikhiyya, *Registre Civil* (31 December 1930–25 August 1932) (Damascus), pp. 191–200. The estimate in 1913 of the value of 'Izzat Pasha al-'Abid's landed property in the Ottoman Empire was reported as high as £T400,000 gold. Among the items composing this figure were a new large building begun in 1907 which was designed to combine with a large European hotel (The Victoria), the offices of the Ottoman Bank, Public Debt, etc. The Ottoman Bank at that time was proposing to rent its office space for the phenomenal sum of £T900 gold annually, but when al-'Abid's property was placed under sequester in August 1908 after the CUP coup (see next chapter), completion of the building was suspended. Nearly all his property seems to have been assigned

before 1908 as *waqf* to the Haram of Medina, to be held for his heirs in trust for ever. FO 371/1848, file 58138, Devey to Mallet, 9 December 1913.

84 Conversation with Wajiha al-Yusuf (Beirut, 15 August 1975).

85 Conversation with Wajiha al-Yusuf (Beirut, 15 August 1975); al-Shatti, *A'yan Dimashq,* pp. 369–72. Actually the man who moved to Damascus from Diarbakir was called Muhammad ibn Yusuf. Eventually the family name became al-Yusuf.

86 Al-Shatti, *A'yan Dimashq,* pp. 369–72; al-Husni, *Kitab muntakhabat,* Vol. 2, pp. 851–3.

87 Al-Shatti, *op. cit.,* pp. 369–72; al-Husni, *op. cit.,* pp. 851–3.

88 *Salname,* 1309–10/1892–93, p. 102.

89 Salibi, 'The 1860 Upheaval,' p. 189, quoting Abu'l Su'ud al-Hasibi.

90 Ma'oz, *Ottoman Reform in Syria,* p. 234.

91 Salibi, 'The 1860 Upheaval,' p. 189.

92 Al-Husni, *Kitab muntakhabat,* Vol. 2, p. 899.

93 Conversation with Wajiha al-Yusuf (Beirut, 15 August 1975).

94 Markaz al-watha'iq al-ta'rikhiyya, *Registre commercial* (1 April 1937–31 March 1938). For an interesting contemporary account of life in al-Salhiyya in the first quarter of the twentieth century see Ahmad Hilmi al-'Allaf, *Dimashq fi matla' al-qarn al-'ashrin,* ed. 'Ali Jamil Nu'iysa (Damascus, 1976).

95 Conversation with Wajiha al-Yusuf (Beirut, 29 August 1975).

96 Al-Husni, *Kitab muntakhabat,* Vol. 2, pp. 891–2.

97 Conversation with Salma Mardam-Beg (London, 7 December 1974); al-Shatti, *A'yan Dimashq,* p. 329.

98 *Salname,* 1296/1878–79, p. 103.

99 Conversation with Wajiha al-Yusuf (Beirut, 29 August 1975).

100 *Salname,* 1296/1878–79, p. 140; Shatti, *A'yan Dimashq,* p. 329.

101 *Salname,* 1302/1884–85, pp. 57, 92.

102 Muslim merchants from Baghdad had been prominent traders in Damascus for generations. In the eighteenth and nineteenth centuries they conducted the long-distance caravan trade across the Syrian desert between Baghdad and Damascus. In Damascus, they were revered for their trading abilities, particularly those who traded at the Khan As'ad Pasha [al-'Azm.] However, with the shift in trade routes owing to the opening of the Suez Canal in 1869, Baghdad merchants gradually lost their important role in the economy of Damascus and the region.

103 Al-Husni, *Kitab muntakhabat,* Vol. 2, pp. 861–2. For instance, Muhammad ibn As'ad, head of the third generation of the Quwwatlis in Damascus, was already a wealthy merchant in the first half of the nineteenth century. Meanwhile, Sa'id al-Quwwatli (d. 1874) erected a famous waterway to the Umayyad Mosque.

104 *Salname,* 1288/1871–72, p. 72.

105 *Ibid.,* 1308–09/1890–91, p. 66; 1309–10/1892–93, pp. 102, 124; 1312/1894–95, p. 71.

106 *Ibid.,* 1309–10/1892–93, p. 124; 1312/1894–95, p. 91; Brunton, 'Who's

Who,' p. 6; al-Husni, *Kitab muntakhabat*, Vol. 2, pp. 861–2; al-Shatti, *A'yan*, p. 425.

107 *Salname*, 1312/1894–95, p. 88.
108 Al-Zirikli, *Al-A'lam*, Vol. 3, pp. 147–8; al-Muradi, *Silk al-durar*, Vol. 3, p. 156.
109 Conversation with Hasan [Abu 'Ali] al-Kilawi (Damascus, 14 February 1976).
110 Al-Husni, *Kitab muntakhabat*, Vol. 2, p. 870; *Salname*, 1296/1878–79, p. 103; 1302/1884–85, pp. 49, 57, 59; 1312/1894–95, p. 102.
111 *Salname*, 1312/1894–95, p. 78. Yusuf was judge on the Commercial Court in 1894.
112 Al-Husni, *Kitab muntakhabat*, Vol. 2, p. 863.
113 *Salname*, 1296/1878–79, p. 140; 1302/1884–85, p. 92.
114 *Salname*, 1288/1871–72, p. 80.
115 Al-Husni, *Kitab muntakhabat*, Vol. 2, p. 863; al-Shatti, *A'yan Dimashq*, p. 347; Ma'oz, *Ottoman Reform in Syria*, p. 12.
116 Al-Shatti, *A'yan*, p. 347; Fakhri al-Barudi, *Mudhakkirat al-Barudi* Vol. 1 (Beirut, 1951).
117 The Hamzas and the Ustwanis were middle-sized landowners. The Muradis, however, sold their lands to the Yusufs in the late nineteenth century. Conversation with Wajiha al-Yusuf (Beirut, 15 August 1975).
118 Conversation with Wajiha al-Yusuf (Beirut, 29 August 1975). For example the Bakris, Malkis and Maydanis were middle-sized landowners. The Maydanis were also moneylending grain merchants. The 'Umaris were industrialists; and the Ayyubis were neither landowners nor merchants though in the early twentieth century they intermarried with the landowning family of al-Jaza'iri.
119 Salibi,'The 1860 Upheaval,' p. 199. Only the Rikabi family seems to have been fairly well-established in politics around 1860.
120 Owen, *The Middle East*, p. 261. On this revival also see Swedenburg, 'The Development of Capitalism in Syria,' pp. 56–61.
121 In the last third of the nineteenth century the Haffars and Jallads emerged as prominent center-city merchants involved in textiles. The Jallads were also landowners. Muhammad Rashid Jallad and Rashid al-Haffar became members of the Chambers of Commerce and Agriculture in the early 1890s. *Salname*, 1308–09/1890–91; al-Husni, *Kitab muntakhabat*, Vol. 2, pp. 902, 910; al-Shatti, *A'yan*, p. 166. The Sukkars, Nuris, Mahaynis, Hakims, Tabba's and Rijlihs, were influential merchant-moneylending *aghawat* in the grain or livestock trade with Hawran peasants and beduins. Only the Tabba's and Nuris were not landowners at this time. Markaz al-watha'iq al-ta'rikhiyya, Register of *al-Mahkama al-tijara al-Sham*, 1302/1884–85; various *Salname*; conversation with Hasan al-Hakim (Damascus, 12 March 1976); al-Husni, *Kitab*, Vol. 2, pp. 859, 863–4, 883. The Agribuz and Buzu families were Kurdish chieftains in the Hayy al-Akrad. Both were ranking Ottoman administrators, the Agribuz family holding the title of *bey*. Both families were landowners and the Buzu were also livestock merchants.

Markaz, Register of *al-Mahkama al-tijara al-Sham*, 1302/1884–85; various *Salname*; al-Husni, *Kitab*, Vol. 2, p. 897. The 'Azmas, apparently of Turcoman origin, were *aghawat* of local garrisons in the eighteenth century, who became Ottoman civil servants in the nineteenth century after the disbanding of garrisons by the State. They, too, were *beys*, residing in the Shaghur quarter. *Salname* 1309–1310/1892–93; communication from Aziz al-Azmeh (Oxford, 23 November 1976); al-Bitar, *Hilyat al-bashar*, Vol. 1, p. 243; al-Husni, *Kitab*, Vol. 2, pp. 638, 849.

122 In the last third of the nineteenth century the leading Christian political families of Damascus included the Asbir, Jubran, Najri, Shalhub, Shamiyya, 'Akhrawi, Qudsi, 'Absi, Siba', Shawi, Abu Sha'r, Asfar, Mishaqa, Abu Hamad, and Ghanaja. The leading Jewish families were the Linyadu, Lizbuna, Totah, and 'Adis. These four families resided in the ancient Jewish quarter of the southeast corner of the old city.

123 Safuh Khayr, *Madinat Dimashq. Dirasa fi jughrafiyya al-mudun* (Damascus, 1969); Danger, 'L'Urbanisme,' p. 137.

124 Owen, *The Middle East*, pp. 171–2; Shamir, 'The Modernization of Syria,' pp. 379–80.

125 For instance, in 1871, 'Ajami Asbir and Jubran Najri were members of the Administrative Council of the Province. Hanna Shalhub and Antun Salim were on the District Council. In 1878, Musa Qudsi and Musa Linyadu were members of the Bureau of Property Taxation. Jurji Shalhub was a judge on the Court of Appeals. Rufa'il Shamiyya was a member of the Court of Summary Justice. 'Abdullah Shakush and Rufa'il 'Akhrawi were judges on the Commercial Court. In 1884, Khalil Bey Qudsi was a member of the Commission of Public Works as well as a member of the Chamber of Agriculture. His cousin, Musa, was a member of the Bureau of Property Taxation along with Musa Lizbuna. Ibrahim 'Absi and Asbir Siba' were judges on the Court of Appeals. Salim Shawi was a judge on the Commercial Court. Jibra'il Shamiyya and Ilahu Totah were members of the District Council. In 1892, the Administrative Council of the Province included Salim Ayyub, Jubran Asbir, and Mayir Lizbuna. The Court of Appeals had four Christian judges: Mikha'il Sidih, Salim Shawi, Nu'man Abu Sha'r, and Jurji Shalhub. The Commercial Court included Yahya Linyadu and Rufa'il 'Akhrawi. The Court of Summary Justice included Milhim Abu Hamad and Rufa'il Shamiyya. *Salname*, 1288/1871–72, pp. 71, 72; 1296/1878–79, pp. 103, 108, 109, 140, 142, 144; 1308/1884–85, pp. 58–9, 60, 64, 92; 1309–10/1892–93, pp. 102, 107, 109, 110.

126 In 1884, Salim Mishaqa, a lay leader of the Protestant Community, served as Dragoman at the British Consulate. At the same time two cousins, 'Abduh and Khalil Qudsi, were Dragomans respectively of Holland and Belgium. In 1890, Nasif Mishaqa, cousin of Salim, was the American Consul in Damascus. Bishara Asfar, the wealthiest Catholic entrepreneur and moneylender in Damascus was Dragoman at the German Consulate. Yusuf Siba', lay leader of the Russian Orthodox Community in Bab Tuma, served as Dragoman at the Russian Consulate. Khalil Ghanaja, another wealthy

Catholic merchant-moneylender, was one of the Dragomans at the French Consulate. *Salname*, 1302/1884–85, pp. 98–9; 1308–09/1890–91, pp. 130–1.

127 Markaz al-watha'iq al-ta'rikhiyya, Register of *al-Mahkama al-tijara: al-Sham*, 1302/1884–85. Two of the most prominent Christian moneylenders were Bishara Asfar and 'Abduh Qudsi. Asfar, Qudsi and other Christians began manipulating usurious capital at this time to indebt peasants and ultimately to foreclose on their lands.

128 *Ibid.*, and conversation with Jubran Shamiyya (Beirut, 29 July 1975).

129 Hourani, 'Ottoman Reform,' p. 46.

130 Weulersse, *Paysans*, p. 116. He claims that in the countryside around the city usury was the main tool used to conquer the area economically and to acquire lands. In Damascus, the extension of usurious capital by merchant-moneylenders in the Ghuta and Hawran was a common feature.

131 Daghestani, *Étude sociologique sur la famille*, pp. 190–2.

132 The Quwwatli family had a reputation for not allowing daughters to marry if no male cousins could be found. Conversation with Wajiha al-Yusuf (Beirut, 29 August 1975). For a detailed study of the Syrian marriage system see K. Chatila, *Le mariage chez les Musulmans en Syrie* (Paris, 1934).

133 Daghestani, *Étude sociologique sur la famille*, pp. 184–5.

134 The author would like to thank Dr Max Gross for passing on this information which he gleaned from the Quai d'Orsay archives (Paris) on Syria in the 1890s. Some individuals did purchase titles solely for the sake of enhancing their prestige. For example, Sami Mardam-Beg, son of Hikmat, bought the title of *pasha*. Conversation with Wajiha al-Yusuf (Beirut, 29 August 1975).

135 See R. Thoumin, *La Maison syrienne dans la plaine hauranaise, le bassin du Barada et sur les plateaux du Qalamoun* (Paris, 1932).

136 The information on intermarriages was collected from two interviews conducted with Wajiha al-Yusuf, daughter of 'Abd al-Rahman Pasha al-Yusuf (Beirut, 15 and 29 August 1975).

137 For example, the 'Abids intermarried with the Muradis, and the Barudis with the 'Ajlanis.

138 Owen, *The Middle East*, p. 172.

139 The Dalati family's sugar and preservatives concern dated from 1830, and catered to pilgrimage demands for preserved fruits and sweets, as well as local demand. *Al-Dalil al-jumhuriyya al-Suriyya 1939–1940* (Damascus, n.d.), pp. 473–4.

140 Hourani, 'The Ottoman Background,' pp. 12–18.

3 Damascus notables and the rise of Arab nationalism before World War I

1 Elie Kedourie, 'The Impact of the Young Turk Revolution in the Arabic-Speaking Provinces of the Ottoman Empire,' in *Arabic Political Memoirs and Other Studies* (London, 1974), pp. 124–5; A. L. Tibawi, *A Modern History of Syria* (London, 1969), pp. 168–9; Shimon Shamir, 'The

Modernization of Syria: Problems and Solutions in the Early Period of Abdülhamid,' in W. R. Polk and R. L. Chambers (eds.), *Beginnings of Modernization in the Middle East* (Chicago, 1968), p. 367; 'Abd al-'Aziz Muhammad 'Awad, *Al-Idara al-'Uthmaniyya fi wilayat Suriyya 1864–1914* (Cairo, 1969), p. 56. On the settlement of the Syrian tribes in the second half of the nineteenth century see my 'The Tribal Shaykh, French Tribal Policy and the Nationalist Movement in Syria Between Two World Wars,' *Middle Eastern Studies* 18 (April 1982), pp. 180–93.

2 Tibawi, *A Modern History*, p. 171.

3 *Ibid.*, pp. 158, 161–3. For discussions and differing points of view on the degree of separatist feelings found in Syria in the 1880s see: George Antonius, *The Arab Awakening* (London, 1938); Zeine N. Zeine, *The Emergence of Arab Nationalism with a Background Study of Arab-Turkish Relations in the Near East* (Beirut, 1966); Shimon Shamir, 'Midhat Pasha and the Anti-Turkish Agitation in Syria,' *Middle Eastern Studies*, 10 (May 1974), p. 115 *et passim*; Jacob M. Landau, 'An Arab Anti-Turk Handbill, 1881,' *Turcica Revue d'Études Turques* 9 (1977), pp. 215–27.

4 Feroz Ahmad, *The Young Turks: The Committee of Union and Progress in Turkish Politics, 1908–1914.* (Oxford, 1969); Tibawi, *A Modern History* p. 199.

5 Kedourie, 'The Impact,' p. 128.

6 Tibawi, *A Modern History*, p. 199.

7 Lutfi al-Haffar, *Dhikriyyat*, Vol. 1 (Damascus, 1954), p. 8.

8 Kedourie, 'The Impact,' p. 137; FO 371/560, file 37930. Devey to Lowther, Damascus, 1 October 1910.

9 FO 371/560, file 37930. Devey to Lowther, 1 October 1908; Tag E. A. Harran,'Turkish–Syrian Relations in the Ottoman Constitutional Period (1908–1914)' (Ph.D. diss., University of London, 1969), pp. 37–8, 50.

10 FO 371/560, file 37930. Devey to Lowther, 1 October 1908; Harran, 'Turkish–Syrian Relations,' p. 46; K. S. Salibi, 'The 1860 Upheaval in Damascus as Seen by al-Sayyid Muhammad Abu'l Su'ud al-Hasibi, Notable and later *Naqib al-Ashraf* of the City,' in Polk and Chambers (eds.), *Beginnings of Modernization in the Middle East*, p. 188. In the fall of 1913 there were rumors to the effect that the CUP had approached 'Izzat Pasha al-'Abid to invite him to return to Turkey with the rank of Senator and other favors provided he would contribute the sum of £T100,000 (possibly to the Public Treasury or to the CUP's fund) but he refused, replying that 'if needed, he would be ready to contribute £T20,000 for military equipment.' The CUP were vexed by his response and in retaliation advised the Sultan to issue an *irade* (decree) confiscating his property in Turkey. This reportedly came after a *fatwa* had been procured from the *Shaykh al-Islam*. 'Izzat Pasha had fled the country at the time the Constitution was outlawed, but his property was not confiscated. Rather, it was put under sequester, which too was removed in 1910. In 1912, he visited Damascus and stayed several weeks, looking after his property and interests, and keeping a low profile visiting relatives and friends. He owned so much that

both the French and the British were interested in the material value of his property as a possible investment opportunity. FO 371/1848, file 58138. Devey to Mallet, 9 December 1913.

11 FO 371/560, file 37930. Devey to Lowther, 1 October 1910; Harran, 'Turkish–Syrian Relations,' p. 50.

12 Kedourie, 'The Impact,' p. 148; Harran, 'Turkish–Syrian Relations,' p. 71.

13 FO 371/1002, file 3391. Devey to Lowther, 2 January 1910; Rashid I. Khalidi, *British Policy towards Syria and Palestine 1906–1914: a Study of the Antecedents of the Hussein–McMahon Correspondence, the Sykes–Picot Agreement, and the Balfour Declaration* (London, 1980), Table: 'Syrian Deputies 1908–1914'; Shaykh 'Abd al-Razzaq al-Bitar, *Hilyat al-bashar fi ta'rikh al-qarn al-thalith 'ashar* (Damascus, 1961), Vol. 1, p. 440.

14 Harran, 'Turkish–Syrian Relations,' p. 57.

15 FO 371/767, file 15583. Devey to Lowther, 3 April 1909.

16 Kedourie, 'The Impact,' p. 148; Harran, 'Turkish–Syrian Relations,' pp. 79–81.

17 Khalidi, *British Policy*, p. 204.

18 By mid-1910, the British Consul in Damascus had already observed: 'It seems that under the present administration much odium is being accumulated both against the vali and his officials, while the antagonistic sentiment as between Arab and Turk has been greatly fomented during the past 3 or 4 months, whether by hasty or somewhat autocratic behaviour on the part of office holders, or by the over-advanced views of those connected with the Young Turks party who are manifesting themselves in a distinct tendency towards xenophoby. The antagonistic sentiment between Turk and Arab is beginning to permeate downwards to the lower classes; and will soon be no longer confined to the ulama, notables and grandees and official circles. The most sore point of all is the attempt of Young Turks to propagate the use of Turkish in exclusion of Arabic in all official circles; and while all verbal evidence is in Arabic at the law courts, judgements, sentences, decrees, and sundry orders are put into Turkish often to the confusion of the applicant or the litigant. In the Judicial Department again most of the higher offices such as the Procurer-General, Presidents of Courts, know scarcely any Arabic or indeed none at all and in fact out of some thirty or more, only half have a fair colloquial knowledge of the language of the country, these being mainly the clerks and assessors; of the three Mustantiks (examining magistrates) one knows very little Arabic, whereas it is absolutely essential for his investigation.' FO 371/1002, file 28562. Devey to Lowther, 4 April 1910.

19 FO 371/1002, file 3391. Devey to Lowther, 2 January 1910; Amin Sa'id, *Al-Thawra al-'Arabiyya al-kubra* (Cairo, 1934), Vol. 1, p. 4.

20 The Ministry of Justice abolished the old system of assigning judicial membership in Damascus to natives elected for two-year terms, and appointed permanent members to fill these posts. Only four of the newly appointed members were from Damascus while the other eight were Turks.

The same procedure was applied to the four *qada's* of Homs, Ba'labakk, the Biqa', and al-Salt. FO 371/1002, file 14066. Devey to Lowther, 4 April 1910.

21 Shaykh Tahir came from an Algerian religious family. His father had emigrated to Damascus in 1844. For further details on his contribution to intellectual developments in Syria see: Adham al-Jundi, *A'lam al-adab wa al-fann* (Damascus, 1954), Vol. 1, pp. 223–4; Albert Hourani, *Arabic Thought in the Liberal Age, 1798–1939* (London, 1962), p. 222.

22 Harran, 'Turkish–Syrian Relations,' pp. 86–8.

23 'Abd al-Rahman Shahbandar, *Al-Thawra al-Suriyya al-wataniyya* (Damascus, 1933), pp. 2–3.

24 Khalidi, *British Policy*, pp. 239–41. Also see Philippe de Tarazi's collection of first issues of Syrian newspapers at the *Bibliothèque nationale* in Beirut, Lebanon, and *A Post-War Bibliography of the Near Eastern Mandates* (Beirut, 1933), pp. 43–51.

25 Kurd 'Ali was tried and acquitted for printing an 'heretical' article calling 'guardedly' for an Arab Caliphate. FO 371/1002, file 3391. Devey to Lowther, 2 January 1910.

26 Harran, 'Turkish–Syrian Relations,' pp. 127–9. Most Syrian deputies, according to Harran, lacked a proper knowledge of Turkish. This may well have encouraged their silence.

27 *Ibid.*, p. 131.

28 *Ibid.*, p. 146.

29 Khalidi, *British Policy*, pp. 227–8.

30 Harran, 'Turkish–Syrian Relations,' pp. 155–6.

31 FO 371/1246, file 41662. 'Quarterly Report on the Affairs of Syria for the Quarter ended September 30, 1911.'

32 Khalidi, *British Policy*, pp. 234–5.

33 *Ibid.*, pp. 241–3.

34 Harran, 'Turkish–Syrian Relations,' p. 158; Khalidi, *British Policy*, Table: 'Syrian Deputies 1908–1914.'

35 Elie Kedourie, 'The Politics of Political Literature: Kawakibi, Azoury and Jung,' in *Arabic Political Memoirs and Other Studies* (London, 1974), p. 107.

36 Khalidi, *British Policy*, pp. 274–6. Rida did so for a variety of personal reasons and perhaps on behalf of the Khedive in Egypt.

37 *Ibid.*, pp. 285–7; Harran, 'Turkish–Syrian Relations,' pp. 196–7.

38 Elie Kedourie, 'Political Parties in the Arab World,' in *Arabic Political Memoirs and Other Studies*, pp. 42–3. Rafiq and Haqqi al-'Azm had headed the local branch of the Turkish Decentralization Movement. See Harran, 'Turkish–Syrian Relations,' p. 200. Before 1908, the 'Liberal Union' and the CUP were linked in opposition to 'Abd ul-Hamid.

39 FO 371/1002, file 39460. Devey to Lowther, 11 October 1910. The Turks could place whomever they wanted in local administrative posts. For instance in the municipal elections in 1910, Ghalib Bey Zaliq received the most votes for the Presidency of the Municipality of Damascus but the Turkish *wali* chose Muhammad Fawzi Pasha al-'Azm instead. In fact, the Turks had some trouble finding suitable Damascenes for the Council.

Between January and July 1910, four different Presidents were selected and then replaced. FO 371/1002, file 28562. Devey to Lowther, 12 July 1910.

40 Khalidi, *British Policy*, pp. 269–70, 276.

41 For example, Rafiq, Haqqi and Shafiq (Mu'ayyad) al-'Azm were 'Arabists' and all were cousins of Muhammad Fawzi al-'Azm, a pro-CUP 'Ottomanist.'

42 Harran, 'Turkish–Syrian Relations,' pp. 276–7.

43 *Ibid.*, p. 289.

44 Al-Haffar, *Dhikriyyat*, Vol. 1, p. 8; Kedourie, 'Political Parties,' p. 40. Known members of the Renaissance Party included 'Abd al-Hamid al-Zahrawi, Muhammad Kurd 'Ali, Faris al-Khuri, Shukri al-'Asali, Salim al-Jaza'iri, Salah al-Din al-Qasimi, 'Uthman Mardam-Beg, Lutfi al-Haffar, Jamal al-Quwwatli, Sami al-'Azm, Rushdi al-Hakim, Ahmad Kurd 'Ali. Its founders were Muhibb al-Din al-Khatib and 'Arif al-Shihabi. See Zafir al-Qasimi, *Maktab 'Anbar* (Beirut, 1967), p. 99.

45 Harran, 'Turkish–Syrian Relations,' p. 187; Kedourie, 'Political Parties,' p. 42.

46 For a partial membership list of *al-Fatat* see, C. Ernest Dawn, 'The Rise of Arabism in Syria,' in *From Ottomanism to Arabism* (Urbana, 1973), p. 74. For the founding members see Kedourie, 'Political Parties,' p. 42.

47 Harran, 'Turkish–Syrian Relations,' pp. 290–1; Khalidi, *British Policy*, pp. 358–9; Zeine, *The Emergence of Arab Nationalism*, pp. 104–5.

48 Harran, 'Turkish–Syrian Relations,' pp. 290–4, 302–6.

49 Al-Yusuf attacked the Union and Liberal Party in Paris in a speech delivered in Damascus at the time. In retaliation, al-'Asali and 'Abd al-Wahhab al-Inglisi got hundreds of signatures on a telegram which was sent to the Paris Party endorsing the reforms demanded by the Paris group. FO 371/1884, file 41182. Nasif Meshaka to Marling, Constantinople, 10 July 1913.

50 Zeine, *The Emergence of Arab Nationalism*, p. 106; Harran, 'Turkish–Syrian Relations,' p. 332; William I. Shorrock, *French Imperialism in the Middle East* (Madison, 1976), pp. 96–8.

51 Harran, 'Turkish–Syrian Relations,' p. 337.

52 *Ibid.*, p. 338. 'Abd al-Rahman al-Yusuf was also appointed a Senator in 1914.

53 Khalidi, *British Policy*, Table: 'Syrian Deputies 1908–1914;' FO 371/3103, file 6453.

54 The analysis in this section depends heavily on the framework provided by C. Ernest Dawn in his essays *From Ottomanism to Arabism*. Also see Hourani, '*The Arab Awakening* Forty Years After,' *The Emergence of the Modern Middle East* (London, 1981), pp. 193–215.

55 On the ideological development of Ottomanism and the idea of Ottoman nationhood see Şerif Mardin, *The Genesis of Young Ottoman Thought* (Princeton, 1962).

56 Of the 126 known members of the pre-1914 'Arab Movement' listed by

Dawn, 40 percent were Syrians. Syria is defined here by its post-independence boundaries. Dawn, *From Ottomanism to Arabism*, pp. 152–4.

57 Damascenes were approximately 80 percent of the total Syrian membership in the pre-1914 'Arab Movement' *Ibid.*, pp. 159, 165, 174–5. Before the War Beirut was also very active in promoting the 'Arab Movement' and in some senses rivalled Damascus in terms of its contribution to activating the idea of 'Arabism.' Khalidi's *British Policy* clearly supports this point. Also see his 'The Press as a Source for Modern Arab Political History: 'Abd al-Ghani al-Uraisi and Al-Mufid,' *Arab Studies Quarterly* 3 (Winter 1981), pp. 22–42.

58 United States National Archives, *Syria*, 890d, 01/47. US Consul (Damascus) to Secretary of State, 7 September 1921; Jurj Faris, *Man huwa fi Suriyya 1949* (Damascus, 1950), p. 302.

59 Khayr al-Din al-Zirikli, *Al-A'lam* (Cairo, 1954–57), Vol. 3, p. 246; Shaykh Muhammad Jamil al-Shatti, *A'yan Dimashq* (Beirut, 1972), p. 441; Muhammad Adib Taqi al-Din al-Husni, *Kitab muntakhabat al-tawarikh li-Dimashq* (Damascus, 1928), Vol. 2, pp. 883–4; Khalidi, *British Policy*, pp. 224–6.

60 Three al-Bakri brothers–Fawzi, Nasib and Sami–were members of *al-Fatat*. See France: Ministère de la Défense, *Service Historique de l'Armée*, 7N 2141 (Arabie 1917–18–19), 'La Famille de Bakri,' Akaba, 20 June 1918.

61 The most popular 'political' café in Damascus before 1920 was called the Quwwatli café. Al-Haffar, *Dhikriyyat*, Vol. 1, p. 8.

62 Dawn, *From Ottomanism to Arabism*, pp. 162, 174–6.

63 Sami Dahhan, *Muhammad Kurd 'Ali: Hayat wa atharuhu* (Damascus, 1955), pp. 15–20. Shahbandar was a graduate of the Syrian Protestant College's Medical Faculty in Beirut, class of 1906. American University of Beirut, *Directory of Alumni, 1870–1952* (Beirut, 1953), p. 42.

64 Maktab 'Anbar, was originally the home of a wealthy Damascus Jew ('Anbar), and was converted into a secondary school in the late nineteenth century. It was located in the Kharrab quarter. Al-Qasimi, *Maktab 'Anbar*. Conversation with Zafir al-Qasimi (Beirut, 26 July 1975).

65 Conversation with Salma Mardam-Beg (London, 7 December 1974).

66 Dawn, *From Ottomanism to Arabism*, pp. 167, 178.

67 *Ibid.*, p. 178.

68 *Ibid.*, p. 167.

69 Al-Husni, *Kitab Muntakhabat*, Vol. 2, pp. 883–4; the 'Asali family according to one source only achieved political prominence with the rise of Shukri. Conversation with Hasan al-Hakim (Damascus, 12 March 1976).

70 Al-Husni, *Muntakhabat*, Vol. 2, p. 901; Dahhan, *Muhammad Kurd 'Ali*, pp. 15–20.

71 Dawn, *From Ottomanism to Arabism*, pp. 171–2.

72 Rafiq came from the Hafiz branch of the 'Azm family. Haqqi came from an even less established branch. Furthermore, their Syrian landholdings were relatively insignificant when compared to those of Muhammad Fawzi. Conversation with Wajiha al-Yusuf (Beirut, 15 August 1975).

73 Conversations with Salma Mardam-Beg (London, 25 November and 7 December 1974). Al-Husni, *Kitab Muntakhabat*, Vol. 2, pp. 891–2; al-Shatti *A'yan Dimashq*, pp. 318–19. Adham al-Jundi, *Shuhada' al-harb al-'alamiyya al-kubra* (Damascus, 1960), p. 175.

74 Conversation with Wajiha al-Yusuf (Beirut, 13 August 1975).

75 Dawn, *From Ottomanism to Arabism*, pp. 173–4.

4 Notables, nationalists and Faysal's Arab government in Damascus, 1918–1920

1 For the leading pro-Ottomanist notables of Damascus and other Syrian towns, collaboration with the CUP was the natural thing. Indeed, it was a very comfortable choice, even during the war years. The wives and daughters of the Damascus notability were in full agreement. In early March 1916, the Syrian Harim Philanthropic Society held a tea party in the Society's hall in Damascus in honor of the two viziers, Enver Pasha and Jamal Pasha. However, Enver could not attend though Jamal did. The Society presented to Enver a beautifully framed picture of an Ottoman girl wrapped in the Ottoman flag and holding in her right hand the photo of Enver Pasha. Another picture was presented to Jamal showing the Suez Canal with Egypt in front imploring Jamal to save her from what had befallen her, and above this the figure of an angel holding the photo of Jamal Pasha himself. Three speeches were given. First the daughter of Muhammad Fawzi Pasha al-'Azm stood up and delivered a speech in Turkish welcoming the 'two great Commanders.' She was followed by the secretary of the Society, the sister of Sami Pasha Mardam-Beg, who made a speech in Arabic in which she stated that the city of Damascus was enjoying a tranquility that guaranteed its advancement, in spite of the thundering guns and rifles which were heard in the distance. She added that in the meantime the women of Damascus had begun their own advancement! When she finished, the daughter of Ahmad Effendi Ibish stood up and made a speech in Arabic also, praising the 'grand Caliph' and the 'two noble Commanders' and thanked them for having founded a school for orphans and the poor, adding that being herself the President of the School, she pledged to fulfill the duties of that post in obedience to the wish of the 'two beloved Commanders.' The party ended with Jamal subscribing £T200 on behalf of Enver and a similar sum on his own to the Society. *Al-Muqtabas* (8 March 1916), cited in FO 371/2768, file 938, No. 88001.

2 Djemal Pasha, *Memoirs of a Turkish Statesman – 1913–1919* (London, 1923), p. 59. He wrote '...judging from the views of these leaders, the Arabian reforms meant nothing more than satisfying the ambitions of a few persons who were hankering after offices and dignities.'

3 *Ibid.*, pp. 59, 198–9; Dawn, *From Ottomanism to Arabism*, p. 156.

4 Turquie: IVème Armée, *La Vérité sur la question syrienne* (Stamboul, 1916), pp. 158–9, 161, 163. Also see Dawn, *From Ottomanism to Arabism*, p. 155. For the most detailed biographical data on the 'martyrs' see al-Jundi, *Shuhada'*, pp. 89–135.

5 Turqie: IVème Armée, *La Vérité*, pp. 165–6.
6 C. Ernest Dawn, 'The Amir of Mecca al-Husayn ibn-'Ali and the Origin of the Arab Revolt,' in *From Ottomanism to Arabism*, pp. 3–5; Butrus Abu Manneh, 'Sultan Abdülhamid II and the Sharifs of Mecca,' *Asian and African Studies* 9 (1973), pp. 1–21.
7 Dawn, 'The Amir of Mecca,' pp. 49–50.
8 *Ibid.*, p. 51. For an interesting interpretation of Sharif Husayn's theological attitudes towards Wahabism and Shi'ism, see the interview with T. E. Lawrence made by Capitaine Saint-Quentin in Cairo, in France: Ministère de la Défense, *Service Historique de l'Armée*, 16N 3200, Dossier 3, No. 4, 26 August 1917.
9 C. Ernest Dawn, 'Ideological Influences in the Arab Revolt,' in *From Ottomanism to Arabism*, pp. 84–5; Dawn, ''Abdullah ibn al-Husayn, Lord Kitchener and the idea of an Arab Revolt,' in *From Ottomanism to Arabism*, p. 56. For a recent detailed analysis of these promises and their different impacts see, Elie Kedourie, *In the Anglo-Arab Labyrinth. The McMahon–Husayn Correspondence and its Interpretations, 1914–1939* (Cambridge, 1976). Perhaps the most balanced and perceptive, yet brief, interpretation of what these promises and others such as the Sykes–Picot Agreement of 1916 and the Balfour Declaration of 1917 meant in the broader context of European wartime diplomacy is in Albert Hourani's '*The Arab Awakening* Forty Years After,' in his *The Emergence of the Modern Middle East*, pp. 206–12.
10 Kedourie, however, argues that Husayn was driven by personal ambition to seek the Caliphate of all Muslims. Elie Kedourie, *England and the Middle East* (London, 1956), pp. 48–56.
11 Dawn, 'The Amir of Mecca,' p. 49.
12 Dawn, *From Ottomanism to Arabism*, pp. 155–6.
13 Suleiman Mousa, 'The Role of Syrians and Iraqis in the Arab Revolt,' *Middle East Forum* 43 (1967), pp. 5–17.
14 In particular, the most influential Damascene notables: Muhammad Fawzi al-'Azm, and 'Abd al-Rahman al-Yusuf. See Khalid al-'Azm, *Mudhakkirat Khalid al-'Azm* (Beirut, 1972), Vol. 1, pp. 90–2.
15 Angus M. Mundy, 'The Arab Government in Syria from the Capture of Damascus to the Battle of Meisalun (30 September 1918–24 July 1920)' (MA diss., American University of Beirut, 1965), p. 36. Also see al-Amir Muhammad Sa'id al-Jaza'iri, *Mudhakkirati*, 2nd ed. (Algiers, 1968).
16 Shukri Pasha al-Ayyubi, who was fifty years old in 1918, had been a general in the Turkish Army and the director of an important carpet factory near Istanbul. He was also supposed to have been one of the heads of the Hamidian spy system. During the War he was imprisoned by the Turks for pro-Arab intrigue and 'suffered considerably.' He either escaped or was released and joined Faysal's army. He was later to be appointed *wali* of Aleppo by Faysal, but because of his incompetence during the Armenian massacre in February 1919 he was transferred to Medina. He was a member of the Ayyubi al-Ansari family which descended from one of the Medina men who fought with the Prophet at the Battle of Badr. Israel State

Archives: 2/file 15. Brunton (General Staff Intelligence in Palestine) to Acting Civil Secretary, 13 August 1921. I would like to thank Mary Christina Wilson for this information.

17 Elie Kedourie, 'The Capture of Damascus, 1 October 1918,' *Middle Eastern Studies* (October 1964), pp. 66–83. For a recent account of the confusing events surrounding the surrender of Damascus and particularly the role of T. E. Lawrence see John E. Mack, *A Prince of our Disorder: The Life of T. E. Lawrence* (London, 1976), Chapter 13, pp. 166–74.

18 Stephen Longrigg, *Syria and Lebanon under French Mandate* (London, 1958), p. 64; Ahmad Qadri, *Mudhakkirati 'an al-thawra al-'Arabiyya al-kubra* (Damascus, 1956), p. 74.

19 Muhammad Kurd 'Ali, *Al-Mudhakkirat* (Damascus, 1948), Vol. 1, p. 231; Khayriyya al-Qasimiyya, *Al-Hukuma al-'Arabiyya fi Dimashq bayn 1918–1920* (Cairo, n.d.), p. 64; Kedourie, *England and the Middle East,* p. 161.

20 Kedourie, *op. cit.,* p. 157.

21 Conversation with Yusuf al-Hakim (Damascus, 21 February 1976). Al-Hakim, a Christian Ottoman official and judge, served in Faysal's last two governments in 1920.

22 *Ibid*; Also see France: Ministère de la Défense, *Service Historique de l'Armée*: Georges Picot Telegrams to Paris, 1919, in 16N 3202, Dossiers 18–22.

23 Kedourie, *England and the Middle East,* pp. 160–1.

24 George Hakim, 'Industry,' in Sa'id B. Himadeh, *Economic Organization of Syria* (Beirut, 1936), pp. 119–22.

25 Sa'id B. Himadeh, 'Monetary and Banking System,' in *Economic Organization of Syria,* p. 264.

26 Mundy, 'The Arab Government,' p. 52.

27 Safuh Khayr, *Madinat Dimashq : Dirasa fi jughrafiyya al-mudun* (Damascus, 1969), p. 213.

28 Mundy, 'The Arab Government,' p. 52.

29 Kedourie, *England and the Middle East,* p. 157.

30 Al-Qasimiyya, *Al-Hukuma al-'Arabiyya,* p. 64; A revisionist interpretation of Faysal's administration suggests that it was becoming increasingly efficient, despite the many pressures upon it. It was only after the British withdrew their subsidy in the fall of 1919 that this trend was reversed. See Malcolm Bruce Russell, 'The Birth of Modern Syria: Amir Faysal's Government in Damascus' (Ph.D. diss., Johns Hopkins University, 1977).

31 United States National Archives, *Syria,* 890d, 00/89. W. K. Prentice, 'The Political Solution in Syria.' 14 October 1918; William L. Cleveland, *The Making of an Arab Nationalist. Ottomanism and Arabism in the Life and Thought of Sati' al-Husri* (Princeton, 1971), p. 49.

32 Kedourie, *England and the Middle East,* pp. 150–1.

33 *Ibid.,* pp. 151–2. Kedourie claims that all sides (English, French, Faysal) considered the Zionist question a secondary matter (p. 151), and that the Hashemites only began to raise strong objections to the Balfour Declaration after the British withdrew their support for Faysal in the fall of 1919. Up

until then they had been willing not to press the question of Palestine and Zionist immigration too hard in the hope of being able to use the British to counter or check French designs in Syria. Also see Kedourie, *In the Anglo-Arab Labyrinth*, pp. 233–4 and Hourani, '*The Arab Awakening*,' pp. 210–11.

34 See Neville Mandel, *The Arabs and Zionism before World War I* (Berkeley, 1976).

35 Kedourie, *England and the Middle East*, pp. 152–6.

36 Y. Porath, *The Emergence of the Palestinian–Arab National Movement, 1918–1929* (London, 1974), p. 77; FO 371/13211, file 5040. GHQ to Curzon, 18 October 1920; FO 371/2915, file 5034. Rowland to Curzon, 27 March 1920. Al-Qasimiyya, *Al-Hukuma al-'Arabiyya*, pp. 69–70; Hisham Nashabi, 'The Political Parties in Syria, 1918–1933' (MA diss., American University of Beirut, 1952), pp. 41–2.

37 Kedourie, 'Political Parties,' p. 45.

38 Mundy, 'The Arab Government,' pp. 61–2.

39 Al-Qasimiyya, *Al-Hukuma al-'Arabiyya*, pp. 68–9. At one time the *Istiqlal* Party claimed to have enrolled 250,000 members. This seems unlikely.

40 Kedourie, 'Political Parties,' p. 45.

41 *Ibid.*, p. 44.

42 Mundy, 'The Arab Government,' pp. 62–3.

43 FO 371/12237, file 5040. Scott to Curzon, 10 September 1920.

44 For details see Porath, *The Emergence*, pp. 70–122.

45 FO 371/12237, file 5040. Scott to Curzon, 10 September 1920.

46 *Ibid.*

47 Al-Qasimiyya, *Al-Hukuma al-'Arabiyya*, p. 71.

48 Kedourie, *England and the Middle East*, p. 159. Kedourie cites Gertrude Bell, 'Syria in October 1919,' in which she claimed that of the 300 Iraqi officers in Faysal's service only one or two belonged to influential Iraqi families.

49 Philippe David, *Un Gouvernement arabe à Damas. Le Congrès syrien* (Paris, 1923), p. 48. Especially before the 'United States Commission of Inquiry' (King–Crane Commission) which visited Syria in the summer of 1919.

50 Kedourie, *England and the Middle East*, p. 148; Mundy, 'The Arab Government,' p. 82.

51 Al-'Azm, *Mudhakkirat*, Vol. 1, pp. 90–2.

52 FO 371/767, file 15583, Devey to Lowther, 3 April 1909; Dawn, 'The Amir of Mecca,' p. 7; al-'Azm, *Mudhakkirat*, Vol. 1, p. 90.

53 Al-'Azm, *Mudhakkirat*, Vol. 1, pp. 94–5.

54 Among the old guard notables elected to the Congress from Damascus were al-'Azm, al-Yusuf, Mahmud al-Barudi (whose son Fakhri was a nationalist and close to Faysal), Shaykh 'Abd al-Qadir al-Khatib, and 'Awni al-Qudamani. For a complete list see Yusuf al-Hakim, *Suriyya wa al-'ahd al-Faysali* (Beirut, 1966), p. 91, and E. Baldissera, 'Note di storia siriana: gli ultimi giorni del regno siriano di Faisal Ibn Husein,' *Oriente Moderno* 52 (1972), pp. 341–56.

55 Yusuf al-Hakim, *Suriyya wa al-'ahd al-Faysali*, p. 92; FO 371/13211, file

5040, Scott to Curzon, 18 October 1920. The Christian community of Damascus had two representatives and the Aleppo community had one. The Jewish community in Damascus also had one representative. Delegates from the Hawran, Jabal Druze and Latakia numbered thirteen.

56 Dawn, *From Ottomanism to Arabism*, p. 175. On the attitudes of the Aleppo notability toward Arab nationalism and Damascus see my 'Politics of Nationalism,' Chapter 5.

57 Mundy, 'The Arab Government,' p. 93.

58 Al-Qasimiyya, *Al-Hukuma al-'Arabiyya*, p. 123.

59 Mundy, 'The Arab Government,' p. 93.

60 France: Ministère de la Défense, *Service Historique de l'Armée*, 16N 3203, Dossier 23 (1919); Kedourie, *England and the Middle East*, pp. 165–6.

61 Kedourie, *op. cit.*, p. 169; Dawn, *From Ottomanism to Arabism*, p. 176. The Committee included the two most prominent merchants of the Maydan quarter, 'Abd al-Qadir Agha Sukkar and As'ad Agha al-Mahayni.

62 *Documents on British Foreign Policy, 1919–39*, ed. E. L. Woodward and R. Butler, 1st series, Vol. 4 (London, 1952), pp. 625–7. For recent interpretations of French aims and activities in the postwar diplomacy over Syria, see Jan Karl Tannenbaum, 'France and the Arab Middle East, 1914–1920,' *Transactions of the American Philosophical Society* 68 (October 1978); my 'Politics of Nationalism,' Chapter 3; and Christopher M. Andrew and A. S. Kanya-Forstner, *The Climax of French Imperial Expansion 1914–1924* (Stanford, 1981), which is also the most perceptive analysis of the governmental and extra-governmental interests encouraging France to occupy Syria (and to maintain and buttress her overseas Empire in general) after the Great War. On the development and consolidation of French cultural, economic and political spheres of influence in Syria before the War, see Jacques Thobie, *Intérêts et impérialisme français dans l'empire ottoman (1895–1914)* (Paris, 1977) and William I. Shorrock, *French Imperialism in the Middle East: The Failure of French Policy in Syria and Lebanon 1900–1914* (Madison, 1976). Finally, the French attitude to British designs on Syria as World War I drew to a close can be found in France: Ministère de la Défense, *Service Historique de l'Armée*, 7N 1658, 'Arabie,' Defrance (Cairo) to Pichon (Paris), 9 March 1918.

63 Kedourie, *England and the Middle East*, p. 168.

64 Captain C. D. Brunton, 'Who's Who in Damascus, 1918–19,' (Brunton File, Middle East Centre, St Antony's College, Oxford), pp. 3–6. France: Ministère des Affaires Étrangères, Série Levant, 1918–1929, *Syrie-Liban*, Massignon Report, November 1920, Vol. 235, pp. 134–5. For example, Haqqi al-'Azm was one of the nationalist turncoats who defected as early as 1917, because of his poor personal relations with the family of Sharif Husayn. See *Al-Qibla* (Mecca), No. 264 (13 March 1919).

65 Mundy, 'The Arab Government,' pp. 63–4, 67.

66 Al-'Azm, *Mudhakkirat*, Vol. 1, p. 101.

67 Porath, *The Emergence*, pp. 78, 328.

68 Adham al-Jundi, *Ta'rikh al-thawrat al-Suriyya fi 'ahd al-intidab al-faransi*

(Damascus, 1960), p. 173; Dawn, *From Ottomanism to Arabism*, p. 174; Mundy, 'The Arab Government,' p. 64.

69 Mundy, *op. cit.*, pp. 100–2; Kedourie, *England and the Middle East*, p. 172; al-Jundi, *Ta'rikh*, p. 173.

70 Yusuf al-Hakim, *Suriyya wa al-'ahd al-Faysali*, pp. 168–9; on the role of rebel bands in Syria from 1919–21 see my 'Politics of Nationalism,' Chapter 4 and France: Ministère de la Défense, *Service Historique de l'Armée*, 7N 4192. 'L'Effort militaire français au Levant 1er Novembre 1919–18 Août 1921.'

71 Kedourie, *England and the Middle East*, p. 172; Hasan al-Hakim, *Mudhakkirati* (Beirut, 1966), Vol. 2, p. 153; al-Qasimiyya, *Al-Hukuma al-'Arabiyya*, p. 179; al-Jundi, *Ta'rikh*, p. 168.

72 Kedourie writes of Faysal: 'He was no leader, and could not impose his will. His history shows that he yielded to the strongest pressure exerted on him at any particular moment' (*England and the Middle East*, p. 169). A different picture of Faysal, one that points to rather remarkable leadership qualities in the highly complex and treacherous conditions of political and social life in Iraq after 1920, can be found in Hanna Batatu, *The Old Social Classes and the Revolutionary Movements of Iraq* (Princeton, 1978), pp. 25–7, 89–92, 99–101, 188–92, 194–202, 321–37.

73 France: Ministère de la Défense, *Service Historique de l'Armée*, 7N 4186, L'effort militaire français au Levant 1er Novembre 1919–18 Août 1921,' Dossier 1; United States National Archives 800.d/ Beirut Consul to Bristol, 25 May 1920; Kedourie, *England and the Middle East*, pp. 169–70.

74 Kedourie, *England and the Middle East*, p. 173.

75 Sati' al-Husri, *Yawm Maysalun* (Beirut, 1947), pp. 122–3.

76 Kedourie, *England and the Middle East*, p. 173.

77 Al-Husri, *Yawm Maysalun*, p. 129. For the activities and strategies of the French Ministries of Foreign Affairs and War in the two months prior to the French occupation of Damascus, see France: Ministère de la Défense, *Service Historique de l'Armée*, 7N 4179, 'Operation contre Fayçal,' Dossier 3 (1920).

78 France: Ministère de la Défense, *op. cit.*, 7N 4192, 'Khan Maisalun,' 24 July 1920; al-Husri, *Yawm Maysalun*, pp. 148–9.

79 Kedourie, *England and the Middle East*, p. 174.

80 Hasan al-Hakim, *Mudhakkirati*, Vol. 2, p. 153.

81 Kedourie, *England and the Middle East*, p. 174.

82 FO 371/13211, file 5040. Scott to Curzon, 18 October 1920.

83 For what happened to the nationalist leadership in Syria and the ways in which nationalists organized themselves in the aftermath of the French occupation, see my 'Factionalism among Syrian Nationalists during the French Mandate,' *International Journal of Middle Eastern Studies* 13 (November 1981), pp. 441–69.

Conclusion

1 Albert Hourani, 'Ottoman Reform and the Politics of Notables,' p. 46.
2 On the debate surrounding this interpretation see Chapter 2, n. 14.
3 William L. Cleveland, 'Sources of Arab Nationalism: An Overview,' *Middle East Review* 11 (Spring 1979), p. 27. The best example of such a Muslim reformer is the Aleppine, 'Abd al-Rahman al-Kawakibi. On al-Kawakibi's social thought see Hanna Batatu, *The Old Social Classes and the Revolutionary Movements of Iraq*, pp. 367–70.
4 Dawn, *From Ottomanism to Arabism*, pp. 122–47; Hourani, '*The Arab Awakening* Forty Years After,' p. 204; Hanna Batatu, 'The Arab Countries from Crisis to Crisis: Some Basic Trends and Tentative Interpretations,' in American University of Beirut (ed.), *The Liberal Arts and the Future of Higher Education in the Middle East* (Beirut, 1979), pp. 5–7.
5 Hourani, '*The Arab Awakening* Forty Years After,' p. 206.
6 Beirut was the only other town in Greater Syria in which the Arab movement can be said to have had a pronounced impact before 1914. See Rashid Khalidi, *British Policy Towards Syria and Palestine 1906–1914*.
7 Sylvia G. Haim, *Arab Nationalism: an Anthology* (Berkeley, 1962), p. 35.
8 Albert Hourani, *Arabic Thought in the Liberal Age, 1798–1939* (London, 1962), p. 308.
9 *Ibid.*, p. 290.
10 This point has been made by Elie Kedourie in *England and the Middle East* (London, 1956).
11 Hourani, *Arabic Thought*, p. 308.
12 Zeine N. Zeine, *The Struggle for Arab Independence* (Beirut, 1960), pp. 265–8.
13 Hourani, *Arabic Thought*, pp. 290–1.
14 This argument, among others, I have developed and elaborated in a sequel to this book which I am currently preparing for publication entitled *The Politics of Nationalism: Syria and the French Mandate*. Some light on this argument is also shed in my 'Factionalism among Syrian Nationalists during the French Mandate,' *International Journal of Middle Eastern Studies* 13 (November 1981), pp. 441–69.

Bibliography

The books and articles of several authors mentioned in the Bibliography were indispensable to my understanding of notables and class, socioeconomic change, political leadership and the emergence of Arab nationalism in Syria. They include Albert Hourani's essays, the 'Politics of Notables' and '*The Arab Awakening* Forty Years After;' Hanna Batatu's studies on class formation in Iraqi-Arab society; Roger Owen's *The Middle East in the World Economy*; and C. Ernest Dawn's essays on Ottomanism and Arabism. I should add that Elie Kedourie's numerous books and articles on Arab politics have always provided useful and eye-opening correctives while Rashid Khalidi's book and Tag Harran's doctoral dissertation helped to fill a yawning gap in my knowledge of political life in Syria in the early twentieth century. Finally there are two M.A. dissertations which need special mention: Ramez Tomeh's 'Landowners and Political Power in Damascus' (of which I read an early draft) and Theodore Swedenburg's 'The Development of Capitalism in Syria.'

Archival sources

France
Centre de Hautes Études Administratives sur l'Afrique et l'Asie Modernes (CHEAM, Paris). Syria (Mémoires en stage).
Ministère des Affaires Étrangères (Quai d'Orsay, Paris), Série Levant, 1918–1929, *Syrie-Liban*.
Ministère de la Défense (Vincennes), *Service Historique de l'Armée*, Série N: 7N, 16N, 17N.

Great Britain
Public Record Office (London). FO 371 (post-1905, Turkey).
Middle East Centre, St Antony's College, University of Oxford (Private Papers Collection).

Syria
Mudiriyyat al-watha'iqiyya al-ta'rikhiyya, Markaz al-watha'iq al-ta'rikhiyya (Directorate of Historical Documentation, Center for Historical Documents) (Damascus):
Mahakim al-shari'a (Shari'a Court records) Ottoman Period/Damascus.

Bibliography

Mahakim al-tijara (Commercial Court records) Ottoman Period/Damascus.
Al-Dawla: Al-Intidab al-Faransi (The State: Records of the French
Mandate).

United States
The National Archives of the United States (Washington, D.C.). Records of the
Department of State Relating to Internal Affairs of Asia, 1910–1929. Record
Group (R.G.) 59. Syria (890.d 00/01 ...)

Works in Arabic

al-'Allaf, Ahmad Hilmi. *Dimashq fi matla' al-qarn al-'ashrin* (Damascus at the
Beginning of the Twentieth Century). Ed. 'Ali Jamil Nu'iysa. Damascus,
1976.
'Awad, 'Abd al-Aziz Muhammad. *Al-Idara al-'Uthmaniyya fi wilayat Suriyya
1864–1914* (Ottoman Administration in the Province of Syria 1864–1914).
Cairo, 1969.
al-'Azm, 'Abd al-Qadir. *Al-Usra al-'Azmiyya* (The Azm Family). Damascus,
1951.
al-'Azm, Khalid. *Mudhakkirat Khalid al-'Azm* (Memoirs of Khalid al-Azm).
Vol. 1. Beirut, 1973.
al-Barudi, Fakhri. *Mudhakkirat al-Barudi* (Memoirs of al-Barudi). Vol. 1.
Beirut, 1951.
al-Basha, Qustantin, ed. *Mudhakkirat ta'rikhiyya* (Historical Memoirs). Harisa,
n.d.
al-Bitar, Shaykh 'Abd al-Razzaq. *Hilyat al-bashar fi ta'rikh al-qarn al-thalith
'ashar* (The Decoration of Mankind in the History of the Thirteenth
Century). Ed. Muhammad Bahjat al-Bitar. 3 vols. Damascus, 1961–63.
al-Budayri al-Hallaq, Shaykh Ahmad. *Hawadith Dimashq al-Yawmiyya
1154–1175/1741–1762* (Daily Events in Damascus 1154–1175/1741–1762).
Ed. Ahmad 'Izzat 'Abd al-Karim. Cairo, 1959.
Dahhan, Sami. *Muhammad Kurd 'Ali: Hayat wa atharuhu* (Muhammad Kurd
'Ali, His Life and His Influence). Damascus, 1955.
Dalil al-jumhuriyya al-Suriyya 1939–40 (Handbook of the Syrian Republic
1939–40). Damascus, n.d.
Darwaza, Muhammad 'Izzat. *Hawl al-haraka al-'Arabiyya al-haditha* (On the
Modern Arab Movement). 6 vols. Sidon, 1950.
Faris, Jurj. *Man huwa fi Suriyya 1949* (Who's Who in Syria 1949). Damascus,
1950.
al-Ghazzi, Najim al-Din. *Al-Kawakib al-sa'ira bi-a'yan al-mi'a al-'ashira*
(Wandering Stars with the Notables of the Tenth Century). Ed. Jibra'il
Sulayman Jabbur. 3 vols. Beirut, 1945–59.
al-Haffar, Lutfi. *Dhikriyyat* (Reminiscences). 2 vols. Damascus, 1954.
al-Hakim, Hasan. *Mudhakkirati: safahat min ta'rikh Suriyya al-haditha* (My
Memoirs: Pages from the History of Modern Syria). 2 vols. Beirut,
1965–1966.

al-Hakim, Yusuf. *Suriyya wa al-'ahd al-Faysali* (Syria and the Faysal Era). Beirut, 1966.

Suriyya wa al-'ahd al-'Uthmani (Syria and the Ottoman Era). Beirut, 1966.

Hanna, 'Abdullah. *Al-Qadiyya al-zira'iyya wa al-harakat al-fallahiyya fi Suriyya wa Lubnan (1820–1920)* (The Agrarian Problem and Peasant Movements in Syria and Lebanon [1820–1920]). Beirut, 1975.

al-Husni, Muhammad Adib Taqi al-Din. *Kitab muntakhabat al-tawarikh li-Dimashq* (Selected Passages from the Histories of Damascus). 3 vols. Damascus, 1927, 1928, 1934.

al-Husri, Sati'. *Yawm Maysalun* (The Day of Maysalun). Beirut, 1947.

al-Jaza'iri, al-Amir Muhammad Sa'id. *Mudhakkirati* (My Memoirs). 2nd ed. Algiers, 1968.

al-Jundi, Adham. *A'lam al-adab wa al-fann* (Eminent Personalities in Literature and the Arts). 2 vols. Damascus, 1954, 1958.

Shuhada' al-harb al-'alamiyya al-kubra (Martyrs of the Great World War). Damascus, 1960.

Ta'rikh al-thawrat al-Suriyya fi 'ahd al-intidab al-Faransi (The History of the Syrian Revolts in the Era of the French Mandate). Damascus, 1960.

al-Kawtharani, Wajih. *Bilad al-Sham* (Greater Syria). Beirut, 1980.

Khayr, Safuh. *Madinat Dimashq: Dirasa fi jughrafiyya al-mudun* (The City of Damascus. Studies in the Geography of Cities). Damascus, 1969.

Khoury [Khuri], Philip. 'Tabi'at al-sulta al-siyasiyya wa tuwazzi'ha fi Dimashq 1860–1908' (The Nature and the Distribution of Political Power in Damascus 1860–1908), in *Al-Mu'tamar al-dawli al-thani li-ta'rikh Bilad al-Sham*. Vol. 1. Damascus, 1980, 437–84.

Kurd 'Ali, Muhammad. *Khitat al-Sham* (The Plan of Damascus). 6 vols. Damascus, 1925–28.

Al-Mudhakkirat (Memoirs). 4 vols. Damascus, 1948–51.

Mardam-Beg, Khalil. *A'yan al-qarn al-thalith 'ashar fi al-fikr wa al-siyasa wa al-ijtima'* (Notables of the Thirteenth Century in Ideas, Politics and Society). Beirut, 1971.

al-Muhibbi, Muhammad al-Amin. *Khulasat al-athar fi a'yan al-qarn al-hadi 'ashar* (Excerpt from the Traditions of the Notables of the Eleventh Century). 4 vols. Cairo, 1867.

al-Muradi, Muhammad Khalil. *Silk al-durar fi a'yan al-qarn al-thani 'ashar* (The String of Pearls of the Notables of the Twelfth Century). 4 vols. Cairo, 1874, 1883.

al-Mu'tamar al-dawli al-thani li-ta'rikh Bilad al-Sham ([Proceedings of the] Second International Congress on the History of Greater Syria). 2 vols. Damascus, 1980.

Qadri, Ahmad. *Mudhakkirati 'an al-thawra al-'Arabiyya al-kubra* (My Memoirs on the Great Arab Revolt). Damascus, 1956.

al-Qasatli, Nu'man. *Kitab al-rawda al-ghana' fi Dimashq al-fayha'* (The Book of the Rich Garden in Damascus). Beirut, 1879.

al-Qasimi, Muhammad Sa'id. *Qamus al-sina'at al-Shamiyya* (Dictionary of Damascus Crafts). Ed. Zafir al-Qasimi. 2 vols. Paris, 1960.

Bibliography

al-Qasimi, Zafir. *Maktab 'Anbar* ('Anbar School). Beirut, 1967.
al-Qasimiyya, Khayriyya. *Al-Hukuma al-'Arabiyya fi Dimashq bayn 1918–1920* (The Arab Government in Damascus 1918–1920). Cairo, n.d.
Rafeq [Rafiq], 'Abd al-Karim. *Al-'Arab wa al-'Uthmaniyyun* (The Arabs and the Ottomans). Damascus, 1974.
Sa'id, Amin. *Al-Thawra al-'Arabiyya al-kubra* (The Great Arab Revolt). 3 vols. Cairo, 1934.
Schilcher, L[inda Schatkowski]. 'Ba'd muthahir ahwal al-a'yan bi-Dimashq fi awakhir al-qarn al-thamin 'ashar wa awa'il al-tasi' 'ashar' (Aspects of Notables' Status in Late Eighteenth and Early Nineteenth Century Damascus), in *Al-Mu'tamar al-dawli al-thani li-ta'rikh Bilad al-Sham.* Vol. 1. Damascus, 1980, 323–56.
Shahbandar, 'Abd al-Rahman. *Al-Thawra al-Suriyya al-wataniyya* (The Syrian National Revolt). Damascus, 1933.
al-Shatti, Shaykh Muhammad Jamil. *A'yan Dimashq fi al-qarn al-thalith 'ashar wa nisf al-qarn al-rabi' 'ashar, 1201–1350 A.H.* (Notables of Damascus in the Thirteenth and the First Half of the Fourteenth Century). 2nd ed. Beirut, 1972.
al-Siba'i, Badr al-Din. *Adwa' 'ala al-rasmal al-ajnabi fi Suriyya 1850–1958.* (Lights on Foreign Capital in Syria 1850–1958). Damascus, 1958.
Smilianskaya, I. *Al-Harakat al-fallahiyya fi Lubnan* (Peasant Movements in Lebanon). Beirut, 1972. Translated from the Russian.
al-Zirikli, Khayr al-Din. *Al-A'lam; qamus tarajim li-ashhar al-rijal wa al-nisa' min al-'Arab wa al-musta'ribin wa al-mustashriqin* (Eminent Personalities; A Biographical Dictionary of Noted Men and Women among the Arabs, the Arabists and the Orientalists). 10 vols. Cairo, 1954–57.

Ottoman Turkish sources

Salname
  Suriye vilayeti (Ottoman Government Yearbook: Syrian Province) 1288 A.H./1871–72 A.D.; 1289/1872–73; 1296/1878–79; 1302/1884–85; 1308–09/1890–91; 1309–10/1892–93; 1312/1894–95
  Vilayet-i Halab (Ottoman Government Yearbook: Aleppo Province) 1309 A.H./1891–92 A.D.; 1310/1892–93; 1314/1896–97; 1324/1906–07; 1326/1908–09; 1329/1911

Works in European languages

Abu-Lughod, Janet L. *Cairo: 1001 Years of the City Victorious.* Princeton, 1971.
Abu Manneh, B. 'Sultan Abdülhamid II and the Sharifs of Mecca,' *Asian and African Studies* 9 (1973), 1–21.
Ahmad, Feroz. *The Young Turks: The Committee of Union and Progress in Turkish Politics, 1908–1914.* Oxford, 1969.
American University of Beirut. *Directory of Alumni, 1870–1952.* Beirut, 1953.
Amin, Samir. *The Arab Nation.* London, 1978.

Andrew, Christopher M. and A. S. Kanya-Forstner. *The Climax of French Imperial Expansion 1914–1924*. Stanford, 1981.

Antonius, George. *The Arab Awakening*. London, 1938.

Baedeker, Karl. *Palestine and Syria. Handbook for Travellers*. Leipzig, 1894, 1898, 1912.

Baer, Gabriel. 'The Evolution of Private Landownership in Egypt and the Fertile Crescent,' *The Economic History of the Middle East*. Ed. Charles Issawi. Chicago, 1966, 80–90.

'Village and City in Egypt and Syria–1500–1914.' Paper presented to the Conference on the Economic History of the Near East, Princeton University, 17–20 June, 1974. A published version of this paper can now be found in Baer, *Fellah and Townsman in the Middle East*. London, 1982, 49–100.

Baldissera, E. 'Note di Storia siriana: gli ultimi giorni del regno siriano di Faisal ibn Husein,' *Oriente Moderno* 52 (1972), 341–56.

Barbir, Karl. *Ottoman Rule in Damascus, 1708–1758*. Princeton, 1980.

Batatu, Hanna. 'The Arab Countries From Crisis to Crisis: Some Basic Trends and Tentative Interpretations,' *The Liberal Arts and the Future of Higher Education in the Middle East*. Ed. American University of Beirut. Beirut, 1979, 3–15.

'Class Analysis and Iraqi Society,' *Arab Studies Quarterly* 1 (Summer 1979), 229–40.

The Old Social Classes and the Revolutionary Movements of Iraq. Princeton, 1978.

Bell, Gertrude Lowthian. *Syria. The Desert and the Sown*. London, 1907.

Bianquis, Anne-Marie. 'Damas et la Ghouta,' *La Syrie d'aujourd'hui*. Ed. André Raymond. Paris, 1980, 359–84.

Bodman, Herbert L. *Political Factions in Aleppo, 1760–1826*. Chapel Hill, 1963.

Bowen, H. 'A'yan,' *Encyclopedia of Islam* (new ed.). Vol. 1, 778.

Bowring, John. *Report on the Commercial Statistics of Syria*. London, 1840.

Brunton, C. D. 'Who's Who in Damascus, 1918–19' Brunton File, Middle East Centre, St Antony's College, University of Oxford.

Buheiry, Marwan R., ed. *Intellectual Life in the Arab East, 1890–1939*. Beirut, 1981.

Chatila, K. *Le Mariage chez les musulmans en Syrie*. Paris, 1934.

Chevallier, Dominique. 'Á Damas. Production et société à la fin du 19ᵉ siècle,' *Annales. Économies, Sociétés, Civilisations* 11 (1964), 966–72.

'Lyon et la Syrie en 1919. Les Bases d'une intervention,' *Revue Historique* 224 (1960), 275–320.

La Société du Mont Liban à l'époque de la Révolution industrielle en Europe. Paris, 1971.

Cleveland, William L. *The Making of an Arab Nationalist. Ottomanism and Arabism in the Life and Thought of Sati' al-Husri*. Princeton, 1971.

'Sources of Arab Nationalism: An Overview,' *Middle East Review* 11 (Spring 1979), 25–33.

Cuinet, Vital. *Syrie, Liban et Palestine: Géographie administrative statistique descriptive et raisonée*. Paris, 1896.

Daghestanti, Kazem. *Étude sociologique sur la famille musulmane contemporaine en Syrie*. Paris, 1932.

Danger, René. 'L'Urbanisme en Syrie: La ville de Damas,' *Urbanisme (Revue mensuelle)* (1937), 123–64.

David, Philippe. *Un Gouvernement arabe à Damas. Le Congrès syrien*. Paris, 1923.

Dawn, C. Ernest. *From Ottomanism to Arabism: Essays on the Origins of Arab Nationalism*. Urbana, 1973.

Dettmann, K. *Damaskus. Eine orientalische Stadt zwischen Tradition und Moderne*. Nürnberg, 1967.

Djemal Pasha. *Memoirs of a Turkish Statesman–1913–1919*. London, 1923.

Documents on British Foreign Policy, 1919–1939. Eds. E. L. Woodward and R. Butler. 1st series, IV, London, 1952.

Epstein, E. 'Notes from a Paper on the Present Conditions in the Hauran,' *Journal of the Royal Central Asian Society* 23 (1936), 594–613.

Firestone, Ya'kov. 'Production and Trade in an Islamic Context: Sharika Contracts in the Transitional Economy of Northern Samaria, 1853–1943,' *International Journal of Middle Eastern Studies* 6 (1975), Part 1, 185–209.

[Gaulmier, J.] 'Note sur la propriété foncière dans la Syrie centrale,' *l'Asie française* (April 1933), no. 309, 130–7.

Gibb, H. A. R. and Harold Bowen. *Islamic Society and the West*. Vol. 1, Pts. 1, 2. London, 1950, 1957.

Haddad, Robert. *Syrian Christians in Muslim Society*. Princeton, 1970.

Haddad, William W. and William L. Ochsenwald, eds. *Nationalism in a Non-National State*. Columbus, 1977.

Haim, Sylvia. *Arab Nationalism: An Anthology*. Berkeley, 1962.

Harran, Tag E. A. M. 'Turkish–Syrian Relations in the Ottoman Constitutional Period (1908–1914).' Ph.D. dissertation, University of London, 1969.

Himadeh, Sa'id B., ed. *Economic Organization of Syria*. Beirut, 1936.

Hofman, Yitzhak. 'The Administration of Syria and Palestine under Egyptian Rule (1831–1840),' *Studies on Palestine during the Ottoman Period*. Ed. Moshe Ma'oz. Jerusalem, 1975, 311–33.

Hourani, Albert. '*The Arab Awakening* Forty Years After,' *The Emergence of the Modern Middle East*. London, 1981, 193–215.

Arabic Thought in the Liberal Age, 1798–1939. London, 1962.

'The Changing Face of the Fertile Crescent in the Eighteenth century,' *Studia Islamica* 8 (1957), 89–122.

The Emergence of the Modern Middle East. London, 1981.

Europe and the Middle East. London, 1980.

'The Ottoman Background of the Modern Middle East,' *The Ottoman State and its Place in History*. Ed. Kemal H. Karpat. Leiden, 1974, 61–78.

'Ottoman Reform and the Politics of Notables,' *Beginnings of Modernization in the Middle East: The Nineteenth Century*. Eds. William R. Polk and Richard L. Chambers. Chicago, 1968, 41–68.

'Revolution in the Arab Middle East,' *Revolution in the Middle East and other Case Studies*. Ed. P. J. Vatikiotis, London, 1972, 65–72.

Syria and Lebanon: A Political Essay. London, 1946.

Hourani, A. H. and S. M. Stern, eds. *The Islamic City*. Oxford, 1970.

Howard, Harry N. *The King–Crane Commission*. Beirut, 1963.

Ibish, Y. 'Elias Qudsi's Sketch of the Guilds of Damascus in the Nineteenth Century,' *Middle East Economic Papers* (1967), 51–66.

Inalcik, Halil. *The Ottoman Empire. The Classical Age 1300–1600*. New York, 1973.

L'Indicateur Libano-syrien. Beirut, 1928–29.

Issawi, Charles, ed. *The Economic History of the Middle East, 1800–1914*. Chicago, 1966.

Kalla, Mohammad Sa'id. 'The Role of Foreign Trade in the Economic Development of Syria, 1831–1914.' Ph.D. dissertation, American University, 1969.

Karpat, Kemal H. 'The Land Regime, Social Structure, and Modernization in the Ottoman Empire,' *Beginnings of Modernization in the Middle East: The Nineteenth Century*. Eds. W. R. Polk and R. L. Chambers. Chicago, 1968, 69–90.

Kedourie, Elie. *In the Anglo-Arab Labyrinth. The McMahon–Husayn Correspondence and its Interpretations, 1914–1939*. Cambridge, 1976.

'The Capture of Damascus, 1 October 1918,' *Middle Eastern Studies* (October 1964), 66–83.

The Chatham House Version and Other Middle Eastern Studies. London, 1970.

England and the Middle East. London, 1956.

'The Impact of the Young Turk Revolution in the Arabic-Speaking Provinces of the Ottoman Empire,' *Arabic Political Memoirs and Other Studies*. London, 1974, 124–61.

Islam in the Modern World. New York, 1981.

'Political Parties in the Arab World,' *Arabic Political Memoirs and Other Studies*. London, 1974, 28–58.

'The Politics of Political Literature: Kawakibi, Azoury and Jung,' *Arabic Political Memoirs and Other Studies*. London, 1974, 107–23.

Khalaf, Samir. *Persistence and Change in Nineteenth-Century Lebanon*. Beirut, 1979.

Khalidi, Rashid I. *British Policy Towards Syria and Palestine 1906–1914: A Study of the Antecedents of the Hussein–McMahon Correspondence, the Sykes–Picot Agreement and the Balfour Declaration*. London, 1980.

'The Press as a Source for Modern Arab Political History: 'Abd al-Ghani al-Uraisi and Al-Mufid,' *Arab Studies Quarterly* 3 (Winter 1981), 22–42.

Khoury, Philip S. 'Factionalism among Syrian Nationalists during the French Mandate,' *International Journal of Middle Eastern Studies* 13 (November 1981), 441–69.

'The Politics of Nationalism: Syria and the French Mandate, 1920–1936.' Ph.D. dissertation, Harvard University, 1980.

'The Tribal Shaykh, French Tribal Policy and the Nationalist Movement in Syria between Two World Wars,' *Middle Eastern Studies* 18 (April 1982), 180–93.

Klat, Paul J. 'The Origins of Landownership in Syria,' *Middle East Economic Papers* (1958), 51–66.

Kremer, A. von. *Mittelsyrien und Damaskus*. Vienna, 1853.

Landau, Jacob M. 'An Arab Anti-Turk Handbill, 1881,' *Turcica Revue d'Études Turques* 9 (1977), 215–27.

Lapidus, Ira M. *Muslim Cities in the Later Middle Ages*. Cambridge, Mass., 1967.

Lewis, Norman N. 'The Frontier of Settlement in Syria, 1800–1950,' *International Affairs* 31 (1955), 48–60.

Longrigg, Stephen H. *Syria and Lebanon under French Mandate*. London, 1958.

Mack, John E. *A Prince of Our Disorder. The Life of T. E. Lawrence*. London, 1976.

Mandel, Neville. *The Arabs and Zionism before World War I*. Berkeley, 1976.

Mantran, Robert and Jean Sauvaget. *Règlements fiscaux ottomans, les provinces syriennes*. Beirut, 1951.

Ma'oz, Moshe. *Ottoman Reform in Syria and Palestine, 1840–1861 : The Impact of the Tanzimat on Politics and Society*. Oxford, 1968.

    ed. *Studies on Palestine during the Ottoman Period*. Jerusalem, 1975.

    'Syrian Urban Politics in the Tanzimat Period between 1840–1861,' *Bulletin of the School of Oriental and African Studies* 29 (1966), 277–301.

    'The 'Ulama' and the Process of Modernization in Syria during the mid-nineteenth century,' *Asian and African Studies* 7 (1971), 77–88.

Mardin, Şerif. *The Genesis of Young Ottoman Thought*. Princeton, 1962.

Martin, B. G. 'A Short History of the Khalwati Order of Dervishes,' *Scholars, Saints and Sufis, Muslim Religious Institutions in the Middle East since 1500*. Ed. Nikki Keddie. Berkeley, 1972, 275–305.

Migdal, Joel S. 'Urbanization and Political Change: The Impact of Foreign Rule,' *Comparative Studies in Society and History* 19 (July 1977), 328–49.

Monroe, Elizabeth. *Britain's Moment in the Middle East, 1914–1956*. London, 1963.

Montagne, R. 'Le Pouvoir des chefs et les élites en Orient,' *Centre de Hautes Études Administratives sur l'Afrique et l'Asie Modernes* (CHEAM, Paris), no. 17 (12 May 1938).

Mousa, Suleiman. 'The Role of the Syrians and Iraqis in the Arab Revolt,' *Middle East Forum* 43 (1967), 5–17.

Mundy, Angus. 'The Arab Government in Syria from the Capture of Damascus to the Battle of Meisalun (30 September 1918–24 July 1920).' MA dissertation, American University of Beirut, 1965.

Naff, Thomas and Roger Owen, eds. *Studies in Eighteenth-Century Islamic History*. Carbondale and Edwardsville, 1977.

Nashabi, Hisham. 'The Political Parties in Syria 1918–1933.' MA dissertation, American University of Beirut, 1952.

Ochsenwald, William. *The Hijaz Railroad*. Charlottesville, 1980.

    'The Vilayet of Syria 1901–1914: a re-examination of diplomatic documents as sources,' *Middle East Journal* 22 (1968), 73–87.

Owen, Roger. *The Middle East in the World Economy 1800–1914*. London, 1981.

Pascual, Jean-Paul. 'La Syrie à l'époque ottomane (le XIXᵉ siècle), ' *La Syrie d'aujourd'hui*. Ed. André Raymond. Paris, 1980, 31–53.

Porath, Y. *The Emergence of the Palestinian-Arab National Movement, 1918–1929*. London, 1974.

A Post-War Bibliography of the Near Eastern Mandates. Beirut, 1933.

Qudsi, Iliya. 'Notice sur les corporations de Damas,' *Actes du VIème Congrès des Orientalistes.* Leiden, 1885.

Rafeq, Abdul-Karim. 'The Local Forces in Syria in the Seventeenth and Eighteenth Centuries,' *War, Technology and Society in the Middle East.* Ed. V. J. Parry and M. E. Yapp. London, 1975, 277–307.
   The Province of Damascus, 1723–1783. Beirut, 1966.

Raymond, André. *Artisans et commerçants au Caire au XVIIIe siècle.* 2 vols. Damascus, 1973, 1974.

Ruppin, A. *Syrien als Wirtschaftsgebiet.* Berlin, 1917.

Russell, Malcolm B. 'The Birth of Modern Syria: Amir Faysal's Government in Damascus, 1918–1920.' Ph.D. dissertation, Johns Hopkins University, 1977.

Saad, Elias N. 'The Damascus Crisis of 1860 in Light of "Kitab al-Ahzan," an Unpublished Eye-Witness Account.' MA dissertation, American University of Beirut, 1974.

Saliba, Najib. 'The Achievements of Midhat Pasha as Governor of the Province of Syria,' *International Journal of Middle Eastern Studies* 9 (1978), 307–23.
   'Wilayat Suriyya, 1876–1909.' Ph.D. dissertation, University of Michigan, 1971.

Salibi, K. S. *The Modern History of Lebanon.* London, 1965.
   'The 1860 Upheaval in Damascus as Seen by al-Sayyid Muhammad Abu'l Su'ud al-Hasibi, Notable and later *Naqib al-Ashraf* of the City,' *Beginnings of Modernization in the Middle East: The Nineteenth Century.* Eds. W. R. Polk and R. L. Chambers. Chicago, 1968, 185–202.

Sauvaget, Jean. *Alep. Essai sur le développement d'une grande ville syrienne des origines au milieu du XIXe siècle.* 2 vols. Paris, 1941.
   'Esquisse d'une histoire de la ville de Damas,' *Revue des Études Islamiques* 8 (1934), 421 bis-480.

Schilcher, L. Schatkowski. 'The Hauran conflicts of the 1860s: A Chapter in the Rural History of Modern Syria,' *International Journal of Middle Eastern Studies* 13 (May 1981), 159–79.

Seikaly, Samir. 'Damascus Intellectual Life in the Opening Years of the 20th Century: Muhammad Kurd 'Ali and *al-Muqtabas*,' *Intellectual Life in the Arab East, 1890–1939.* Ed. Marwan R. Buheiry. Beirut, 1981, 125–53.

Shamir, Shimon. 'As'ad Pasha Al-'Azm and Ottoman Rule in Damascus (1743–1758),' *Bulletin of the School of Oriental and African Studies* 26 (1963), 1–28.
   'Midhat Pasha and the Anti-Turkish Agitation in Syria,' *Middle Eastern Studies* 10 (May 1974), 115–41.
   'The Modernization of Syria: Problems and Solutions in the Early Period of Abdülhamid,' *Beginnings of Modernization in the Middle East: The Nineteenth Century.* Eds. W. R. Polk and R. L. Chambers. Chicago, 1968, 351–82.

Shaw, Stanford J. 'The Ottoman Census System and Population, 1831–1914,' *International Journal of Middle Eastern Studies* 10 (August 1978), 325–38.

Bibliography

Shorrock, William I. *French Imperialism in the Middle East. The Failure of Policy in Syria and Lebanon 1900–1914.* Madison, 1976.

Smilianskaya, I. M. 'The Disintegration of Feudal Relations in Syria and Lebanon in the Middle of the Nineteenth Century,' *The Economic History of the Middle East.* Ed. Charles Issawi. Chicago, 1966, 227–47.

Spagnolo, John P. *France and Ottoman Lebanon, 1861–1914.* London, 1977.
  'French Influence in Syria prior to World War I: The Functional Weakness of Imperialism,' *Middle East Journal* 23 (Winter 1969), 45–62.

Steppat, Fritz. 'Some Arabic Manuscript Sources on the Syrian Crisis of 1860,' *Les Arabes par leurs archives (XVI–XXe siècles).* Eds. Jacques Berque and Dominique Chevallier. Paris, 1976, 183–91.

Swedenburg, Theodore Romain. 'The Development of Capitalism in Greater Syria, 1830–1914: An Historico-Geographical Approach.' MA dissertation, University of Texas at Austin, 1980.

Tannenbaum, Jan Karl. 'France and the Arab Middle East, 1914–1920,' *Transactions of the American Philosophical Society* 68 (October 1978), 1–50.

Tamari, Salim. 'Factionalism and Class Formation in Recent Palestinian History,' *Studies in the Economic and Social History of Palestine in the Nineteenth and Twentieth Centuries.* Ed. Roger Owen. Carbondale and Edwardsville, 1982, 177–202.

Thobie, Jacques. *Intérêts et impérialisme français dans l'empire ottoman: 1895–1914.* Paris, 1977.

Thoumin, R. *La Maison syrienne dans la plaine hauranaise, le bassin du Barada et sur les plateaux du Qalamoun.* Paris, 1932.

Tibawi, A. L. *A Modern History of Syria including Lebanon and Palestine.* London, 1969.
  'Some Misconceptions about the Nahda,' *Middle East Forum* 47 (Autumn and Winter 1971), 15–22.

Tibi, Bassam. *Arab Nationalism. A Critical Inquiry.* New York, 1981.

Tomeh, Ramez George. 'Landowners and Political Power in Damascus, 1858–1958.' MA dissertation, American University of Beirut, 1977.

Tresse, R. *Le Pèlerinage syrien aux villes saintes de l'Islam.* Paris, 1937.

Turquie: IVème Armée. *La Vérité sur la question syrienne.* Stamboul, 1916.

Verney, Nöel and Georges Daubmann. *Les Puissances étrangères dans le Levant, en Syrie et au Palestine.* Paris, 1900.

Voll, John. 'Old "Ulama" Families and Ottoman Influence in Eighteenth-Century Damascus,' *American Journal of Arabic Studies* 3 (1975), 48–59.

Warriner, Doreen. *Land Reform and Development in the Middle East: A Study of Egypt, Syria and Iraq.* 2nd ed. London, 1962.

Weulersse, Jacques. *Paysans de Syrie et du Proche-Orient.* Paris, 1946.
  'Régime agraire et vie agricole en Syrie,' *Bulletin de l'Association de Géographes français* No. 113 (April 1938), 58–61.

Williams, S. L. 'Ottoman Land Policy and Social Change: The Syrian Provinces,' *Acta Orientalia Academiae Scientiarum Hungaricae* 35 (1981), 89–120.

Wirth, Eugen. *Syrien Eine Geographische Landeskunde.* Darmstadt, 1971.

Woodward, E. L. and R. Butler. See *Documents on British Foreign Policy, 1919–1939.*
Young, George. *Corps de droit ottoman.* Vol. 6. Oxford, 1906.
Zeine, Zeine N. *The Emergence of Arab Nationalism with a Background Study of Arab–Turkish Relations in the Near East.* Beirut, 1966.
    The Struggle for Arab Independence. Beirut, 1960.
Ziadeh, Nicola A. *Urban Life in Syria under the Early Mamluks.* Beirut, 1953.

Interviews*

Munir al-'Ajlani (Beirut, 2 September 1975)
Nadim Demichkie (London, 25 June 1975)
Hasan al-Hakim (Damascus, 12 and 21 March 1976)
Yusuf al-Hakim (Damascus, 21 February 1976)
Hani al-Hindi (Beirut, 21 August 1975)
Wajiha al-Yusuf [Ibish] (Beirut, 15 and 29 August 1975)
Yusuf Ibish (Beirut, 4 July 1975)
Hasan [Abu 'Ali] al-Kilawi (Damascus, 14 February, 3 March and 15 May 1976)
Salma Mardam-Beg (London, 25 November and 7 December 1974)
Zafir al-Qasimi (Beirut, 25 and 26 July 1975)
Edmond Rabbath (Beirut, 21 and 27 August, 3 September 1975)
Jubran Shamiyya (Beirut, 29 July 1975)
Qustantin Zurayq (Beirut, 10 January 1976)

*Several interviews in Beirut were conducted jointly with Ramez Tomeh.

Glossary of Arabic, Persian and Turkish terms

(A) = Arabic; (P) = Persian; (T) = Turkish

agha (pl. *aghawat*) (T)	Ottoman title meaning 'chief'; in reference to the head of the local janissaries (*yerlıyye*) (q.v.)
ahl al-'ird (A)	'honorable citizenry' or notables
'alim (pl. *'ulama'*) (q.v.) (A)	one learned in the Islamic sciences
amir (A)	commander, prince
amir al-hajj (A)	Commander of the Pilgrimage
'arada (pl. *'aradat*) (A)	demonstration, parade
asnaf (A)	artisanal corporations
a'yan (A)	'notables'
defterdar (T)	accountant or treasurer
defterkhane (T)	public record office
diwan (A)	council
fatwa (A)	legal opinion issued by a *mufti* (q.v.)
Hanafi (A)	follower of the Orthodox (*Sunni*) school of law (*madhhab*) (q.v.) named after Abu Hanifa
Hanbali (A)	follower of the Orthodox school of law named after Ahmad ibn Hanbal
iltizam (T)	Ottoman system of tax farming, prevalent in the Arab provinces
jihad (A)	holy war
ketkhuda (P, T)	steward in a great man's household
khan (T)	large building for travelers and merchandise; caravanserai
khatib (A)	preacher; one who delivers the Friday-noon sermon or *khutba* in Islam
liwa' (A)	district in a province
madhhab (A)	*Sunni* legal school
madrasa (A)	secondary school that teaches the Islamic sciences
majlis (A)	council
majlis al-baladiyya (A)	Municipal Council
majlis al-idara (A)	administrative council
maktab (A)	elementary school that teaches the Islamic sciences

144

malikane (T)	hereditary tax farm
miri (A)	state-owned property
mufti (A)	person trained in the religious law or *shariʿa* (q.v.) who gives a non-binding legal opinion or *fatwa* (q.v.)
muhtasib (A)	market inspector who also enforced public morality
mukhtar (A)	village headman
mulk (A)	private property
multezim (T)	holder of a tax farm or *iltizam* (q.v.)
mutasarrif (A)	provincial governor
nahda (A)	renaissance
Naqib al-Ashraf (A)	doyen of the descendants of the Prophet
nazir al-waqf (A)	trustee of a *waqf* (q.v.) or religious endowment
pasha (T)	Ottoman honorary title of high rank
qaʾimaqam (A)	District Commissioner
qadi (A)	Muslim judge whose decisions are legally binding
salname (T)	Ottoman government yearbook
Shafiʿi (A)	follower of the *Sunni* (q.v.) school of law named after al-Shafiʿi
shariʿa (A)	Islamic law
sharif (pl. *ashraf*) (A)	descendant of the Prophet
Shaykh al-Islam (A)	title of the leading religious figure (aside from the Caliph) in a Muslim state; in the Ottoman state, appointed *mufti* (q.v.) of Istanbul
sipahi (P)	cavalryman in the Ottoman Empire who often held a *timar* (q.v.)
sufi (A)	Muslim mystic
suq (A)	market
Tanzimat (T)	term used to describe the period of Ottoman reform and modernization in the nineteenth century; literally 'reorganization'
timar (T)	Ottoman grant of income from a tax source, usually land, in return for the military service of a cavalryman or *sipahi* (q.v.)
tajir (pl. *tujjar*) (A)	merchant
ʿulamaʾ (A)	'Muslim clergy'
wajih (pl. *wujahaʾ*) (A)	a notable or eminent personality
wali (A); *vali* (T)	governor of a province
waqf (pl. *awqaf*) (A)	endowment fund whereby the revenues from a particular source are permanently allocated for a pious purpose
waqf ahli (A)	family endowment; estate in mortmain whose proceeds accrue to the members of the donor's family
wazir (A); *vezir* (T)	vizier or minister, such as a prime minister
wilaya (A); *vilayet* (T)	Ottoman administrative unit or province
yerlıyye or *yerlı kulları* (T)	local janissaries or Ottoman infantrymen (as opposed to the *kapıkulları* or imperial janissaries)

Index

'Abduh, (Shaykh) Muhammad, 62
'Abd ul-Hamid II (Sultan), 56, 63, 64;
and pan-Islamic policy, 38, 54, 96; and
'Izzat al-'Abid, 38; and extension of
reforms, 53; and moderation of
religious discontent, 55; deposition of,
57–8
al-'Abid (family), 35, 36, 37–9, 40, 47–8,
69, 116–17 (n. 83)
al-'Abid, 'Abd al-Qadir bin 'Umar, 38
al-'Abid, Ahmad 'Izzat, 56; and Hijaz
Railway, 38; and Sultan 'Abd
ul-Hamid, 38; British views of, 116 (n.
79, n. 80), 121 (n. 10)
al-'Abid, Hawlu, 39, 42, 49
al-'Abid, Mahmud, 38
al-'Abid, Muhammad, 38
al-'Abid, Muhammad 'Ali ibn Ahmad
'Izzat, 39, 81
al-'Abid, Mustafa, 38
al-'Abid, 'Umar Agha, 25, 37
Acre, 39, 40
Administrative Council of the Province,
see *majlis al-idara al-wilaya*
aghawat, 18, 26; as component of
notables, 11; sociopolitical power
before 1860, 12, 13; in the economy,
19–23; in peripheral quarters, 19–23;
and Kurds, 35; see also notables,
yerlıyye
agrarian commercialization, in Syria, 5, 94
Agribuz (family), 35, 44
Agricultural Bank of Syrian Province, 42
al-'Ahd (Society of the Covenant), 85,
86; see also notables
ahl al-'ird, 9; see also notables
al-'Ajlani (family), 14, 31–2, 34, 36, 50
al-'Ajlani, (Shaykh) Ahmad Darwish, 33
al-'Ajlani, 'Ata, 32, 81
al-'Ajlani, Muhammad ibn Ahmad
Darwish, 31, 57, 61, 70

Aleppo, 6, 18, 19, 20, 82, 87, 88, 91, 100,
101 (n. 1)
Amir al-Hajj, 30, 39–40, 48, 87; see also
pilgrimage, al-Yusuf (family)
Amirate, 77; see also Husayn (Sharif)
'Anjar, 39
Arab Congress (Paris, 1913), and goals,
65–6
Arab Kingdom (Damascus, 1920), 91, 92;
see also Arab state, Faysal
Arab nationalism (Arabism): rise of, 1, 7,
62, 67, 78, 85; as political movement, 1,
7, 61, 80, 85, 88, 92, 95, 97, 98–100;
goals of, 63, 98; and secularism, 64, 71,
95–6, 98–9; impact on *al-Fatat*, 64–5;
British influence on, 64; and conflict
with Ottomanism, 64, 66, 67–74, 88;
contribution of Damascus to, 68, 92,
98; as Syrian-inspired movement, 68;
and Islam, 71, 98; contribution of
Syrian Christians to, 95–96;
contribution of Syrian Muslim
reformers to, 98; see also Arab
nationalists, notables, Ottomanism
Arab nationalists (Arabists): as
distinguished from Ottomanists, 67–74;
perceptions of CUP, 68; arrest and
executions of, 76, 92; possibilities for
revolt, 76
Arab Renaissance Society, see *jam'iyyat
al-nahda al-'Arabiyya*
Arab Revolt (1916), 90, 98, 99; and
impact on Arab nationalism, 76–8
Arab state (Syria 1918–20), 78, 80
Arabia, 53, 77, 78
Arabic language, 2, 50, 58; and *nahda*, 29,
95–6
'aradat, 56
Armenians, 82
Army of the Levant, 91
artisans, role in 1860 Crisis, 23

146

al-'Asali, Shukri, 60, 61–2, 63, 69, 70, 72–3, 76, 85

ashraf, as component of notables, 11, 19, 104–5 (n. 12); *see also Naqib al-Ashraf*, *'ulama*'

al-Atasi (family), 87

al-Atasi, Hashim, 91

al-'al'Attar (family), 34, 44, 113 (n. 59)

a'yan, 10; *see also* notables

al-Ayyubi (family), 34, 44, 114 (n. 60)

al-Ayyubi, 'Ata, 92

al-Ayyubi, Shukri, 79

al-Azhar, 90

al-'Azm (family), 9, 18, 19, 35, 36–7, 40, 42, 43, 74, 95

al-'Azm, 'Abdullah Bey, on *majlis* of 1860, 36

al-'Azm, 'Abdullah Pasha, 43

al-'Azm, Haqqi, 69, 70, 72, 73, 76, 78

al-'Azm, Ibrahim, 18

al-'Azm, Isma'il, 18

al-'Azm, Khalid ibn Muhammad Fawzi, 37

al-'Azm, Muhammad 'Ali, 36

al-'Azm, Muhammad Fawzi ibn Muhammad 'Ali, 48, 74, 81; rise to family leadership, 36–7; and election of 1912, 62; and opposition to Arab nationalists, 63, 65, 70; conflict with Faysal, 86–7; death of, 90

al-'Azm, Muhammad Pasha (d. 1783), 18

al-'Azm, Sulayman, 18

al-'Azma (family), 44

al-'Azma, Yusuf, 91, 92

al-Bakri (family), 34–5, 44, 45, 49, 50, 56, 69, 73, 87

al-Bakri, 'Ata, 35, 49

al-Bakri, Fawzi, 35, 65, 70, 87

al-Bakri, Nasib, 35, 65, 70, 84

al-Bakri, Sami, 70

al-Barazi (family), 87

al-Barudi (Damascus family), 35, 36, 43, 49, 50

al-Barudi, Fakhri ibn Mahmud, 43, 65, 70, 84

al-Barudi, Hasan Agha, 43

al-Barudi, Mahmud ibn Muhammad, 43

al-Barudi, Muhammad ibn Hasan, 43, 49

beduin, 1, 6, 8, 21, 49, 53, 77, 78

Beirut: growth of, 6; and missionary education, 38; and opposition to Sultan, 54; Christian community compared with that of Damascus, 54; contribution to Arab nationalist movement, 98; *see also* Damascus

Beirut Reform Society, 65, 66

Biqa', 26, 89

al-Bitar (family), 114 (n. 59)

Britain: commerce with Syria, 16; influence on Arab nationalism and Arab Revolt, 64, 66, 77, 98; and subsidy to Faysal government, 83, 89; withdrawal of army of occupation from Syria, 89

Buzu (family), 35, 44

Cairo, 62–4, 65, 76, 77, 85

Caliphate, 62, 63, 76, 80, 99

Chamber of Agriculture (Damascus), 33, 36, 38, 42, 46

Chamber of Commerce (Damascus), 36, 42, 46

Christian Arabs: and Crisis of 1860, 8, 9, 23; as chroniclers, 9; as commerical bourgeoisie 6, 19, 54, 96; in Bab Musalla, 37; as intellectuals, 54; in Bab Tuma, 89; and birth of Arab nationalism, 95–6; and secularism, 99; *see also* minorities

civil service, *see* Ottoman bureaucracy

class conflict, and intra-class conflict, 4, 70, 74, 94, 95

class formation in Syria, 4–5, *see also* landowning-bureaucratic families

Clemenceau, (Georges), 89

Commercial Court (Damascus), 36, 41, 46

Committee of National Defense, (Damascus) 89, 90

Committee of Union and Progress (CUP): impact of 1908 Revolt, 55–74; and opposition to Sultan 'Abd ul-Hamid, 55; class and professional background, 55, 58; Damascus branch, 56; and Damascus opposition, 56–7, 58–67; elections, 57, 62; and reforms, 59; campaigns against Arab nationalist organizations and leadership, 65, 75; ideology, 69; conflict with Sharif Husayn, 76–7; *see also* Arab nationalism, notables, Young Turks

Constituent Assembly (1876), 31, 42

consular officials, 3, 6, 10, 46; as notables, 102 (n. 7)

Council of the *Awqaf* (Damascus), 30, 36, 42

Council of Directors (Damascus), 88, 90

Court of Appeals (Damascus), 35, 36, 38, 46

Index

Court of Summary Justice (Damascus), 36, 46
Crisis of 1860 (Damascus), impact on notables, 13, 23, 25, 26, 37, 40, 46, 93; *see also* minorities, *Tanzimat*

al-Dalati (family), 49–50
Damascus: and 1860 crisis, 1–11, 13; political configuration, 12, 93; and *Tanzimat*, 17; demography, 21; Christian community, 54; and Arab nationalism, 56, 59, 61, 67–74, 88; and elections of 1908, 57; condition at end of World War I, 79; and Allied–Arab occupation, 79; trade with Palestine and Iraq, 85; and Syrian Congress, 86–7; and Aleppo, 88, 101 (n. 1); and French occupation, 92; *see also* Arab nationalism, Committee of Union and Progress, Faysal, notables
Darwaza, 'Izzat, 84
defterdar, 30
District Council (Syrian Province), *see majlis al-idara al-liwa'*
Druzes, 8, 21, 23, 89
Duma, 32, 33, 39, 43
al-Durubi, 'Ala al-Din, 92

econony (Syria); commericalization of, 6, 12, 26, 27, 34; and commercial depression of late eighteenth century, 21; of 1870s, 27, 53; European competition and impact on, 19, 46, 22, 23, 25, 49; role of religious minorities in, 46; conditions during and after World War I, 81–2, 86; *see also* European influence, minorities
education: and religious establishment, 29; and secularization, 30, 53; and Ottoman professional schools, 30, 50; and Arab nationalism, 70–1
Egyptian occupation (1831–1840), impact on Syria, 16, 17, 47
elections, to Ottoman Parliament, 56, 57, 61, 62, 66–7; to Syrian Congress, 86
entente libérale, 61–2, 63, 64, 67, 69, 70
European influence in Syria 5, 6, 19, 22, 23, 25, 29, 49

families: and patron–client networks, 13, 35–6, 47, 48, 94–5; and religious establishment, 13–15, 30–4; and marriages, 22, 47; and landowning-bureaucrats, 35–44; and wealth, 40, 41, 42, 44, 47; and social

mobility, 41; and Ottoman lifestyle, 50–1; intra-familial competition, 73–4; *see also* class conflict, notables
al-Fatat : and Arab nationalism, 64–5, 69–70; membership, branches, 65, 84, 85; political behavior, 70; contribution to Arab Revolt, 78; relations with *Istiqlal* Party, *al-Nadi al-'Arabi* and *al-'Ahd*, 84, 85–6; and Syrian Congress, 88; and Faysal's government, 90–1
Faysal (King), 78–92; and nationalism, 80; and notables, 80–1, 89–90; and Army, 82, 92; and administration, 82–3; and European diplomacy, 82, 83, 89–90; and Arab nationalists, 84–6; and Zionist movement, 84; and 1919 elections, 86; and Syrian Congress, 88, 90; and French, 89–90, 91; elected King, 90; leaves Damascus, 92; and political leadership, 131 (n. 72)
Faysal–Clemenceau Agreement, 90
France: and Arab nationalists, 76, 92; ambitions in Syria, 83, 91; political agents, 81, 86; negotiations with Faysal, 89; and Mandate, 91; and occupation of Damascus, 92
Fu'ad Pasha, 8, 9, 25, 31

al-Gaylani, 'Abd al-Qadir, 32; *see also* al-Kaylani (family)
al-Ghazzi (family), 31, 34, 36, 50
al-Ghazzi, 'Abd al-Rahman, 32
al-Ghazzi, (Shaykh) Husayn, 32
al-Ghazzi, Salih, 32
al-Ghazzi, 'Umar, 32
al-Ghuta, 19, 32, 35, 36, 39, 40, 41, 42, 43, 73; *see also* Damascus, economy (Syria), landownership
Gouraud, General (Henri), 91, 92

al-Hakim (family), 44
al-Hakim, Hasan, 108 (n. 57)
al-Halabi (family), 34, 44, 114 (n. 60)
Hama, 18, 32, 36, 37, 38, 40, 61, 82, 87, 88, 100
al-Hamza (family), 14, 31, 34, 44, 113, (n. 59)
al-Hamza, Nasib, 63
Hananu (family), 87
harim, 41
Hashemites, 78, 79, 87; *see also* Faysal, Husayn
al-Hashimi, Yasin, 84, 88
al-Hasibi (family), 15, 31, 33–4, 36, 50

al-Hasibi, Abu'l Su'ud, 9, 10, 12, 13, 17, 19, 26, 33
al-Hasibi, Ahmad, 15, 16, 33, 34
Hawran, 10, 21, 26, 34, 36, 39–40; *see also* *aghawat*, landownership
Hijaz, 76, 77, 78, 80
Hijaz Railway, 33, 36, 54, 77
al-Hiraki (family), 87
Hizb al-Istiqlal al-'Arabi, see Istiqlal Party
Hizb al-lamarkaziyya al-idariyya al-'Uthmani, see Ottoman Party of Administrative Decentralization (Cairo)
Hizb al-watani, see National Party
Holy Cities, 19, 77; *see also* Hijaz, Hijaz Railway, pilgrimage
Homs, 15, 82, 87, 88, 100
'honorable citizens', *see ahl al-'ird*
Husayn (Sharif): and conflict with CUP, 76–7; and interpretations of Ottomanism, Islam and Arabism, 77; conflicts with Damascus notables, 87
Husayn–McMahon Correspondence, 77

Ibrahim Pasha, 16, 17, 23; *see also,* Egyptian occupation, Muhammad 'Ali
iltizam, 19, 107 (n. 44); *see also* landownership, *malikane*
al-'Imadi (family), 14
industry, 49; *see also* economy (Syria)
intra-class conflict, *see* class conflict
Iraq, 53, 85, 86, 92, 100
Iraqis, 80, 85, 88; *see also* al-'Ahd
Islam: revivalism, 77, 96; and Arab nationalism, 98; and politics, 99
Istanbul, 2, 9, 13, 14, 15, 17; and Ottoman centralization, 38; and notables, 44, 50–1; and Arab provinces, 53; *see also* education, Ottoman reform, Ottomanism, *Tanzimat*
Istiqlal Party, 84, 85; *see also* al-Fatat

al-Jabiri (family), 87
al-Jallad (family), 44, 49–50
Jamal Pasha, 75
al-jam'iyya al-Qahtaniyya (Qahtan Society), 64
jam'iyyat al-'Ahd, see al-'Ahd
jam'iyyat al-nahda al'Arabiyya (Arab Renaissance Society), 59, 60, 61, 64, 71, 74, 124 (n. 44)
jam'iyyat al-umumiyya al-islahiyya fi Bayrut, see Beirut Reform Society
janissaries, 18, 19; *see also kapıkulları, yerlıyye,*
al-Jaza'iri (family), 34, 36

al-Jaza'iri, (Amir) 'Abd al-Qadir (Algerian resistance leader), 34
al-Jaza'iri, (Amir) 'Abd al-Qadir (grandson of above), 79
al-Jaza'iri, 'Ali, 67
al-Jaza'iri, (Amir) Sa'id, 79
al-Jaza'iri, (Shaykh) Tahir, 59, 71
al-Jaza'iri, (Amir) 'Umar, 76
Jewish community (Damascus), 19, 23, 119 (n. 122) *see also* minorities
Jewish 'national home', 83, 90
al-Judayda, 33
judicial system: and *'ulama'*, 29–30; and *mahakim al-shari'a*, 30–1

Kamal, Mustafa (Atatürk), 81, 91
kapıkulları, 21; *see also* janissaries, *yerlıyye*
al-Kaylani (family), 31, 32–3, 34, 36, 87
al-Kaylani 'Abd al-Latif, 33
al-Kaylani, 'Attallah, 33
al-Kaylani, Faris, 33
al-Kaylani, Ibrahim, 33
al-Kaylani, Muhammad, 33
al-Kaylani, Sa'id, 33
al-Kayyali (family), 87
ketkhuda, 43
Khalwatiyya, 15
khan, 18
Khan Maysalun, 92
khatib, 13, 14
al-Khatib (family), 14, 73
al-Khatib, (Muhibb al-Din), 65, 70
al-Khuri, Faris, 67
al-Kikhiyya (family), 87
Kurd 'Ali, Muhammad, 60, 70, 72, 73, 75
Kurds, 8, 10, 21, 39–40; *see also* al-Yusuf (family)

La La Mustafa Pasha, *see* Mardam-Beg (family)
Land Code (Ottoman) of 1858, 27–8, 37
landownership: and private property, 26–7, 47, 94; and formation of big landowning class, 27–8; and political power, 28
landowning-bureaucratic families, 35–46; as a class, 5, 7, 46, 53, 74, 79, 87, 94, 95, 97–8; identification with Istanbul and Ottomanism, 44, 50, 51, 52; and landowning-scholars, 44; and patron–client networks, 48; *see also* class conflict, families, notables
landowning-scholars, 30–5, 44, 50; *see*

landowning-scholars (*cont.*)
also families, notables, religious
establishment, '*ulama*'
Latakia, 91
Lebanon, 8, 23, 39, 83, 86, 90, 91, 100;
see also Beirut

Ma'arrat al-Nu'man, 18
madhhab, 14, 15
madrasa, 29
mahakim al-shari'a, 16, 29, 41
al-Mahasini (family), 34, 44, 113 (n. 59)
al-Mahasini, Khalil, 14
al-Mahasini, Taj al-Din, 13
al-Mahayni (family), 35, 44
al-Mahayni, Salih Agha, 25
al-Mahayni, Salim Agha, 25
majlis: and Crisis of 1860, 9, 15, 17, 19,
23, 36; and landownership, 27–8
majlis al-balidiyya, 30, 32, 33, 35, 36, 38,
46
majlis al-idara al-liwa', 30, 35, 36, 38, 41,
42, 43, 46
majlis al-idara al-wilaya, 30, 35, 36, 38,
40, 41, 42, 46
majlis shura, 16
maktab, 29
Maktab 'Anbar, 71
malikane, 14, 15, 19; *see also iltizam*,
landownership, tax farms
al-Malki (family), 34, 44, 114 (n. 60)
al-Mar'ashli (family), 87
Mardam-Beg (family), 35, 41, 42, 43,
47–8, 73–4
Mardam-Beg, 'Abd al-Qadir, 73
Mardam-Beg, 'Abdullah, 49
Mardam-Beg, 'Ali, 41, 42, 73
Mardam-Beg, Hikmat, 41, 49, 73
Mardam-Beg, Jamil, 65, 70, 71, 73–4, 84,
85, 87, 88
Mardam-Beg, Sami, 49, 73
Mardam-Beg, 'Uthman, 41, 42, 73
Mardam-Beg, 'Uthman ibn 'Abd
al-Qadir, 73–4
marriages: al-Yusuf–Shamdin alliance,
40; al-Quwwatli network, 42;
intermarriage, 48–50; *see also* families,
landowning-bureaucratic families,
landowning-scholars, notables
al-Maydani (family), 34, 44, 114–15 (n.
60)
merchants: Muslim, 6, 16; Christian, 6;
grain and livestock, 21; and
moneylenders, 22, 46; *see also* Christian
Arabs, economy (Syria), minorities
minorities, 6, 16, 19, 23; and early

Tanzimat, 17; and education, 29;
position in political élite, 45–6; and
European commercial interests, 46; and
Muslim landowning class, 46; and
Muslim religious establishment, 54;
national awakening, 95; *see also* Arab
nationalism, Christian Arabs, economy
(Syria), European influence, Jews,
missionaries
miri, 27
missionaries: and Europe and America, 6;
and education, 29, 38, 54, 69, 70; and
nahda, 95–6
Mixed Courts, 32
Mosul, 38, 40
Mu'ayyad al-'Azm (family), 35, 36; *see
also* al-'Azm (family)
Mu'ayyad al-'Azm, Badi' 67, 81, 90, 92
Mu'ayyad al-'Azm, Shafiq, 57, 61, 62, 63,
69, 70, 72, 76
al-Mudarris (family), 87
Muhammad 'Ali, 16; *see also* Egyptian
occupation, Ibrahim Pasha
Muhammadan Union (Damascus), and
CUP, 57
al-Muqattam, 63
al-Muqtabas, 60
al-Muradi (family), 14, 34, 44, 114 (n.
59)
mutasarrif, 38, 39

al-Nadi al-'Arabi, 84, 85–6
nahda, 29, 95–6, 110 (n. 14)
Naqib al-Ashraf, 13, 14, 30–1, 33, 56; *see
also ashraf*, notables, religious
establishment
Naqshabandiyya, 14, 15
National Party, 90, 92; *see also* notables
al-Nayyal (family), 87
notables: as urban leaders, 2–3, 46; in
religious establishment, 3; and Crisis of
1860, 8, 9; changing relations with
Ottoman state, 10–11, 12–13; as
political and sociological concept, 11; as
a class, 11; and Egyptian occupation,
16; and resistance to early *Tanzimat*,
17; and rural élites, 27, 43; residences
of, 48; political culture of, 52;
factionalism, 52, 63; post-1860
realignment with Ottoman state, 53–4;
reactions to CUP revolt and reforms,
56, 59; and elections of 1908, 57;
interpretation of Ottomanism, 58;
attraction to Istanbul, 69; attitude to
military 72; attitude to Hashemites,
79–80; attitude to Faysal, 80–1, 89–90;

notables: as urban leaders (*cont.*)
    attitude to Arab nationalists, 80–1, 82;
    political survival after War, 81, 92, 100;
    as consuls, 102 (n. 7); *see also Aghawat*,
    Arab nationalsim, class conflict,
    families, Istanbul,
    landowning-bureaucratic families,
    landowning-scholars, Ottomanism,
    secular dignitaries, '*ulama*'
Nuri, Sa'id Agha, 25

Ottoman bureaucracy, 5, 12, 39, 44, 82,
    93, 96
Ottoman Constitution of 1876, 55, 56, 57
Ottoman Customs Tariff, 49
Ottoman Empire, 53, 75, 87; structural
    changes, 95
Ottoman governors, *see wali*
Ottoman Land Code, *see* Land Code
    (Ottoman) of 1858
Ottoman Law Codes, 82
Ottoman Law of the Provinces (1864), 30
Ottoman Ministry of *Awqaf*, 59
Ottoman Ministry of Foreign Affairs, 39
Ottoman Ministry of Justice, 59
Ottoman Parliament, 32, 61, 62, 69, 84
Ottoman Party of Administrative
    Decentralization (Cairo), 63, 64 65, 66,
    76
Ottoman reform: and centralization, 5,
    25; and notables, 28; and CUP, 58–9;
    see also Tanzimat
Ottoman rule in Syria, 2, 3, 6, 9;
    application of *Tanzimat*, 1841–60, and
    reimposition of authority in 1860, 17;
    impact on local political leadership, 34,
    38; *see also wali*
Ottoman Senate, 66, 75
Ottomanism: and Damascus political
    leadership, 39, 51–2; CUP
    interpretation of, 55; rival
    interpretations of, 58; and Arabism,
    64–74; obsolescence of, 75, 81, 98; and
    persistence of loyalty to, 96; *see also*
    Arab nationalism, Committee of Union
    and Progress, notables

Palestine Question, 85
Palestinians: and reaction to
    Faysal–Weizmann negotiations, 83; and
    reaction to Arab Revolt, 84; and
    al-Nadi al-'Arabi, 84
Pan-Islam: and Sultan 'Abd ul-Hamid,
    38, 40, 55; reaction of Christians to, 54
patronage networks, *see* families, notables
peasants: and landownership, 5, 27–8;

and exploitation by big landowners, 47;
    see also Land Code (Ottoman) of 1858,
    landowning-bureaucratic families
pilgrimage (to Holy Cities), 2, 18, 19, 20,
    48, 50, 87; *see also Amir al-Hajj*,
    Damascus, Hijaz Railway
political élite (leadership) of Damascus:
    and 1860 Crisis, 23, 25; and
    secularization, 28, 54; membership,
    size, and status, 31, 32, 34–5, 43–4,
    68–9, 73; changes in behavior, 46–52;
    changing relations with Istanbul, 46–7;
    and Arab nationalist societies, 85;
    metamorphosis, 93–4; *see also* Arab
    nationalism, families,
    landowning-bureaucratic families,
    notables, Ottoman rule in Syria
private property, 27–8; 92; *see also* Land
    Code (Ottoman) of 1858

al-Qabas, 60, 61
qadi, 30
Qadiriyya, 15, 32
Qadri, Ahmad, 70, 71, 84, 85, 87, 88
qa'imaqam, 38
al-Qassab, (Shaykh) Kamil, 90
al-Qudamani, 'Awni, 67
al-Qudsi (Aleppo Muslim family), 87
al-Qudsi (Damascus Christian family), 46
al-Qunaytra, 34
al-Quwwatli (family), 35, 36, 41–2, 43,
    49, 50
al-Quwwatli, 'Abd al-Ghani, 42
al-Quwwatli, Ahmad, 42
al-Quwwatli, Hasan, 42
al-Quwwatli, Muhammad, 41
al-Quwwatli, Muhammad 'Arif, 81
al-Quwwatli, Murad, 42, 49
al-Quwwatli, Shukri, 84, 85, 87, 88

Rafeq, Abdul-Karim, on history of
    eighteenth-century Damascus, 103–4
    (n. 9)
Raslan (family), 87
religious establishment, 11, 13–17, 26, 44;
    composition of, 13–15; mobility of
    members, 15; impact of Egyptian
    occupation on, 16; and marriages with
    landowning-bureaucratic families, 49;
    opposition to Sultan, 54; reaction to
    CUP Revolt, 56; role in growth of Arab
    nationalism, 98; *see also, ashraf*,
    landowning scholars, notables, '*ulama*'
Rida, (Shaykh) Rashid, 62, 63, 76
al-Rifa'i (family), 87
al-Rijlih (family), 44

Index

al-Rikabi (family), 9, 44
al-Rikabi, 'Ali Rida, 88, 90, 91
rushdiyya, 29

Salam, Salim 'Ali, 66
al-Sayyadi, Abu'l Huda, 38; *see also*
  Sultan 'Abd ul-Hamid II
secret societies, 56, 64–5, 84, 85, 99
secular dignitaries, 18–20, 26; *see also*
  al-'Azm (family), notables
Shahbandar, 'Abd al-Rahman, 60, 70, 72,
  73, 75, 91
al-Sham'a (family), 35, 36, 42–3
al-Sham'a, Ahmad Rafiq, 42–3, 63
al-Sham'a, Rushdi ibn Ahmad Rafiq, 42,
  57, 61, 62, 63, 69, 72, 76
al-Sham'a, Yusuf, 42
Shamdin (family), 35, 39–40, 49; *see also*
  al-Yusuf (family)
Shamdin Agha, 40
Shamdin Pasha, Muhammad Sa'id, 40, 49
al-Shamiyya (family), 46
shari'a, 9, 13, 57
shari'a courts, see *mahakim al-shari'a*
Sharif Husayn, *see* Husayn (Sharif)
Sharif Pasha, 43
Shaykh al-Mashayikh, 31, 48
shaykhs, see '*ulama*'
al-Shihab, Amir Bashir, 39
al-Shihabi, Fa'iz, 87
sufi orders, 14, 15, 32; *see also*
  Khalwatiyya, Naqshabandiyya,
  Qadiriyya, '*ulama*'
al-Sukkar (family), 35, 44
Sykes–Picot Agreement, 89
Syria: and classes, 1, 2, 4, 5; and
  Egyptian occupation, 10, 16, 23; and
  British trade, 16; return of Ottoman
  rule, 17; and *Tanzimat*, 17, 23–5,
  26–30; Ottoman conquest of 1516, 19;
  and the Young Turks, 53–67;
  contribution to Arab nationalism,
  67–74, 95–100; *see also* Damascus,
  notables
Syrian Congress (Damascus), 86–7, 88,
  89, 90, 91, 100
Syrian Protestant College, and Arabism,
  54, 98
Syrians, and Christians, 7; émigrés, 62;
  contribution to Arab nationalism,
  67–74, 95–100; and Arab Revolt of
  1916, 78

al-Tabba' (family), 44
Tanzimat, 30, 93; early reforms, 17; and

Crisis of 1860, 23; application after
  1860, 45, 47; *see also* Ottoman reform
Tarazi, Amin, 62
tax farms, 3, 10, 11, 12, 18–19; *see also*
  iltizam, landownership, *malikane*
tujjar, see merchants
'Turkification', in Arab provinces, 11, 58,
  59, 71, 75, 95; *see also* Arab
  nationalism, Committee of Union and
  Progress, notables
Turkish language, 50, 58, 59, 122 (n. 18)
Turkish liberal reformers, 55

'*ulama*': as component of the notables,
  11; and religious establishment, 13–17;
  adjustment to Ottoman pressures before
  1830, 16; reaction to early *Tanzimat*,
  17; and Crisis of 1860, 23, 25; hostility
  to post-1860 reforms, 28; and
  education, 29; and secularization, 54;
  and opposition to Sultan, 54–5;
  reaction to CUP Revolt, 56–7; *see also*
  Arab nationalism, *ashraf*,
  landowning-scholars, notables, religious
  establishment
al-'Umari (family), 34, 44, 114 (n. 60)
al-Ustwani (family), 34, 44, 113–14 (n.
  59)
al-Ustwani, 'Abd al-Muhsin, 62
wali, 2, 17, 30, 43, 48, 56; *see also*
  Ottoman rule
waqf, pl. *awqaf*, 13
waqf ahli, 41, 30, 32, 41, 47
Weizmann, Chaim, 83–4; *see also* Faysal
women's dress code movement
  (Damascus), 56–7; *see also* Committee
  of Union and Progress, Muhammadan
  Union, '*ulama*'
wujaha', 80; *see also* notables

yerlıyye, 20, 21; *see also* *aghawat*,
  kapıkulları
Young Turks, 11, 55, 95, 97, 98–9; *see*
  also Committee of Union and Progress
al-Yusuf (family), 35, 36, 37, 39–40, 42,
  43, 47–8; *see also* Amir al-Hajj, Arab
  nationalism, Ottomanism, Shamdin
  (family)
al-Yusuf, 'Abd al-Rahman ibn
  Muhammad: as *Amir al-Hajj*, 48, 87;
  marriage relations, 49; and election to
  Ottoman Parliament, 57, 62; opposition
  to Arab nationalists, 63, 65, 70; attitude to
  Faysal, 86–7, 90, 92
al-Yusuf, Ahmad Agha, 39

al-Yusuf, Muhammad ibn Ahmad, 39, 40, 49

Zahla, 23

al-Zahrawi, (Shaykh) 'Abd al-Hamid, 61, 63, 66, 75, 76
Zionist movement, 62, 83–4

12.